Shakespeare's House

RELATED TITLES

Shakespeare's House

A Window onto his Life and Legacy

Richard Schoch

THE ARDEN SHAKESPEARE
LONDON • NEW YORK • OXFORD • NEW DELHI • SYDNEY

THE ARDEN SHAKESPEARE
Bloomsbury Publishing Plc
50 Bedford Square, London, WC1B 3DP, UK
1385 Broadway, New York, NY 10018, USA
29 Earlsfort Terrace, Dublin 2, Ireland

BLOOMSBURY, THE ARDEN SHAKESPEARE and the Arden Shakespeare logo are
trademarks of Bloomsbury Publishing Plc

First published in Great Britain 2024

Cover design: Elena Durey
Illustration © Elena Durey
Photograph of Paper texture © Kiwihug / Unsplash

A catalogue record for this book is available from the British Library.

Library of Congress Cataloging-in-Publication Data
Names: Schoch, Richard W., author.
Title: Shakespeare's house : a window onto his life and legacy / Richard Schoch.
Description: London ; New York : The Arden Shakespeare, 2024.
| Includes bibliographical references and index.
Identifiers: LCCN 2023002764 (print) | LCCN 2023002765 (ebook) |
ISBN 9781350409354 (hardback) | ISBN 9781350409361 (epub) |
ISBN 9781350409378 (pdf)
Subjects: LCSH: Shakespeare, William, 1564–1616–Homes and haunts–England--Stratford-
upon-Avon. | Shakespeare, William, 1564-1616–Childhood and youth. |
Dramatists, English–Homes and haunts–England–Stratford-upon-Avon. |
Dramatists, English–Early modern, 1500–1700–Biography. | Stratford-upon-Avon
(England–Buildings, structures, etc. | Stratford-upon-Avon (England–Biography.
Classification: LCC PR2916 .S136 2024 (print) | LCC PR2916 (ebook) |
DDC 822.3/3 [B—dc23/eng/20230329
LC record available at https://lccn.loc.gov/2023002764
LC ebook record available at https://lccn.loc.gov/2023002765

ISBN: HB: 978-1-3504-0935-4
         ePDF: 978-1-3504-0937-8
         eBook: 978-1-3504-0936-1

Typeset by RefineCatch Limited, Bungay, Suffolk

To find out more about our authors and books visit www.bloomsbury.com
and sign up for our newsletters.

for Sir Stanley Wells, magister omnium nostrum

CONTENTS

ILLUSTRATIONS

13. Exterior of Shakespeare's Birthplace, Stratford-upon-Avon, watercolour drawing by Phoebe Dighton, 1834. Folger Shakespeare Library, ART Vol. d61 no.22a.

14. 'The Birthplace of Shakspere', Stratford-upon-Avon, drawn by John Brandard, printed in Leamington, England, by C. Elston, c. 1830s. Folger Shakespeare Library, ART File S899h1 no.3.

15. 'The Room in which Shakespere was Born', drawn and printed by George Rowe, published by F. & G. Ward, Stratford-upon-Avon, c. 1840s. Folger Shakespeare Library, ART File S899h1 no.40.

16. Shakespeare's Birthplace, Stratford-upon-Avon, exterior, photographed and published by Samuel E. Poulton, London and Reading, England, c. 1840s. Folger Shakespeare Library, ART File S899h1 no.58.

17. Broadside, auction of Shakespeare's Birthplace, Stratford-upon-Avon, held at the Auction Mart in Covent Garden, London, on 16 September 1847, printed by Alfred Roberts, London. Folger Shakespeare Library, Y.d.1147.

18. View of Henley Street, Stratford-upon-Avon, looking northeast, photograph, c. 1870. Folger Shakespeare Library, ART File S899h1 no.57 part 18.

19. Attic staircase, Shakespeare's Birthplace, Stratford-upon-Avon, pencil and watercolour sketch by John Thomas Blight, 1864. Folger Shakespeare Library, ART Vol. d69 no.13b.

20. Birthroom, Shakespeare's Birthplace, Stratford-upon-Avon, pencil and watercolour sketch by John Thomas Blight, 1864. Folger Shakespeare Library, ART Vol. d69 no.13a.

21. Birthroom, Shakespeare's Birthplace, Stratford-upon-Avon, photograph by Francis Bedford, c. 1870s. Folger Shakespeare Library, ART File S899h1 no.60 part 12.

22. Interior, Shakespeare's Birthplace, Stratford-upon-Avon, pencil and watercolour sketch by John Thomas Blight, 1864. Folger Shakespeare Library, ART Vol. d69 no.23a.

23. Desk and chair, Shakespeare's Birthplace, Stratford-upon-Avon, pencil and watercolour sketch by Paul Braddon, late-nineteenth century. Folger Shakespeare Library, ART Box B798 no.23.

24. Exterior, Shakespeare's Birthplace, Stratford-upon-Avon, photograph, c. 1900. Folger Shakespeare Library, ART File S899h1 no.57 part 7.

25. Henry Wallis, 'Shakespeare's House, Stratford-upon-Avon', oil painting, c. 1854, as repainted by Sir Edwin Landseer. Victoria and Albert Museum, London, accession number F.38. © Victoria and Albert Museum, London.

Illustration 25 is reproduced courtesy of the Victoria and Albert Museum, London. All other illustrations are reproduced courtesy of the Folger Shakespeare Library, Washington, DC, under a Creative Commons Attribution-ShareAlike 4.0 International License.

Prologue

Tradition claims that William Shakespeare was born in the two-storey, half-timbered house owned by his father on the north side of Henley Street in the Warwickshire market town of Stratford-upon-Avon. He was born in 1564, but his family home still stands.

That Shakespeare's birthplace has survived is not in itself remarkable. In Stratford alone, other places are equally old, or older still: the former Falcon Hotel on Chapel Street – around the corner from Falcon Cottage on Scholars Lane, where I lived while writing this book – was built around 1500, while the nearby Guild Chapel, grammar school and intact row of eleven almshouses all date from the 1420s. What's remarkable is that an ordinary house in an ordinary town has become the most popular place in the world devoted to Shakespeare. Before the Covid pandemic slammed the brakes on Stratford tourism, nearly four hundred thousand people from more than 100 countries visited Shakespeare's birthplace each year.

Its unmistakable Tudor façade appears on the heaps of postcards mailed from Stratford to everywhere and brands the T-shirts piled high in the town's abundance of giftshops. The Birthplace – we all know whose, no identifying name needed – supplies the picturesque background for countless Facebook and Instagram selfies. Attracting a hundred thousand more visitors a year than Stratford's Holy Trinity Church, where Shakespeare's bones crumbled into dust long ago, or the Globe on London's Bankside, the replica of the playhouse that made him famous, this house remains the focal point of the global cult of Shakespeare.

During the Covid lockdowns, when the Birthplace was shut, some of the cult's more energetic members stole tiles from the porch roof, determined to get their hands on a Shakespeare souvenir. Spoiler alert: the tiles aren't original. Yet did they know, as they leaned over the iron railings to seize their plunder, that pilfering has been part of the house's history? Visitors back in the eighteenth century were positively encouraged to take home a slice of the chair that belonged – or, more likely, didn't belong – to Shakespeare himself. Once that sacred chair had been whittled down to nothingness, a fresh one appeared, ready to surrender itself to the wielding of yet more eager pocketknives. Don't try it today.

I'm sympathetic to the desire to get your hands on a piece of Shakespeare's house. After all, the surviving documentary records about Shakespeare fail to enthuse. Property deeds and parish registers do not beguile the reader. The plays themselves, however majestic on the page, however moving in the theatre, are phantom imaginings, not assured revelations of the author's soul. Fire destroyed the original Globe Theatre in Shakespeare's own lifetime. New Place, the large house in Stratford that Shakespeare bought for himself and his family, and where he died, was torn down in the eighteenth century. Only its stone foundations remain, buried, like Shakespeare's corpse, in the receiving earth. But the Birthplace – well, it's right there, on Henley Street, where it's always been, big as life. Big enough not to miss a small tile or two.

Shakespeare would be stunned. Because never did it occur to him, not even as he lay dying in the early spring of 1616, that multitudes would seek out the site where he was born, let alone that his house would become his chief monument and memorial. Yet that's what happened.

Others made it happen, and not overnight. It took generations. Shakespeare's birthplace, so fixed, so bulkily emphatic, appears as if it has survived the centuries intact and unchanged, floating down the river of time from his age to ours. The truth is rather more turbulent: the Birthplace as we know it is nothing like the Birthplace as it once was, including as it was to Shakespeare himself.

How the Birthplace *became* the Birthplace – how an ordinary family home was transformed into the worldwide centre of the Shakespeare trade – is a singular and fascinating story. And it's the story I tell in this book. Having studied and taught Shakespeare for three decades, I am struck by how the changing fortunes of the Birthplace mirror perfectly the changing attitudes toward Shakespeare over the past four hundred years. The house was neglected in the seventeenth century, just as Shakespeare's life story was then neglected. It didn't attract tourists until well into the eighteenth century, when new editions of the plays made Shakespeare more popular. In the late nineteenth century, it turned into a museum, just as Shakespeare himself turned into the god of Victorian idolatry. Now, it's a costumed history theme park with a light touch of pedagogy, the anchor site in the well-known Shakespeare tourist trail.

In the pages ahead, I want to reveal the hidden story of Shakespeare's house, the story of how a Tudor family home was turned into the tourist-thronged heritage site that we know it as today. This unlikely yet enduring transformation was more or less achieved by the start of the twentieth century, which is where this book logically ends. The years since have witnessed not so much further evolution in the house's identity but rather a growing professionalism in how the Birthplace and its adjacent library and archival collection are run and made accessible to the public. Though it now presents itself as merely factual, the Birthplace has never been a neutral place. One way or another, sometimes by design, and sometimes by neglect, this house has constructed different versions of Shakespeare and sanctioned our relationship to them.

This strange eventful history, much of it concealed for centuries, is appealing purely as a tale of wild improbability: Shakespeare's descendants turned the house ramshackle, posterity's cold indifference, fake relics – the sword Shakespeare brandished while acting in *Hamlet*, the quill pen he used to write it – peddled to the first gullible tourists, devout pilgrims either defaced or adorned the Birthplace's walls (depending on your point of view) with their scribbled signatures, P.T. Barnum threatened to dismantle the house and rebuild it in his 'American Museum' on Broadway and, in a last humiliation, Shakespeare's house was sold at auction like dairy cattle from a Warwickshire farm.

Yet this same history, I believe, also tells a larger story, the story of how Shakespeare understood the world and how the world has understood Shakespeare. That is why so many millions have journeyed to this one particular old house, stood on its doorstep, knocked on the door and, in a collapsing moment of past and present, waited hopefully for Shakespeare to let them inside. Let us, in this book, do the same. Please don't steal anything.

PART ONE

Shakespeare and the World

1

On the Right Hand of Avon

'Will we return unto thy father's house'
THE TAMING OF THE SHREW (4.3.55)

In the 1530s, late in Henry VIII's reign, a farmer named Richard Shakespeare lived in the English hilltop village of Snitterfield. A husbandman – master of his own household, not somebody else's ward or hireling – he rented a cottage in the Warwickshire countryside, along with land for growing crops and pastures where his sheep and cattle grazed. The eighty acres he leased ran from Snitterfield's main road down to the stream that flowed through the village before merging with the river Avon. Despite being fined by the village council for skipping a session of the manor court, and for letting his pigs run loose, William Shakespeare's grandfather was known to be an honest and worthy man. More than once he drew up the inventory of a deceased neighbour's household goods, an intimate legal duty entrusted to men of upright character only.

The upright Richard Shakespeare and his wife, Abigail, raised two sons, Henry and John. They were not alike. Henry, content with a farmer's life, tilled the soil at nearby Ingon Meadow, when he wasn't busy getting into fights, being thrown into prison for trespass or refusing to pay his share of the tithe to support the local church of St James the Great. His elder brother, John, preferring town to country, set down his ploughshares for good and, sometime in the 1540s, made his way to Stratford-upon-Avon, an hour's easy walk to the southwest. He knew the route, having journeyed there many times before, to help his father sell oats and cheese at the market held every Thursday, where they could also buy a sack of salt and a jar of honey, or even find a new pair of leather boots to replace the ones John had outgrown.

On one particular day, young John Shakespeare arrived in Stratford to begin his apprenticeship under the tutelage of a local craftsman or trader, in whose house he would live during the customary seven years of training. At the end of his apprenticeship, he would be entitled to make his own living and start his own household. There were plenty of trades he could learn: butcher, grocer, baker, tailor, weaver, shoemaker, blacksmith or ironmonger.

The town needed them all. John learned to become a glover – one of just four in Stratford – with a specialty line as a whittawer, meaning he cured and whitened animal hides. Silk-lined white kid gloves were the height of Tudor fashion for women and men alike, although most gloves were made for people who worked outdoors, like farmers or masons. He might, in later years, have passed on the skills of his craft to William, his eldest son.

In leaving Snitterfield and settling in Stratford, John Shakespeare played his part in a great migration taking place across England in the middle of the sixteenth century. Sons, by the thousands, turned their backs on village life or family farms and moved to towns, where they made new lives as skilled artisans or enterprising traders, found new ways to make and spend money and indulged in the new pleasures that town life so temptingly afforded. As the elder son, John inherited property in Snitterfield after his father's death in 1561. Yet by then he was firmly tied to Stratford. On the rise in local politics, he had just been elected a burgess, or town councillor, having served earlier as a constable and official ale-taster. He felt no desire to leave his adopted hometown. After coming into his father's land, he leased it to his brother-in-law instead of farming it himself.

'On the right hand of Avon'

Settled before the Saxons arrived in England in the fifth century, Stratford-upon-Avon first took shape at the place where the old Roman road from Alcester crossed the river Avon. Indeed, the town's very name signifies the meeting point of the road (*straet* in Old English, from the Latin *strata*) and the shallow ford over the river. The original passage over the Avon was just the ford, but a bridge later spanned the river, built first in wood, risky during floods, and then in sturdy stone. Sir Hugh Clopton, Stratford's greatest benefactor, paid for the stone bridge with fourteen arches – more than a thousand feet long – that was built in 1490. You can walk across it still today.

Favourably sited for travel and transport, Stratford thrived as a market town from the late twelfth century onward, after Richard I (the 'Lionhearted') gave his assent for a market to be held on Thursdays. In the thirteenth century, the bishops of Worcester obtained a royal charter granting approval for fairs to be held in Stratford three or four times a year, the longest running just over two weeks. On market days, local farmers sold eggs, butter, cheese and corn to the townspeople while the town's artisans sold lanterns, knives, saddles and shoes to the farmers. Bound close together in their own commercial ecosystem, town and country depended upon each other for their livelihoods. Protected by the Guild of the Holy Cross and successive bishops of Worcester, the town prospered.

In 1540, a few years before John Shakespeare's arrival, the antiquarian John Leland visited Stratford with a highly focused task in mind. He spent six years travelling to towns and cities throughout the kingdom, recording all that he deemed noteworthy about each site. Leland, founder of English local history, titled his compilation *The New Year's Gift, 1546*, which he presented to his sovereign and patron, Henry VIII. The full manuscript, held in the Bodleian Library at Oxford University since 1632, remained unpublished until 1712. Today, a quick Google search makes Leland's nearly five-hundred-year-old text available to anyone.

What a shame this unique work was not printed earlier, because it offers a panorama of the Stratford that Shakespeare's family knew. Here, in modern English, is what Henry VIII's antiquary saw in that proud old town:

The town of Stratford stands upon plain ground on the right hand . . . of Avon, as the water descends. It has two or three very large streets, besides back lanes . . . The bishop of Worcester is lord of the town. The town is reasonably well built of timber. There is once a year a great fair at Holyrood Day [14 September]. The parish church is a fair large piece of work, and stands at the south end of the town.

. . . There is a right goodly chapel in a fair street toward the south end of the town dedicated to the Trinity. The chapel was newly re-edified by one Hugh Clopton, Mayor of London . . . This Clopton built also by the north side of this chapel a pretty house of brick and timber, where he lay in his latter days and died.

There is a grammar school on the south side of this chapel, of the foundation of one Jolif a master of arts, born in Stratford, whereabouts he had some patrimony; and that he gave to this school.

There is also an almshouse of ten poor folk at the south side of the chapel of the Trinity maintained by a Fraternity of the Holy Cross.

Clopton aforesaid made also the great and sumptuous bridge upon Avon at the east end of the town. This bridge [has] fourteen great arches of stone, and a long causeway made of stone and now walled on each side, at the west end of the bridge.

Anybody reading Leland's text for clues about the Stratford that William Shakespeare knew might focus on one site he briefly described: the pretty house of brick and timber that Hugh Clopton had built opposite the Guild Chapel. Stratford's best houses, those belonging to gentlemen and affluent yeomen, were found on Chapel Street. These six words – 'praty howse of brike and tymbar', to use the original spelling – make up the oldest known description of a house where Shakespeare lived. It's not the birthplace, however, but the house of his later life. Of course, Shakespeare was not yet born when Leland visited Stratford, and it was not until 1597 that he purchased (and then, rebuilt) the grand residence long known to locals as New Place. He knew all the other sites that Leland noted – Holy Trinity Church, the Guild Chapel, the King's New School, the row of almshouses and the magnificent stone-arched Clopton Bridge – because he saw them every day while growing up. When you visit Stratford today, you can see them, too, because they have all survived.

Stratford's grid layout – slightly askew, because it follows the irregular contours of the open meadows on which the town was built – was never intensively reshaped. Anyone walking along the streets and lanes of Stratford today is following pretty much the same routes that Shakespeare followed, turning where he turned, crossing where he crossed and looking where he looked.

Looking, but not quite seeing what he saw. Because the detail of Shakespeare's daily life in Stratford is, apart from the few landmarks that Leland named, largely invisible to us. The spire of Holy Trinity Church, where Shakespeare was baptized and buried, was then wooden; the stone spire we see today was built in 1763. The streets that Shakespeare walked were lined with medieval buildings, long since pulled down or gutted by fire. The market crosses have likewise vanished, along with thatched roofs, barns and pigsties in backyards, communal dunghills, unpaved lanes, horse-drawn carts, the charnel house in the churchyard and the green fields that stretched nearly to the back of Shakespeare's childhood home on Henley Street. The street where Shakespeare first lived marked the route to the neighbouring town of Henley-in-Arden, from which its name derived.

The Stratford that John Leland visited in the final years of Henry VIII's reign was, like all English towns, being radically transformed in the anxious aftermath of the Protestant Reformation. In 1547, the crown suppressed Stratford's Guild of the Holy Cross, the wealthy Roman Catholic medieval institution that ran the local grammar school, kept Clopton Bridge in proper repair (vital for transporting the goods on which the town's prosperity depended) and maintained almshouses for the poor. Such were the major elements of civic life; and they were all properly noted by Leland, a man in the king's own employ. Indeed, the Guild undertook many of the responsibilities and provided most of the services associated with a municipal government. Yet like other Roman Catholic institutions across the land, it was summarily dissolved, its property was seized and its assets forfeited. From a secular perspective, the dissolution of the Guild, under whose auspices so much of public life had been reliably conducted, must have left the people of Stratford feeling adrift and unmoored.

Matters soon improved. In 1553, the boy-king Edward VI (or rather, the Regency Council that acted in his name) granted a royal charter to Stratford-upon-Avon, making it an independent and self-governing town, no longer under the patronage, and thus control, of a bishop or an earl. The charter gave townspeople the right to hold markets and the right to create their own by-laws through an elected council – the 'Corporation', still running the show today – consisting of fourteen aldermen and fourteen burgesses and headed by an annually elected High Bailiff, or mayor. John Shakespeare became an alderman in 1565 and was elected bailiff in September 1568. During his year in office, his son William turned five. The Corporation's silver-and-iron mace, behind which he walked in formal processions throughout Stratford, can now be seen at the Shakespeare Birthplace Trust. Importantly, the charter bestowed upon the new Corporation of Stratford the valuable property that had until recently belonged to the Guild of the Holy Cross, thus giving it the wherewithal needed to discharge its civic duties. Stratford, in short, had made the successful transition from one type of town into another. In the not-too-distant past, a religious organization had governed all aspects of life; but now, as if overnight, a secular and municipal institution controlled the town's assets, passed its laws and generally set the tone for daily life.

On Thursdays, Stratford swelled to bursting, as traders and travellers from as far away as Bristol found their way to the open stalls crowded around the Market Cross, where local glovers held pride of place. Here, in microcosm, was Tudor England in full: the gentry, the parson, the schoolmaster, the innkeeper, the midwives, the rowdy and restless apprentices, the day labourers, the skilled artisans who moonlighted as town worthies, the wives who kept their households running, the girls who learned at their mothers' side and the boys who crept unwillingly to school. The whole town whirled with a sense of its own worth and freedom. For an ambitious, entrepreneurial and civic-minded artisan like John Shakespeare of Snitterfield, there was nowhere better to make his way in the world than the prosperous and self-governing town of Stratford-upon-Avon.

'A common muckhill'

For the seven years that he was likely apprenticed to a master glover, John Shakespeare lived in his master's house and formed part of the extended household, along with the master's wife and children, domestic servants and any other apprentices. He had sworn, like every apprentice before him, not to gamble, consort with prostitutes, get married or 'commit any carnal act' with maidservants. His master might have been Thomas Dickson, whose wife, Joan, had also grown up in Snitterfield. But we don't know. What we do know is that once Shakespeare's father was free to set up his own shop, he needed a place to live; and by custom, an artisan's home was also his shop. By 1552, having just attained his majority, the bachelor John Shakespeare was settled in Henley Street, on the town's northern edge. Almost certainly, he then resided in a timber-and-plaster house where, twelve years later, his son William was born.

We know this because on 29 April 1552, the Stratford Court Leet fined him one shilling for dumping faeces into the gutter on Henley Street. There were no drains to carry it away, so it was illegal to let filth accumulate there. John Shakespeare should have carried his slop bucket to the 'common muckhill' at the end of the road. The penalty cost him about two days' earnings – enough to feel the pinch – reflecting the town's concern not just to keep it streets clear but to prevent outbreaks of plague and disease. The document detailing this unsavoury (but not, alas, uncommon) offence lay buried in the archives for nearly three hundred years, until 1845, when antiquarian sleuth Joseph Hunter found it and published it in *New Illustrations of the Life, Studies, and Writings of Shakespeare.*

John Shakespeare must have been talented in the glove trade, because, in October 1556, he acquired two properties in Stratford, a house with garden and croft in nearby Greenhill Street and the eastern wing of the Henley Street house (now presented as the parlour, hall, workshop and rooms above) along with its back garden. Exactly when he bought the western side of the house (now presented as the entrance and back kitchen) we don't know, although likely he acquired it around the same time. Having found himself a roomy house with a large yard in the back, he stayed put in Henley Street until his death, aged about seventy, in 1601. He lived long enough to know that his eldest son had become rich from writing poems and plays and from owning a share in a successful London theatre company, a relatively new form of commercial enterprise.

In 1557, John Shakespeare brought his bride into his new house. She was Mary Arden, daughter of the late Robert Arden, the wealthy farmer from whom his own father had rented a house and surrounding land in Snitterfield. A 'most antient and worthy Family', so commended by William Dugdale, a prominent seventeenth-century antiquary, the Ardens had resided in Warwickshire since before the Norman Conquest. In the social hierarchy of the day, Robert Arden was, at best, minor gentry. Even so, an affluent yeoman farmer like him with such a long lineage would have looked down on the Shakespeare family – his tenants, not his equals – just as he would have looked up to a great landowner like Sir Thomas Lucy of nearby Charlecote Park, whose deer the young William Shakespeare was later alleged to have poached.

Robert Arden died in 1556, and thus never knew that his daughter married into a socially inferior family. In the will he made out shortly before his death, he provided first for his widow and then bestowed upon his daughter Mary the sixty-acre Wilmcote estate known as 'Asbies'. Land was his greatest asset and he left it to his daughter. Doubtless it was intended as her dowry, because not long after her father's death, Mary Arden the Wilmcote heiress wed the up-and-coming Stratford glover John Shakespeare. The precise date remains unknown, because English churches did not then keep marriage registers. What is known is that they made a life together in their home on Henley Street.

'Gulielmus filius Johannes Shakspere'

The newly married man must have felt that he was fortune's favourite. Within a few years of completing his apprenticeship, John Shakespeare owned a house in Henley Street, another one in Greenhill Street and the freehold estate in Wilmcote that formed the chief part of his wife's inheritance. Not yet thirty, he had already surpassed his father's wealth and position. While Mary Arden knew that she had married a little down the social scale, she also knew that her husband was poised to become a man of some importance in Stratford. Before their first wedding anniversary he was named one of the borough's four constables, charged with keeping the peace. It was a big step up from being the official ale-taster, a job that does sound rather more appealing. Greater civic responsibilities soon followed.

Over the next twenty-two years, Mary Shakespeare gave birth in the family home to four sons and four daughters: Joan (1558–1559?), Margaret (1562–63), William (1564–1616), Gilbert (1566–1612), another Joan (1569–1646), Anne (1571–79), Richard (1574–1613) and Edmund (1580–1607). All were christened in nearby Holy Trinity Church and all but one laid to rest there. Edmund, who became an actor, died in London and was buried in St Saviour's Church, now Southwark Cathedral, not far from the Globe and Rose theatres. It was probably his brother William who paid twenty shillings for the tolling of the 'great bell' during the young man's funeral, held in the morning so that his fellow actors, who performed in the afternoon, could attend.

In the Elizabethan age, child mortality was high: one in ten died within a month, one in three before the age of sixteen. Among the eight Shakespeare children, two died in infancy and another in childhood. William, the third child, but the first to survive into adolescence, was baptized on 26 April 1564, as we know from the now-legendary Latin entry in the official parchment copy of the original (but long lost) parish register: '*Gulielmus filius Johannes Shakspere*'. He, too, might have died before his first birthday. The dreaded plague hit Stratford that summer, claiming its first victim, the apprentice Oliver Gunn, when Willian Shakespeare was eleven weeks old. Before the calamity passed, it killed more than two hundred people in Stratford, about one in seven. Deaths from plague clustered in families, because when disease-carrying rats infested a house, few who lived there survived. An entire household could perish in a week. Four of their neighbour Robert Greene's children died, but the Shakespeare family, who lived three doors away, was spared entirely.

John and Mary Shakespeare mourned the loss of three daughters – they paid eightpence for Holy Trinity's bell to be tolled while Anne's coffin was carried to the church graveyard, one penny for each year of her short life – but they would not have felt that death's cold hand rested longer upon their house than any other. Touchingly, their firstborn, Joan, whose span of life numbered months, not years, lived on in a later daughter, also named Joan. This second Joan, who married the hatter William Hart, died in her late seventies and outlived her siblings, resided in one part or another of the Henley Street house all her long life. It was Joan Hart's descendants who also dwelled in the house, came eventually to own it, let it fall into disrepair, rented it out and, facing bankruptcy, sold it early in the nineteenth century. But we are getting ahead of ourselves.

2

To Be Wise in Building a House

.

Sometime around 1485, when Richard III met his death in the Battle of
Bosworth Field, someone built a house on the site where, eighty years later,
William Shakespeare was born. Lived in and refurbished by unknown
owners before Shakespeare's father acquired it in the 1550s, the house in its
earliest state remains forever lost to us. But it was lost to the Shakespeare
family, too. For them, and everyone else at the time, restoring a house to its
original layout and appearance made no sense. Houses were meant to be
improved: advancing with the times, not staying stuck in the past. Though
it's now hard to believe, so easily are we seduced by the nostalgic charm of
old buildings, people in Elizabethan England wanted their houses to be
modern.

Proud of their modernity, each generation left its own refining mark on a
house: a gabled roof, a larger garden, wood panelling on the walls or glass
in the windows. The most visible sign of Elizabethan home improvement
was the 'jetty' – from the French *jeter*, to throw – a cantilevered upper story
that projected over the floor below and out toward the street. These
precarious overhangs, now reproduced on countless postcards, were, to the
people who built them, not quaintly backward-looking but stridently
progressive. The outward thrust of the higher story, with its double or triple
gables, boldly announced that the building, exceeding, as it were, its own
structure, was throwing itself into the future.

There's something anachronistic, then, about the desire to restore the
Birthplace to what it was like when William Shakespeare lived there, for the
plain reason that the house was itself rebuilt, renovated, updated and
improved over the years, including by Shakespeare's own family. Its material
history was always dynamic, never static. The architectural historian
Nicholas Molyneux has recently claimed that the Birthplace in its current
form dates from the 1580s at the earliest, and more likely from the 1590s,
meaning that John Shakespeare demolished the house he had bought (or a
fire did the job for him) and then built a new one in its place. If so, then
William Shakespeare never lived in the house long accepted as his birthplace,
although he certainly knew it from when he visited his parents and siblings.
Perhaps he even paid for it, using his new wealth to enhance or enlarge his

father's house. This blurred architectural history puts nothing in jeopardy. Because restoring the house on Henley Street has been *our* way to preserve the Elizabethan past, an exercise in nostalgia-filled fantasy that appealed but little to Elizabethan people, Shakespeare included.

Wattle-and-daub

The Middle Ages bequeathed to the Tudor period a simple and popular design for a townhouse. Built mainly of timber, it had a narrow frontage to the street, front and back rooms on each floor, with a long court or garden to the rear. The front door opened directly into the 'hall', which was not a corridor (as we use the word today) but a formal space, a household's main dining and living area. Other rooms led off of the hall, including the kitchen and workspaces. Bedchambers were found upstairs, one room connecting to another, leaving little space for privacy. If the house had a loft, it was used for storing grain or bacon, or possibly rough sleeping quarters for servants or apprentices. Sometimes called a 'unit-house', it served as the template for dwellings in all English towns throughout the sixteenth and seventeenth centuries. The Shakespeare family home, like many others of its time and place, elaborated on this basic design.

Situated among a row of similar residences on the north side of Henley Street, John Shakespeare's house stood on a quarter-acre plot, or burbage, as it was then called, about sixty feet wide and 150 feet long, the standard dimensions stipulated in the town charter. A row of elms might be planted between plots to mark the boundary line. At the very least, an earthen ridge divided one property from another. The Shakespeare family home was originally a two-storey, timber frame built upon a cellar and a low foundation wall of stone. It was built not by an architect, but by local artisans: stone masons, bricklayers, carpenters, sawyers, coopers, turners, painters, glaziers and even the humble carter, who each day hauled materials to the building site and at day's end took away the accumulated rubbish.

Once the land was cleared, and the cellar dug, the masons laid a stone base around the house's perimeter, rising to about three feet above the ground. The blue-grey stone was quarried in Wilmcote, where Shakespeare's mother, Mary Arden, grew up. Then the carpenters took over, building the frame from oak trees felled in the nearby Forest of Arden (the name for the green-world setting in *As You Like* It). Visitors to the Birthplace today can see that some of the wood still bears the hack marks left by the broad-axe when the trees were first cut down. Beams varied in length and thickness depending on how much weight they carried. Thick vertical posts, capable of bearing the heaviest load, were anchored in the house's corners to hold up the entire structure. Upstairs, thick horizontal beams spanned the length of each room to support the much thinner floorboards placed over them and running in the opposite direction. The timber shell included window frames and the roof. Windows tended to be small, and often were bare openings – glass cost a great deal of money – with a wooden shutter affixed to the frame with an iron hinge. The roof was covered with wooden boards over which straw thatch or clay tiles were placed.

Like pieces in a puzzle, all the squared-off planks in the house locked tightly together, their joints secured by large wooden pegs, with few iron nails or brackets needed. Craftsmen responsible for securing timber frames in this way were called 'joiners'. The company of rude mechanicals that performs 'Pyramus and Thisbe' in *A Midsummer Night's Dream* includes just such a joiner: the fittingly named 'Snug', whose proficiency, however, never extended beyond making simple joint stools. Cast as the lion, Snug fears that he will forget his lines, which consist mostly of roaring.

Walls were made from a lattice of woven sticks and twigs ('wattle') slotted into the vertical spaces between the oak beams. Once affixed, the wattle was covered ('daubed') with a thick spreadable paste of clay, mud, grass, hair and animal dung. The dried surface was whitewashed to give it an agreeable, if not entirely smooth, appearance. A wall panel in the upstairs birthroom has been removed to reveal the original wattle-and-daub lattice underneath, most of which was removed in the nineteenth century and replaced by brick and cement infill. The same has been done at Anne Hathaway's Cottage. This symmetry of exposed timber beams and plastered surfaces is called 'half-timber': because half the wall surface is wood and the other half plaster. In Stratford, a town ringed by forests, wood was plentiful but still expensive. The closer the beams in a house were spaced – more wood, less plaster – the wealthier its owner. The ones in the Birthplace are nine inches wide and set nine inches apart, about average for an Elizabethan family home.

Once the walls, stairs and roof were in place, the masons returned to build the brick fireplaces (one in each room) and the chimneystacks above them, each made of local blue lias stone. They also laid the paving stones on the ground floor, fitting them together over a timber frame. Wood flooring would have soon rotted away, while stone prevented rising damp from the soil below. Meanwhile, the carpenters busied themselves hanging the wooden doors, among the last features of a house to be installed. Plumbers were then unknown because Tudor houses had neither toilets nor running water. Water was drawn from an outdoor well and carried, bucket by heavy bucket, into the main house or an outbuilding for cooking, cleaning and, sometimes, bathing.

'The Great Rebuilding'

In the 1950s, the historian W.G. Hoskins coined the term 'The Great Rebuilding' to describe a period of dramatic change in housebuilding and domestic habits that occurred in England between 1570 and 1640, a period that started just after Shakespeare's birth and ended a few decades after his death. Hoskins' thesis was that yeomen farmers, town tradesmen and the minor gentry – in short, people like Shakespeare's parents – sold their goods at higher and higher prices, and then invested the additional income in their houses. They did so, he argued, to emulate the upper classes, whose far more comfortable homes offered far greater privacy. Though it has come under recent challenge, the basic insight of 'The Great Rebuilding' still holds. Something decisive happened to the middling classes in Tudor and Jacobean England: they became house-proud.

Traditionally, many parts of a house – shutters, doors, wall panelling, chimney pieces, staircases, floorboards and window frames – moved from one dwelling to another. Detachable, they could be sold separately from the dwelling itself or follow their owners into new houses. But as Elizabethan families lavished more money, and more care, on their homes, they began to think of its various elements as forming a single, integrated whole. Over time, furnishings solidified into fixtures and what previously could have been removed was now secured firmly in place. The simple act of nailing down a floorboard, to use a deceptively trivial example, reveals just how deeply Elizabethans became attached to home improvements. An unfastened floorboard resting on top of ceiling beams was tentative, removeable at any moment. But a board nailed tightly into a cross beam became integral to the house itself; it spoke permanency.

In such ways, people in Shakespeare's time came to regard their homes as personal legacies. Like the land a family owned, its house should remain intact – ideally, be improved – and then passed on to the next generation, not torn apart or sold to the highest bidder. When Shakespeare died, in 1616, he owned two houses in Stratford – New Place and his father's old house on Henley Street – and nowhere does his will mention dismantling, stripping or selling them. Those houses were bequeathed to his daughter and heir Susanna Hall, whole and entire.

'A Spyce Morter of Brasse'

William Shakespeare grew up in a home with six principal rooms: hall, parlour and workshop, all downstairs, with three bedchambers upstairs. Nathaniel Hawthorne, when he visited the house in the 1850s, complained that it was 'smaller and humbler' than he expected. Shakespeare, he felt, deserved a birthplace more palatial (a house of seven gables, perhaps). John and Mary Shakespeare, however, didn't think their house was small and humble, especially after they enlarged it, perhaps in the early 1580s. More rooms in the house meant not just more privacy, but also a more segregated daily life. In a medieval cottage, a whole family lived in one large room. But the Shakespeare family, like their neighbours on Henley Street, used separate rooms for cooking, eating, entertaining and sleeping. By and large, their daily activities were dispersed throughout their house.

You move through houses like the Birthplace not by following corridors – such transitional spaces were found only in much grander homes – but by passing directly from room to room, each dedicated to its own particular purpose. Though roomy, the house does feel like a rabbit warren: smallish spaces, each linked one to another. Indeed, the Birthplace has but a single cross-passage, leading from the front door directly into the back garden. You cannot stride at length through Shakespeare's house, but only wander through it, twisting, turning, peering and ducking as you go. Nor are there long interior vistas to appreciate, but only glimpses of an adjacent room or a few steps on a narrow staircase before it angles out of sight. Now, just as then, Shakespeare's house offers itself only in parts.

Visitors today enter the Birthplace through a side door and step into a small front room that although owned by John Shakespeare was not initially part of his family's home. Known by tradition as 'Joan Hart's cottage' – named after Shakespeare's sister, who later lived there – this small, separate dwelling was not merged with the main house until the 1850s, when the entire site was renovated to give the Birthplace a much grander feel.

From there, visitors move into the parlour, then through to the larger hall and finally over the cross-passage and into what had been John Shakespeare's workshop. The entire lower level has a stone floor, some of it believed to be original. Uneven and rudely squared, it marked, nonetheless, a significant improvement over the traditional ground floor of compacted earth covered with straw rushes. A central staircase leads to the room above the hall. From there, visitors who turn left enter the chamber over the workshop, while those turning right proceed directly into the birthroom. These six rooms – and these six rooms only – form the house where Shakespeare was born and grew up.

A narrow staircase just behind the birthroom leads to rooms added in the early seventeenth century, decades after Shakespeare had lived there. The downstairs room now presented as the back kitchen is where tourists once came to see 'Shakespeare's chair'. The open hearth was large enough to feature an inglenook, where on a cold night one or two people could sit cozily in a recessed space next to the warming fire. And that's where Shakespeare's chair was put on display. This picturesque scene, reproduced in countless engravings made in the eighteenth and nineteenth centuries, was entirely fabricated: the chair never belonged to Shakespeare and the room itself was a later addition.

Back in the original house, the parlour looks barren today, but in Shakespeare's time it was likely crammed with items for cooking and serving food, from brass pots hanging on the wall to pewter plates stored in the cupboard, while salt cellars and brass spice mortars were kept within reach to season any dish cooking over the fire. The messier work of preparing food – gutting fish, dressing meat, shelling peas – was likely done in a timber outbuilding, long since demolished. An adjacent buttery was used for storing liquids, while bread, grains and other dry goods were kept in the pantry.

Provisions not needed throughout the day were stored in the stone cellar, the part of the house that has undergone the least renovation over the past four hundred years. In the sixteenth century, the daily tasks of storing, preparing, cooking and serving food took place in different spaces, extending well beyond our modern idea of a single kitchen distinct from other rooms in the house.

Mary Shakespeare worked hard, but a serving girl would have scrubbed the stone floor, cleaned out the hearth and tended the fire. For the mistress herself, there was butter to churn, fruit to preserve, bacon to cure, beer to brew and pickles and pies to make. Stirring the pot on the open hearth was but the last step in a long, laborious process that began in the garden, the piggery and the hen house.

But there was yet more work to do. Her household's milliner-in-chief, Shakespeare's mother spun wool and flax to make and mend clothing, blankets and tablecloths. When not in use – in the parlour, to avoid spills and food stains – her spinning wheel would have been stowed away down in the cellar or up in the eaves. She kept a medicine chest for 'kitchen physic', its cubby holes and drawers stuffed to capacity with herbs, ointments and potions for treating injuries and illnesses. Passing on the recipes she had learned from her own mother, Mary Shakespeare taught her daughter Joan to make hog's liver pudding and to use mint leaves for an upset stomach.

In medieval times, the open hall with a fireplace was a house's main living and dining space. Despite the constant presence of smoke, it was the largest, warmest, and, hence, most frequently occupied room. For a long time previously there had been chimneys in palaces, monasteries and grand manor houses, giving some warmth and comfort to multiple rooms in those large buildings. But only in the sixteenth century did they appear in the more modest homes of English farmers and town dwellers, people like John and Mary Shakespeare.

The chimney revolutionized domestic life. People of modest means could now live upstairs, instead of using their loft space for storage and meat curing. Without a chimney, the continuous upward drift of smoke made the higher floor uninhabitable but ideal for a smokehouse. Extra room was gained by creating an enclosed space above the hall, which, thanks to the chimney, no longer had to be open to the roof. And because the chimneystack ran up through this new room, it, too, could have a fireplace, making it a coveted sleeping chamber.

'Household stuffe'

Visitors today have to pass through two rooms in the Birthplace before reaching the hall. In Shakespeare's time, however, visitors stepped directly into the hall after entering through the front door on Henley Street. The hall was where Shakespeare's family dined, prayed together, played music, enjoyed backgammon or chess, told stories – 'In winter's tedious nights', Richard II counsels his queen, 'sit by the fire / With good old folks, and let them tell thee tales' (4.1.40–1) – and spent the minimal leisure time they had. As the room where guests were received, it was also where a household openly displayed its wealth, whether through wood panelling, pewter flatware or lead glass windows. Literally and symbolically, it was the house's centre, the only room where everyone gathered.

John Shakespeare was for a time affluent enough to have indulged, if he so wished, in the luxury of a few glass windows: small triangular or diamond-shaped pieces of glass set into a wooden lattice in the surrounding frame, as seen throughout the Birthplace today. His neighbour Anne Hiccox, a tailor's widow, had several glass windows in her house. A tailor earned roughly the same as a glover, so we can safely assume that if the Hiccox family could afford glass windows then so could the Shakespeare family. Glass, being expensive, was likely used only for the front windows, where it could arouse the envy of others. Most windows would have been covered with small strips of much cheaper (and surprisingly translucent) polished cow horn, slotted into a cross-hatched leaden lattice.

Household inventories from the time suggest that ten or so people could easily gather in the hall, most sitting on chairs or joint stools, while others crowded onto benches or perched atop a low chest in which blankets, sheets, tablecloths and table napkins were stored. In *The Taming of the Shrew*, Gremio tries to win Bianca's favour by bragging about the luxury items kept safe in his 'cypress chests': fine linens, pear-studded cushions, gold needlework, pewter, brass and 'all things that belongs / To house or housekeeping' (3.1.355, 360). The chest's inset front panels could be decorated – one surviving chest, from the 1570s, shows the Old Testament story of Judith holding the head of the beheaded Holofernes – but the lid was kept plain so that it could be used for seating. Single chairs were prized, with the best ones reserved for the exclusive use of the house's master and mistress.

Anywhere anybody sat in an ordinary Elizabethan home was, by our standards, uncomfortable, but at least the chairs had backs, however unyieldingly straight. The hard seat of a wooden chair might be softened with a sack of wool or a horsehair-stuffed cushion. Upholstered chairs were a luxury affordable to only the wealthiest households.

In Elizabethan folklore, witches and ghosts disguised themselves as humble joint stools, the better to go about in secret their unearthly business. When Macbeth stares at Banquo's ghost seated at the banquet table, his wife reassures him that nothing is there: 'When all's done, / You look but on a stool' (3.4.63–4). Yet it's not so clear that she's right. Is the joint stool really only a joint stool? Or is it, as her guilty husband fears, possessed by a supernatural spirit? When it came to Elizabethan furniture, you could never be completely certain that it wasn't bewitched.

The entire household – master and mistress, children, apprentices, servants – took their main meal at midday, seated around a large wooden trestle table with detachable parts. If there weren't enough chairs, the lowest members of the household ate standing up. When not used, the table was dismantled and placed against a wall to free up living space. Seated at the head of the table, the master of the house made his authority visible with the simple gesture of resting his arms on the arms of his chair. No other chair in the room had arms. He looked like a king occupying his throne. And in his own house, every master was every inch a king.

For Shakespeare, the idea that people living under the same roof would eat at different times, or somewhere other than at the communal table or while absorbed in doing something else, would have felt utterly alien. This is not to idealize Elizabethan family life but rather to emphasize that an Elizabethan household was meant to function as a rule-obeying, cohesive unit. Family unity was expressed, day after well-ordered day, in how they used the rooms in their house.

Much of the furniture in John Shakespeare's hall – high narrow storage cupboard, dining table, benches – would strike us as massive and crude, but that's a misleading impression. The dark patina of old oak, which deepens over time, obscures the reality that when such furniture was new, it was as light as modern oak. Tables, chests and cupboards may well have been painted, their original bright appearance long since faded. Cushions, table carpets and other textiles would have softened the furniture's hard edges, adding comfort, texture and yet more vibrant colour. Above all, these great blocks of wood symbolized to Elizabethans both durability and long life. Furniture was often inherited, just as the house itself was passed down from father to firstborn son. Or, in Shakespeare's case, from father to firstborn daughter. He bequeathed his 'Household stuffe' – a phrase he had used two decades earlier, in *The Taming of the Shrew* – to his elder daughter Susanna and her husband, John Hall, even though they were hardly penurious.

No one in 1616 would have thought any of that unusual. Indeed, people in Shakespeare's time would be puzzled by our modern compulsion to buy new furniture merely to follow the latest trend. The idea that perfectly useable furniture could somehow fall out of fashion, and thus need replacing, made no sense to them. When Elizabethans bought household goods, it was not so much to acquire new items as to acquire more opulent versions of what they already possessed. To replace a wooden spoon with a silver one, a joint stool with a carved chair or a horsehair mattress with one softened by feathers. That, they understood. Because as soon as a family had enough money to trade up, they did.

'By a painted cloth be kept in awe'

William Shakespeare may well have been raised in a house with no books other than the mass-produced Geneva Bible, the most significant English translation of scripture until the King James version, and maybe a psalter or a copy of Archbishop Cranmer's *Book of Common Prayer*, first published in 1559. Such books would be useful to John Shakespeare, who was probably literate, given his civic duties and business dealings, in his role as the household's spiritual leader and teacher. Other sorts of books – romances, histories, poems, tales from classical mythology – were unlikely to number among his possessions. True, Shakespeare read a great deal in his youth, but mostly at school and mostly in Latin: Ovid's *Metamorphoses*, Virgil's *Aeneid*, the comedies of Plautus and the tragedies of Seneca. That's where his love of poetry and drama started, in the classroom. Also, perhaps, from watching plays occasionally performed by visiting acting companies, like the Earl of Leicester's Men, in the Guildhall or a Stratford innyard. The endearing image of Shakespeare the boy reading book after book at home, eagerly, and perhaps secretly, by the midnight flicker of a lone candle, is a concocted fantasy.

Though it may have sheltered few books, John Shakespeare's house did not lack for decoration. Rich woven tapestries, called an 'arras', hung a foot or two in front of thick stone walls in castles and manor houses, providing ornament and keeping in the fire's warmth. Polonius is stabbed to death by Hamlet through an arras, behind which he had hidden to eavesdrop on the prince and his mother, Gertrude. But in humble town dwellings, like those in Stratford, painted cloths hung from the timber and plaster walls, not just in the main rooms but also in the upper bedchambers. They were not hung in the master's workshop, where wall space was needed for shelves and storage. Linen sheets were stiffened with a glue paste – 'size', made from boiled animal bones – and then cut into strips to fit around doors and windows and to hang from ceiling to floor.

Biblical or classical scenes were painted on the cloths in vivid colours, sometimes with an accompanying moral epigram stencilled at the bottom. One of the few surviving cloths, now in the Shakespeare Birthplace Trust, shows the Old Testament story of Eliezer and Rebecca at the well, a scene doubtless chosen by a husband to promote wifely virtue. In *Love's Labour's Lost*, Costard, a country lad, refers to a painted cloth depicting Alexander the Great, a figure out of historical legend. Other times, they were covered in geometric patterns or depicted the natural world, flowers or forest greenery, bringing the outdoors indoors. It was Flemish tapestry on the cheap. Perhaps it was their artistic inelegance, or their finger-wagging pedantry, that made Shakespeare remember these homespun textiles with a jaded eye in his poem *The Rape of Lucrece*: 'Who fears a sentence or an old man's saw / Shall by a painted cloth be kept in awe' (244–5).

When Mary Shakespeare's father, Robert Arden, died in 1556, the inventory of his Wilmcote farmhouse listed eleven painted cloths, two hanging in the entryway, five in the main hall, with the rest adorning the upstairs bedrooms. In an ordinary Elizabethan home, a home unlikely to be richly decorated, such wall hangings must have been enjoyable, not least because they injected flashes of colour into dark, candlelit rooms dominated by heavy wooden furniture. The prosperous yeoman farmer Robert Arden had money to spend and he spent it on eleven painted cloths.

'Like a glover's paring-knife'

The room in the Birthplace furthest away from the parlour was once John Shakespeare's large, windowed and unheated workshop, where he and his glovers-in-training spent the day, when they weren't in the backyard curing and dying animal hides or selling their wares under the town's market cross on Thursdays. The workshop took up a good deal of space, inside and out. Finished items were placed on a shelf near the front window overlooking Henley Street, to entice any passers-by in a mood to spend money. At the other end of the room, near the back garden, was the busy workshop, where cured animal hides were cut, shaped and stitched into gloves, belts, satchels, purses or leather aprons. Some of those finished products dangled on hooks above the open hatch front door: eye-catching, but hard for any mischievous passer-by to steal. Plenty of knives, shears, rawhide mallets, bevellers, needles, eyelets and threads cluttered the worktables and hung on the walls. Years later, in *The Merry Wives of Windsor*, Shakespeare likens a glover's circular paring-knife – a tool of his father's trade, an object once daily familiar to him – to a 'great round beard' (1.4.19). Outside, and as far back as the Guild Pits, flayed animal skins, sourced from local butchers, were scraped clean of hair on the outer side and blood or gristle on the inner side. Then they were boiled, stretched, dyed and dried. A noxious and messy undertaking, best kept far away from everyone else.

'The birthroom'

Upstairs were three chambers, including the one long accepted as Shakespeare's birthroom. A rough-hewn wooden floor ran the entire length of the upper story. Today, those rooms are open to the roof, except for the birthroom, whose uneven low plaster ceiling was installed some time before the nineteenth century. The unseen attic houses the Birthplace's air conditioning units, installed in 1994. Surviving mortices in the adjacent rooms confirm that they, too, were originally ceilinged and so were used as bed chambers. Yet in Elizabethan times, upper rooms in family homes rarely had a single purpose; a bedroom could easily double as a storage room.

The people who slept under John and Mary Shakespeare's roof weren't just their five children, but also the male apprentices. So that everyone had a place to sleep, beds outnumbered chairs in the upstairs rooms. And those beds were of different kinds, some freestanding, perhaps, but more likely they were bedsteads that could be dismantled and packed up or simple pallets on the floor that could be quickly rolled up, all to make space for using the room in other ways. It was not so hard to convert a bedroom, used mainly at night, into another sort of room during the day. After all, in a bedroom only three items were needed: a bed, a small chest for storing clothes and a pisspot.

John Shakespeare's house was large, but not so large that everyone had their own room. With only three chambers available upstairs, some people likely slept in the downstairs parlour. A four-postered marital bed, adorned with a canopy and embroidered curtains, was frequently the most valuable piece of furniture in an ordinary Elizabethan home. As such, it was often displayed in the parlour, where guests could admire it, in the same way that guests today might admire an expensive Oriental rug or the latest flat-screen television. Wherever the bed was kept, that's where wife and husband slept. Removing the marital bed to an upper floor, a clear sign of the increased valued accorded to domestic privacy, occurred later, in the seventeenth century, and then only gradually.

Marital beds were considered part of a house's fixtures, and so were not counted, as flock and trundle beds were, among the owner's goods and chattel. When Shakespeare left his wife the 'second-best bed', as he famously stipulated in his will, he wasn't insulting her, as some have long believed. Rather, he was looking after her; because the best bed, the one that Anne herself had slept in for years, now belonged to the house's new owner, their daughter Susanna. Shakespeare, far from demeaning his widow, was ensuring that she ended up with the best of the remaining beds.

The Stratford tanner Henry Field died in 1592. A year later, his son Richard, who had entered the book trade in London, printed three non-dramatic poems, including *Venus and Adonis*, written by his childhood friend William Shakespeare. Henry Field's inventory reveals that a feather bed was kept in the parlour, along with a profusion of pillows and bed linen. The house's other rooms contained only flock beds and truckle beds, smaller and less comfortable. The evidence points in one direction only: Henry Field and his wife slept downstairs, while everybody else slept upstairs.

John and Mary Shakespeare may have done just the same. Tradition alone claims that they slept in the upper chamber now shown as the birthroom, a tradition dating only from the 1760s – two centuries after the fact – by which time domestic sleeping arrangements had altered. It's entirely possible, then, that William Shakespeare was born in the downstairs parlour and not in the room that has long since become his natal shrine.

'Fatting like a swine'

Though Stratford was a densely built town, the natural world was fully present within it. Spreading elm trees lined the streets and thorn hedges divided one householder's burbage plot from another. Town dwellings were also small subsistence farms, and so part of the land behind John Shakespeare's house was dedicated to a working garden and orchard, both producing food for the family. It was not a retreat for strolling or quiet meditation. Fruit trees were planted along garden walls to keep space free for vegetables, flowers and herbs, all grown together to ward off pests. Fragrant lavender grown in the garden today was likely once also planted there by Mary Shakespeare, but for a purpose far more practical, lavender tea being a favourite Elizabethan home remedy for headaches. Even flowers were grown with utility in mind. Roses and violets made delicious seasonings for cakes.

At the far end of the backyard plot, near the Guild Pits, stood a barn, for stabling horses and storing grain. Even in town, pigs were easy to keep. Fattened on peelings and food scraps from the slop bucket – nothing went to waste – they provided the family with bacon. In *The Two Noble Kinsmen*, Palamon, nephew of the king of Thebes, urges immediate action lest anyone think him idle, 'fatting like a swine' (3.6.11). Pigs were usually killed in autumn so that they didn't need to be fed in wintertime, when fresh food was scarcer. In those lean winter months, the family lived off preserved meats, fruits and vegetables. Chickens could be kept year-round in the yard, for eggs or extra meat. There may have been a single cow for milking, although many families bought their butter and cheese at the weekly market.

The calfskin and other hides – horse, sheep, deer, goat – that John Shakespeare needed to make leather goods did not come from his own livestock but rather were supplied by local butchers. Hence, the erroneous speculation in later years that he himself was a butcher. Fear of contaminated meat from a slaughterhouse ensured that, by law, glove-making and butchering were separate trades carried out in separate places. No man could do both on the same site. Nor would those different lines of work have suited the same type of person. Butchery was fast, while glove-making was slow. It took six months to turn animal skin into leather and that was just the first step.

'Permit no common pissing place'

Sanitary arrangements were by our standards primitive. During the day, an outhouse ('house of easement') or open pit would be used, both situated as far as possible from the main house. Chamber pots were kept near the beds at night and then emptied first thing each morning. Falstaff, in the second part of *Henry IV*, uses a popular slang term for a chamber pot, calling for a servant to 'empty the jordan' (2.4.33).

Elizabethan people believed that diseases were caused by toxic vapours, no one back then knowing anything of germs or bacterial infections, and so they worried that fumes from urine and faeces would make them ill. There was fresh air and there was pestilential air, and they had to stay separate. That's why faeces were thrown onto the common dunghill and not dumped in the open street. If only John Shakespeare had observed that public health rule. He could have saved himself a shilling.

In 1540, the physician, and former Carthusian monk, Andrew Boorde wrote *The Book for to Learn a Man to be Wise in Building of his House*, urging his readers to 'permit no common pissing place to be about the house ... And beware of ... pissing in chimneys, so that all evil and contagious airs may be expelled, and clean air kept unputrified.' The Tudors were obsessed with ridding their houses of urine. They didn't always succeed; otherwise, Andrew Boorde would not have issued his health warning. If I had to bet whether rascally little William Shakespeare pissed in the chimney or brainy little William Shakespeare kept a stack of bedside books, I'd put my money on pissing.

'This night's great business'

With so much labour needed to keep the household running, in addition to the business of making and selling leather goods, John Shakespeare's home didn't feel peaceful or serene for most of the day and into the night. Wattle-and-daub interior walls provided little sound insulation. Walnut shells were sometimes packed in the spaces between the floor joists, a largely ineffective remedy for what Elizabethans clearly felt was a big problem: their houses were too noisy.

Today, the house's silence is broken only by the visitors who ask questions and the guides who genially answer them. But when Shakespeare lived there, the house was quiet only on Sundays, empty while the family worshipped at Holy Trinity Church. At any other time, it would be full of noises: creaking floorboards, clattering pots and pans, pounding hammers, apprentices shouting, an infant wailing, a fire crackling, a kettle hissing, a father leading his family in prayer, a pig grunting and street life buzzing on the other side of the front door.

Ironically, the more we feel that our homes today have been infiltrated by work, the closer we come to the collapse of boundaries between home and work in Shakespeare's own life. And yet, the comparison isn't quite exact; because letting work come in through the front door, so to speak, or searching for it on one gadget or another, feels like it violates our domestic privacy – we should be better at resisting it – whereas for Shakespeare's family there was no such thing as home life untouched by work.

Their work lives and home lives intertwined, Elizabethan wives and husbands related to each other not just as spouses and parents, but as fellow workers engaged in valuable economic activity. The Macbeths, though their actions are criminal, speak to each other like partners in a law firm. 'You shall put / This night's great business into my dispatch' (1.5.65–6), Lady Macbeth instructs her husband. We know where Shakespeare first got the idea of spousal collaboration: from watching his own parents work as a team.

Friends and neighbours

Ever since the mid-nineteenth century, when its adjacent houses were demolished, Shakespeare's Birthplace has stood out like a landmark, detached from its surroundings, granting to the world's greatest author a befitting, dignified isolation. But the young William Shakespeare did not know that he was destined to become the world's greatest author. Nor did he think that his house was remarkable, because it wasn't. The house where he was born and raised stood in the midst of similarly undistinguished dwellings on the north side of Henley Street. Built mainly of timber and plaster, most of those houses had a ground floor workshop where the master ran his business, some had jetties, some a gable roof or a bay window, a few doubled as inns, but none were more than two or three stories high. Just as tight joinery held together a house's beams, so the houses that lined both sides of Henley Street were held together by their common architecture and appearance.

Most of the people whom John and Mary Shakespeare knew in Stratford lived their entire lives in the town. So perhaps we shouldn't be too surprised that the historical record tells us the names of their Henley Street neighbours, the people that William and his siblings treated, so their parents hoped, with courtesy and respect. To the right of the house, as you face it, were once two small cottages, purchased by Edward Willis in 1575 and later converted into the Bell Inn. The next house over, now the Birthplace's giftshop, belonged to the blacksmith Richard Hornby, whose family remained well-known in Stratford for many years. In the early nineteenth century, Mary Hornby, his descendant by marriage, lived in the Birthplace, where she entertained growing numbers of visitors with bogus relics and equally bogus stories about the house's most famous resident. Much more about her in the pages ahead. Next to Richard Hornby's house stood one owned by the Corporation of Stratford. When Shakespeare was a child, the glover Gilbert Bradley lived there, and then later a whittawer named Wilson. For Shakespeare's father, these two neighbours were also his rivals, because they all made similar goods and competed for the same customers. In 1566, John and Mary named their second son Gilbert. Children were often named after friends of the parents, not just after relatives, and so it seems that the Bradley and Shakespeare families stayed on good terms.

On the left side of the Birthplace stood the home of the draper George Badger. In late January 1597, he paid fifty shillings to John Shakespeare for the toft, a strip of land eighteen inches wide, that ran between their houses from Henley Street back to the Guild Pits, a length of about eighty-four feet. The original deed of conveyance is now part of the Shakespeare Birthplace Trust's collection. We don't know why Badger wanted the extra slice of land; perhaps it was to extend his house or build a low boundary wall between the houses. Either way, John Shakespeare was glad to sell it. By then, he had fallen on hard times and needed the money. Sometime before

1707, Badger's house was converted into the Swan Inn. In 1590, and likely for some years prior, it was the home of one John Ichivar. For many years, the neighbour directly across Henley Street was the shepherd John Cox, who, in 1566, was fined four pence for sheltering a pregnant woman from outside the town. He knew the Shakespeare family well because he lived opposite them until his own house burned down in 1594.

All these families – the Hornbys, the Badgers, the Bradleys, the Ichivars and the Shakespeares – were of the middling sort. They were neighbours who lived side-by-side, and peaceably so, for decades. They weren't as famous, or as wealthy, as Stratford benefactor Sir Hugh Clopton, nor as learned as the local schoolmaster and the parish vicar. But they were self-respecting enough to take an active role in town affairs and prosperous enough to take pride and care in where they lived and what they owned.

3

Epitome of the Whole World

'I will be master of what is mine own'
THE TAMING OF THE SHREW (3.2.232)

On my first morning in Stratford-upon-Avon, as I walked down Church Street, near the grammar school where Shakespeare had been a pupil, I witnessed a modern-day version of the boyish reluctance that he so memorably described in *As You Like It*: 'Then the whining schoolboy, with his satchel / And shining morning face, creeping like snail / Unwillingly to school' (2.7.146–8). The image is, of course, from Jaques' speech on the seven ages of man.

It was plain to see that the boys straggling along Church Street, straggling despite the coldness of a winter's day, were headed to the King Edward VI School, as it's now called. That was their destination. But I started to think about where they were coming from, where they had begun their journey. At home, most likely. And then it hit me, the genius of Shakespeare likening a schoolboy to a snail.

Everyone knows that snails creep; it's their signature style. Yet to start creeping, they must first emerge from within their protective shells. Shakespeare's point, then, isn't that a schoolboy, like a snail, creeps – though he does – but that he has left home. For the first time, his world has enlarged. But there's a twist: a snail's shell remains part of its body, permanently affixed. In the same way, Shakespeare tells us, when we leave home to enter the wider world – starting school, launching a career, falling in love, raising children – we never leave behind the home that first we knew. Like the snail, we remain attached to it, wherever we may go.

'Two households'

When the audience at the Globe heard the melancholy Jaques deliver his now-famous speech, did they stop and think, as I had to, about the deeper significance of the schoolboy and the snail? Probably not. The simile's meaning, no doubt felt more than overtly articulated, would have been apparent to them because it reflected their own life experience; it captured an emotional attachment to their own houses and households.

For the Elizabethans, a 'house' was not just a physical dwelling, not merely brick and timber, but the sign and living symbol of a larger domestic ideal. John Shakespeare's 'house' included not just his wife Mary and their children, but also servants and apprentices, for they all lived or worked under his roof and his rule. His son William grew up in a household with at least nine members. To the nobility, a 'house' signified something yet more elaborate, because it created a lineage, with successors, claimants and hereditary titles. This original meaning still survives in a variety of dynastic clans: fashionistas from the House of Gucci, drag legends in the House of Xtravaganza and Britain's royal family is the House of Windsor. Shakespeare's idea of house and household was much broader and deeper than ours. Broader because it extended beyond his immediate family, and deeper because it entailed reciprocal obligations between husband and wife, parents and children and masters and servants – obligations that created an unusually cohesive, if not always peaceful, domestic world.

The prologue to *Romeo and Juliet* frames the play as the story of two rival houses and not that of the two star-crossed lovers. Or, rather, Shakespeare's play enacts the tragic conflict between the ironclad demands of households and the rebellious, even destructive, impulses of their members. Thus, the Chorus, speaking the prologue, places the unfolding drama of one particular woman and one particular man in its larger social setting, the setting that gives this intimate personal drama its collective meaning: 'Two households, both alike in dignity, / In fair Verona, where we lay our scene, / From ancient grudge break to new mutiny' (1–3).

Romeo and Juliet's love, as we all know, is illicit because the Capulets and the Montagues are enemies. That is the ultimate fact, the one from which all other facts derive. Yet the lovers cannot escape their households, and, deep down, they both know it. Romeo is no more capable of denying his father and refusing his name than Juliet is free to renounce her own parentage. They can run away from Verona, and they do; but they can never run away from the identities, the irreconcilable identities, that their households have branded them with. They cannot be other than who they already are. The tragedy of Juliet and her Romeo is that their yearning for a life independent of their two households can be satisfied only in death.

Fidelity to household, as Shakespeare shows throughout the play, runs up and down the social scale. The wealthy Capulet household includes not just Juliet and her parents, but the Nurse, the page Peter and the servants. On the night of the Capulets' banquet, the poor servants are in meltdown. Run ragged, they greet the guests, arrange napkins on the table, carry food up from the kitchen, prod the scullery maids to scrape the plates and try to be everywhere at once. 'Everything', one harried servant confesses to Lady Capulet, is 'in extremity' (1.4.103). But, somehow, in this scene of comic uproar – a scene that my students love to perform – it all comes together.

Like the performance itself, the 'old accustomed feast' (1.2.19) is a hands-on production, a showstopping number, only the final, flourished efforts of which are visible, but which depends entirely on much unseen labour.

This glimpse of the entire household at work – upstairs, Lord Capulet calling for a dance; downstairs, a servant grabbing a chunk of leftover marzipan – makes Romeo's trespass all the more threatening. The banquet is an intimate event, a way for Lord Capulet to reward his guests for their loyalty and allegiance. It's a party with partisan intent. Romeo, then, isn't merely an annoying gatecrasher; he's the loathed enemy, someone *never* to be made welcome, someone whose alien presence threatens the household's very survival. And yet, Lord Capulet, relenting, allows Romeo to stay, an action that sets the whole tragedy in motion. A tragedy not of two discrete individuals, but of two populated households.

Shakespeare, as far as we know, didn't live in an aristocratic household, let alone take sides in tribal blood feuds; but neither was he a stranger to that elite world. As a young poet, he benefited from the patronage, and, some say, the love, of Henry Wriothesley, third Earl of Southampton. Shakespeare the actor and playwright for the Lord Chamberlain's Men – renamed the King's Men after James I was crowned, in 1603 – found himself close to the Tudor and Stuart courts, the grandest and most powerful houses in all the land. *Romeo and Juliet* took the social fact of the 'house' to its sorrowful extreme, an extreme reached when households act only to reward their friends and rout their enemies. Yet even then, Shakespeare was imaginatively transforming the realities that he encountered in his own life.

'Non Sanz Droict'

In the 1590s, having met with literary and theatrical success, Shakespeare devoted time and money to petition the College of Arms to grant his father a coat of arms. This was not the first time that the heralds in London had received such an application. About two decades earlier, at the height of his career in local politics, Shakespeare's father sought to acquire yet greater status and reputation by being granted a coat of arms. There were several dozen gentlemen in Stratford – some by birth, some by grant – and John Shakespeare wanted to number among them.

Certainly, he had made a name for himself in Stratford, rising quickly through a succession of town offices that culminated in his election as the High Bailiff, or mayor. Still, he hankered after the fabricated lineage depicted in a medieval-style coat of arms. Apart from the blazonry itself, by which he would thereafter be identified, John Shakespeare would be permitted to style himself a 'gentleman' and to wear a ceremonial sword. And he knew full well that a coat of arms was legal property, something he could bequeath to William, his eldest son.

Of course, it was all totally impractical. Nobody, unless they were spoiling for a fight, roamed around Stratford brandishing a sword and a shield. And yet, those same objects, useless to John Shakespeare in one way, were highly coveted by him in another way: because they symbolized that he, the young man from the Snitterfield sticks, had arrived. Not just arrived, but triumphed. Knowing that his wife's family, the Ardens, boasted their own coat of arms must have spurred his resolve to acquire the same for himself. His request, for reasons still mysterious, was denied and not immediately appealed. Perhaps the snub was due to John Shakespeare's debts, for by then he was insolvent. A bankrupt man, no matter if he had once been elected High Bailiff, lacked by definition the good character necessary to receive a heraldic honour.

The family did not forget this rebuff. In October 1596, William Shakespeare relaunched his father's failed campaign, determined that the 'house of Shakespeare' be publicly recognized. As is told in every Shakespeare biography, this second petition, which survives in the College of Arms in London, was successful. John Shakespeare was finally granted a coat of arms, partly in recognition that his 'ancestors were for their valiant and faithful service advanced and rewarded by the most prudent prince King Henry the Seventh'. That's likely a reference to his wife's great-uncle, Sir John Arden, an 'Esquire of the Body' to Henry VII.

The armorial design, roughly sketched in the granting document, was elegant in its simplicity and yet assertive in its courtly symbols: a golden, silver-tipped spear outlined in black, making it gleam all the more, and set diagonally on a golden shield. The surmounted crest showed a silver falcon, its wings spread as if about to take flight – 'shaking', in the idiom of falconry – atop silver laurels and clutching an upright spear. The puns are obvious, unmissable, overdone. A replica now hangs above the front entrance to the Birthplace.

The motto for the coat of arms was *Non Sanz Droict*, chivalric old French for 'not without right'. Although its meaning is obscure, perhaps the motto betrays Shakespeare's injured familial pride that his father had been turned down twenty years earlier. John Shakespeare, so his son and heir believed, had been wronged; and now, at last, that wrong had been set aright. But who knows?

Still, there's no doubt that Shakespeare was anxious to obtain the prestige of being a gentleman. In the 'St Crispin's Day' battlefield speech in *Henry* V, written soon after the Shakespeare coat of arms had been granted, the untested young king promises his 'band of brothers' that, once they return to England, he will make them all gentlemen, no matter how low their reputation back home: 'For he today that sheds his blood with me / Shall be my brother; be he ne'er so vile, / This day shall gentle his condition' (4.3.60, 61–3).

Though it was William Shakespeare who secured the coat of arms, it was to John Shakespeare that it was granted. The honour was specifically not conferred upon the man who by then had written *Richard III*, *A Midsummer*

Night's Dream, and the best-selling poem *Venus and Adonis*. After William Shakespeare inherited the coat of arms, in 1601, upon his father's death, a herald in the College of Arms challenged it on the grounds that a common 'player' was not fit to be called a gentleman. Alas, theatre has always struggled to gain respectability. Renowned historian William Camden, the most senior herald, eventually ruled that Shakespeare the 'player' was fully entitled to the coat of arms – not because of his theatrical and literary fame, and not because the queen had commanded the Lord Chamberlain's Men to perform at court, but because his father had been High Bailiff of Stratford and his great-grandfather had served as a soldier in the reign of Henry VII. Strictly on his own merits, William Shakespeare would have been denied the honour.

His theatrical peers teased him for social climbing. A character in Ben Jonson's comedy *Every Man Out of his Humour* (1599) tells Sogliardo, a country boy transplanted to the city, to adopt the motto 'Not Without Mustard' for his purchased coat of arms. That must have stung. But the chivalric honour was Shakespeare's to use, and he used it. He styled himself 'gentleman' in legal documents, as he was fully entitled to do. He kept his ceremonial sword, and probably wore it when the King's Men marched in the coronation procession for James I in 1603. Although the coat of arms was, oddly, missing from Shakespeare's portrait in the First Folio, published in 1623, seven years after his death, it formed part of his funerary monument in Stratford's Holy Trinity Church, as visitors today can see for themselves.

When the hereditary coat of arms was granted, William Shakespeare relished the symbolic restoration of his father's status in their hometown. But he was also grieving the death of eleven-year-old Hamnet, his only son. A sad irony, indeed, that Shakespeare acquired a coat of arms just weeks after the death of the only child who could inherit it. His daughter Susanna, his firstborn, was not eligible because heraldic insignia passed through the male line only, the line that ended with little Hamnet's death. In his will, Shakespeare gave his ceremonial sword to young Thomas Combe because he had no surviving son to whom he could bequeath it. His sole heir lay buried in the town churchyard, dead before his time. 'Grief fills the room up of my absent child, / Lies in his bed, walks up and down with me' (*King John*, 3.4.93–5). He wrote those lines for Queen Constance, mourning her son Arthur's death, but they feel acutely personal. William Shakespeare, loyal son turned broken-hearted father, found himself in the sad, unforeseen predicament of setting up the house of Shakespeare knowing that it would not survive him.

'The Furniture of Our Houses'

Shakespeare, when writing his English history plays and his tragedies *Macbeth* and *King Lear*, kept at his elbow an open copy of Raphael Holinshed's *Chronicles of England, Scotland, and Ireland*. To judge from the material in those plays, he likely used the 1587 second edition. Holinshed's great work, commissioned near the beginning of Elizabeth I's reign and first printed in 1577, was part of a larger but unfinished publishing venture on the 'universal Cosmography of the whole world', about as big a topic as the human mind can conceive.

One of Holinshed's collaborators in that prodigious effort was the clergyman William Harrison, whose task, close to what we now call 'micro-history', was to convey the details of daily life in ages past, a rag-bag subject that encompassed everything from vegetable gardens to the universities of Oxford and Cambridge, and from outdoor markets to the breeds of English dogs. He tracked down all those details by reading old books and letters, poring over maps, questioning old people, for their memories were the longest, and, most of all, just observing the richness of life surrounding him.

With the modesty befitting a priest, Harrison called his compilation a 'foul frizzled treatise'. But the name under which it was published, also in 1577, gives a truer sense of its sweeping ambition: *An Historicall Description of the Land of Britaine*. The eighth of its eighteen chapters was titled 'Of the Manner of Building and Furniture Of Our Houses'. Did Shakespeare read this one chapter? We don't know. But he could hardly have been unaware of this sprawling social history, given how often and how much he relied upon Holinshed.

Harrison, a bit of a snob, complained that the mania for 'costly furniture' had descended from noblemen to knights, from knights to merchants and from merchants to 'inferior artificers and any farmers'. In other words, all the way down to the bottom of the Elizabethan social hierarchy. Peasants tilling the fields, apprentices learning their craft and servants cooking the meals were, socially speaking, all invisible.

Workaday craftsmen, or 'artificers', occupied the lowest rung on the ladder of men who were masters of their own households, and so who needed to furnish, decorate and sometimes build, the places where they lived. They were day labourers, like Peter Quince the carpenter in *A Midsummer Night's Dream*. One rung up were husbandmen farmers, people like Shakespeare's grandfather Richard. A successful trader ranked higher still, in a respectable class that included merchants, land-owning yeoman farmers and holders of minor political offices. Next were 'gentlemen', an official status conferred on worthy men by dint of birth or family distinction. Here, as Harrison admitted, the categories blurred, because some gentlemen – John Shakespeare, to name one – were also merchants and civic officials. Soaring above them all, in a different realm entirely, were knights, nobles and royalty.

For all his class-inflected carping, Harrison made a valid point. The many surviving household inventories from the Elizabethan age confirm that even modestly well-off families enjoyed their pick of fireplaces by which to keep warm, decorated their beds with bolster pillows and adorned their dining table with green or yellow napkins.

It would surely have irked William Harrison that, as soon as he could afford it, William Shakespeare bought a house with no fewer than twelve chimneys, as has been claimed for New Place. But it would not have surprised him. For it was proof positive that the English mania for domestic comfort really did exceed all delicacy. Yet for Shakespeare himself, such conspicuous consumption was household pride made visible. If you had a gentlemanly coat of arms, then you needed a house worthy of a gentleman.

'An Epitome of the whole World'

On the afternoon of 29 June 1613, the Globe Theatre burned to the ground – in less than one hour – after its thatched roof caught fire during a performance of *All is True*. Today we know the play as *Henry VIII*, jointly written by Shakespeare and John Fletcher. A highlight of this sumptuous production was the entrance of King Henry VIII and his retinue, all disguised as shepherds, during a masked ball given by Cardinal Wolsey in York Place. The audience must have thrilled when the king arrived not just to the sweet music of hautboys, but to the bang and flash of cannons. Alarmingly, touchpaper from one cannon landed on the theatre's thatched roof and set it alight. The audience, captivated by the stage spectacle before them, paid no attention to the smoke rising from the thatch. It really must have been a great show. Within minutes, a ring of fire encircled the theatre's upper story. Panicked, everyone scrambled to get out before the whole theatre was destroyed. No deaths were reported, although one poor soul escaped being broiled alive by dousing his flaming breeches with a bottle of ale. How providential that he was a slow drinker.

Among the audience on that ill-fated day was Henry Wotton, an English diplomat recently returned from his posting to the Republic of Venice. He is best remembered for his wry adage, 'An ambassador is a man sent abroad to lie for the good of his country.' In 1624, eight years after Shakespeare's death, Wotton wrote *The Elements of Architecture*, a handbook for a learned art that was then attracting ever more attention from English scholars and travellers abroad. During his long Venetian sojourn, the author saw for himself many instances of revived classical architecture, a style then only beginning to take hold in England, chiefly through Palladian-style buildings like the Banqueting House at the Palace of Whitehall, designed in 1622 by the architect, and theatrical scene designer, Inigo Jones.

Although his text was a loose paraphrase of *De Architectura*, a treatise composed sixteen centuries earlier by the Roman engineer and architect Marcus Vitruvius Pollio, it spoke directly to how Wotton's fellow countrymen, the proverbial 'Every Man', ought to feel about their homes. Each and every English house – be it vast or cramped, new or old, stone or timber, built in city, town or country – held the whole world in miniature: 'Every man's proper mansion house and home, being the theater of his hospitality, the seat of self-fruition, the comfortablest part of his own life, the noblest of his son's Inheritance, a kind of private princedom; nay, to the possessors thereof, an epitome of the whole world.'

A house, to *be* a house, must nourish its owner's true self. It offers leisure, comfort and privacy, those three desirable alternatives to the grubby world of work. Its owner's greatest asset, the house can be handed down from one generation to the next. Above all, it becomes the master's own kingdom, the realm over which he alone (and it was almost always a 'he') wields total power, a little commonwealth unto itself. Just as a king ruled from his palace, and a lord held sway in his castle, so the humble freeman exercised sovereignty in his home, his own 'private Princedom'. All these commendable attributes crowd into Wotton's final image of a house as the universe in microcosm: 'an *Epitome* of the whole *World*'.

This was how the boy William Shakespeare understood his father's house. This was how, in later years, he understood his own house. This was how Shakespeare understood *all* houses, including the imaginary ones created for his characters. When the innkeeper in *The Merry Wives of Windsor* jests that Sir John Falstaff's rented lodgings are 'his chamber, his house, his castle' (4.5.5), invoking images of successively larger and grander dwellings, he trades on a shared belief that even a temporary and humble abode is, nonetheless, the seat of freedom and authority for whomever is master there. In Falstaff's room at the Garter Inn, there are two beds: a regular one for him and a smaller trundle bed, underneath, where his page will sleep. The larger and higher bed in his room for the night expressed Falstaff's uncompromised authority; in every way, he remained *above* his servant.

'A Godly Form of Household Government'

In the ideal Elizabethan household, so ideal that it may have existed only in pious sermons preached by men, or in hectoring conduct manuals authored by men, the husband earned the money his family needed while the wife, wisely and carefully, spent it. A partnership, yes, but on permanently unequal terms. Anyone in Shakespeare's time needing a reminder about the proper roles of husbands and wives could turn to John Dod and Robert Cleaver's *A Godlie Forme of Householde Government: for the Ordering of Private Families, According to the Direction of God's Word*. Published in 1598, their book sets out the divinely decreed obligations of spouses:

> The duty of the husband is to travel abroad to seek living; and the wife's duty is to keep the house. The duty of the husband is to get money and provision; and of the wife's, not vainly to spend it. The duty of the husband is to deal with many men; and of the wife's, to talk with few ... The duty of the husband is to be a giver; and of the wife, to be a saver.

A wife's duties, although no less essential than her spouse's, were confined largely to the domestic sphere. Conversely, the husband must venture 'abroad' – not to another country, but outside the home and into the larger world of commerce, craft and trade, where he made his living. Husbands leaving their homes and wives staying put was true symbolically, if not always literally. Men who hauled goods or drove cattle to market obviously did travel away from their families, sometimes journeying great distances to provide for them. So did a Warwickshire playwright. Far more typical, however, was the town craftsman, who worked at home.

When John Shakespeare ventured 'abroad' to support his wife and five children, he simply walked a few feet to his glover's workshop at the far end of his house. Separated from the rest of the house by a traditional cross-passage that opened onto the back garden, this room was a dedicated workspace with no other purpose. Animal hides had to be left in place after they were wetted and stretched to make the shape required for gloves, belts or satchels. Glovers used extremely sharp scissors and knives so that the leather wouldn't tear, yet another reason for a separate workshop: to prevent curious children from wandering in and hurting themselves.

Except for the market held on Thursdays, John and his apprentices, one of whom may have been his son William, laboured in the workshop, or out in the backyard, stopping only at midday to join everyone in the hall for their main meal. It was Mary Shakespeare, mistress of the household, who oversaw that communal meal's preparation. Her day revolved around the kitchen, the pantry, the cellar and the garden. Separated by no more than fifty feet, husband and wife were, in terms of their own responsibilities, worlds apart. He was getting money and she was spending it. He was open to the world – literally so, for John Shakespeare sold some of his wares from a hatch door that opened onto Henley Street – and she was closed to it. He trained apprentices, while she minded the children and gave orders to maidservants. Their gender-defined worlds intersected at daily rituals like mealtime, an event mythologized for uniting in sweet harmony the husband who provided for the family and the wife who sustained it.

'Gadding Out and About'

Such was the official story. But never was it the full story. The boundary line that separated masculine and feminine worlds in Elizabethan England, though drawn so clearly in the abstract, grew blurry and vague in practice. Hence, the anxiety to police it: women kept crossing over that dividing line. A woman who could read, write and do some arithmetic might keep her husband's account books, and thus learn exactly how much money was coming in and going out. She might, to add to her husband's earnings, take in washing or sell fresh milk and eggs from an open window overlooking the street. With her family, a woman went to church, fairs and festivals and other communal events; but on her own, she went to the market, visited friends, settled accounts with tradesmen, looked in on a sick neighbour or took on some extra chores to help a new mother.

And so, a more complex picture of home life emerges. Social norms, pronounced by a male ruling elite, drove a wedge, if only a rhetorical one, between a woman's world and a man's world so that households might be well-governed, at least according to patriarchal definitions of domestic tranquillity. Social reality, however, daily eroded any such separation. Elizabethan wives and daughters, just like their husbands, sons and brothers, found and seized opportunities to enlarge their worlds. Sir Edmund Tilney, in his 1568 dialogue *The Flower of Friendship*, cautioned women to be 'wary in going abroad'. His warning was a dead giveaway that many women were already doing just that. Otherwise, why warn? Shakespeare knew Tilney, who served as Master of the Revels, the official who censored plays, organized performances at court and shut down London theatres during outbreaks of plague. Apparently, he also liked to censor and shut down women.

Men who, like Tilney, got jittery when women pursued lives outside their homes, retaliated by declaring that only loose women – harlots, sirens, jezebels – were seen and heard in masculine company. A woman who opened her mouth in front of men other than her husband might open up to them other parts of herself, so the paranoid fears escalated. The Elizabethan man's idea of a proper wife was that she was *closed*: her mouth shut, unlike the nagging shrew and scold; her house locked, to protect her husband's hard-earned property; and her body shielded from everyone but him, to ensure the legitimacy of the children she bore. A woman 'gadding out and about' (Tilney, again) must behave as if she were still inside her own house and under her husband's watch. Even in the great outdoors, a woman was symbolically sequestered.

'Horum, harum, horum'

In *The Merry Wives of Windsor*, Shakespeare comically depicts two 'gadding' housewives, Mistress Page and Mistress Quickly, openly indulging in sexual innuendo as they disrupt an impromptu Latin lesson taught to Mistress Page's son William by his Welsh schoolmaster, Sir Hugh Evans. Readers and critics have long debated whether this schoolboy William is Shakespeare's portrayal of his youthful self, a pupil at the King's New School in Stratford, where he studied Lily's Latin Grammar. Impossible to know. But if so, he hardly cast his mother in a flattering light. It's the other character, Mistress Quickly, who gets the smutty lines, but both women come across as silly chatterboxes. Indeed, the scene's comedy depends on the housewives *not* understanding basic Latin – why would they? Girls back then weren't sent to school – which causes them to misinterpret what they hear, converting a simple grammar lesson into a string of dirty jokes.

Mistress Quickly overhears the schoolmaster ask her friend's son to recite the 'genitive case plural' of the pronoun 'hic', meaning 'this' or 'these'. He starts William off with a few declensions: 'horum, harum, horum'. It's a classroom quiz, and not too surprising. In Latin, nouns change according to their number and function in a sentence. Yet Mistress Quickly, knowing no Latin – it was Greek to her, to paraphrase Casca in *Julius Caesar* – misunderstands what she hears. What she *thinks* she hears offends her mightily. Stopping the tutorial, she insists that the boy not respond to such wicked remarks: 'Vengeance of Jenny's case, fie on her! Never name her child, if she be a whore' (4.2.56–7). In her comic mishearing, 'genitive' is a woman named 'Jenny', 'case' is Elizabethan slang for vagina and 'horum' sounds like 'whore'. So when the schoolmaster speaks innocently of Latin grammar – 'genitive', 'case', 'horum' – what the outraged Mistress Quickly hears is a lewd remark: 'Jenny's vagina, that whore'.

A more obvious pun occurs when Sir Hugh's Welsh accent, in which 'v' is pronounced as 'f', makes the Latin word 'vocative' sound like 'focative', which Mistress Quickly mistakes for a variant of 'fuck'. At first embarrassed, and then exasperated, the schoolmaster wants only to silence these 'foolish Christian creatures' (4.2.67). While it's cumbersome to explain these aural jokes in writing, in performance they were funny the instant they reached the ear, at least the ears of those men in the audience who once had Latin grammar drilled into their schoolboy heads.

This scene cuts both ways. It depicts women speaking in public, and thus resisting the gag order that masculine rule imposes upon them. Yet when they do speak, they get it wrong. They misspeak. Ignorant of what every diligent pupil knows by heart, they convert wholesome words into filth. True, Mistress Quickly and Mistress Page get all the laughs; but those laughs accumulate at their expense. In Shakespeare's theatre, female characters were played by teenage boys, not women, a gender-swap that only accentuates this scene's ambivalence. Neither in the reality of daily life nor in the artifice of the playhouse could women truly speak for themselves.

'My Wife'

Sir Hugh scolds Mistress Page and Mistress Quickly for not understanding the 'genders'. As used in the early modern era, gender was a purely linguistic term, not yet referring, as it now does, to cultural differences between women and men. Even so, when we read that word in a Shakespeare play, or hear it spoken on the stage, we cannot help but interpret it in light of our own understanding of gender. We ask ourselves whether Shakespeare, in his heart, endorsed the patriarchal belief that women had no business outside the home. After all, when Portia, in *The Merchant of Venice*, triumphs over Shylock in the courtroom, she does so in necessarily male disguise, no woman of the time allowed to join the legal profession. But instead of trying to discern Shakespeare's private beliefs by scrutinizing his dramatic characters – a fool's errand – we should look at the circumstances of his own home life in Stratford and London. Or, rather, we should look to his wife.

Anne Hathaway, daughter of Richard, was born in 1556, or thereabouts, at Hewland Farm in the village of Shottery, a little over a mile from Stratford-upon-Avon. In 1582, her name appeared alongside that of her betrothed, William Shakespeare, in their marriage bond. She was older than most brides of the time, he younger than most grooms. For the remainder of her life, Anne was not mentioned by name in any other document, not until the record of her burial, in 1623, at Holy Trinity Church. Even in her own husband's will, drawn up in March 1616, she was referred to only as 'my wife'.

Anne's near invisibility in the annals of recorded history hardly means that she played no role in the world. Indeed, the home truth is that Mistress Shakespeare was, in all likelihood, master of New Place during the nineteen years when her husband lived mainly in London, a two-day's journey on horseback away. Gilbert and Richard Shakespeare may also have been living at New Place, helping to look after their older brother's affairs in Stratford. But if so, and there's no corroborating document, it seems unlikely that Shakespeare would have allowed them to sideline his own wife. Indeed, there may be a simple reason why Anne Shakespeare seems never to have left Stratford after her marriage: she had too much work to do.

Growing up in the house on Henley Street, William Shakespeare the boy was taught to believe that husbands and fathers ruled their households with total and unquestioned authority. No fact of life could be more basic. Yet when it came time for him to play those same leading roles, he had fled the scene. For all we know, when Shakespeare left his wife Anne and their children Susanna, Judith and Hamnet, sometime in the late 1580s, they were still living under his father's roof, along with his mother, Mary, and his four younger siblings. The twins, born in 1585, were named after Stratford residents Hamnet and Judith Sadler, friends of their parents. Nothing to do with *Hamlet*. Only in 1597, when Shakespeare purchased New Place, did it become a certainty that his own family lived in their own house. Though by then the family was a little smaller, Hamnet having died the year before.

The earliest Shakespeare anecdotes, dating from the 1680s, suggest that the playwright returned home to Anne, Susanna and Judith at least once a year. But half a dozen times a year would still not be enough for Shakespeare to run his growing business and property interests in Stratford without help. True, he likely also returned for months at a time when plague shut down theatres in London, but such unwelcome interludes were unpredictable. Shakespeare the landowner and investor must have entrusted his wife with an uncommonly high degree of authority in his absence, a necessary bending of gender rules.

In London, Shakespeare the playwright was never master of his own household because he never lived there in a property he owned. Whether in Bishopsgate, Silver Street or Southwark – he moved around, but never strayed far from the theatres – Shakespeare preferred, so the surviving evidence indicates, to remain a lodger in someone else's home. When he rented a room in the house of the wigmaker Christopher Mountjoy, in Silver Street, the family clearly respected him. He was asked to help settle the terms of Mary Mountjoy's marriage to Stephen Bellott, and later testified in court when matters turned sour. His testimony survives, the only words known to have been spoken by William Shakespeare. Alas, they are not revelatory. Yet being a tenant, even a reliable and well-liked tenant, is the opposite of being your own lord and master, the role a grown man was supposed to perform.

When it comes to houses and households, Shakespeare emerges as a man of paradox. He wanted his father to be honoured in Stratford as a gentleman, but he wanted to make his own name in London. Although wealthier than his father, and more prominent in the world, he wanted nothing to do with civic life in Stratford. It was important that his family lived in a handsome residence in the town centre, but it was not important that he himself ran that household. He was, in defiance of social norms, content for his wife to take on traditionally masculine responsibilities – the Portia of Warwickshire – while he lived nearly a hundred miles away as the itinerant lodger in other men's houses. Shakespeare the boy learned all the right lessons about domestic life, and then Shakespeare the man ignored every one of them.

4

Household Stuff

'Might I but know thee by thy household badge'
HENRY VI, PART 2 (5.1.201)

John Shakespeare's corpse lies in the front hall of his house on Henley Street. It's the first week of September 1601. Three men move silently from room to room. Though mourning their friend's death, and consoling his widow, Mary, they have official business to conduct. 'Men of good credit' – honest, dependable, staunch – they have been charged by the state with listing the contents of this deceased man's home. Pausing in each room, they name aloud every item they find there, agree its value and then one of them, the nominated scribe, records it in a ledger. With three pairs of eyes, they notice everything, down to the number of candlesticks and the colours of the bolster pillows on the four-poster bed. In case something has been overlooked, they add a disclaimer: 'for forgotten goods . . . one shilling'. They add up the value of each individual item, the final figure representing the total worth of the household property. On the ledger's last page, they sign their names or make their mark. Bidding a sorrowful good-bye to the assembled family, their work is finished. So concludes the probate inventory of the late John Shakespeare, gentleman, of Stratford-upon-Avon, in the county of Warwickshire.

'To note the chamber. I will write all down.'

Beginning in 1529, twenty years into Henry VIII's reign, the law required that an inventory of possessions be drawn up after the death of each man or woman in the kingdom before the deceased's last will and testament could be approved. Usually compiled within a week of the testator's death, the inventory enabled debts to be paid or recovered and bequests to be honoured. This task was entrusted to a few good men, usually old friends or trusted neighbours. Yet even when done by friends, drawing up such an inventory must have felt like intruding on a family's grief. The law, with all its rules, impersonal formalities and orders of compliance, forced itself into the home, that most private of spaces, at the worst possible moment.

Around 1608, not long after his mother's death, Shakespeare wrote a play that captures this feeling of violated privacy and turns it to sinister purposes. In *Cymbeline*, Iachimo bets Posthumus that he can seduce his friend's wife, Imogen, whom her husband has praised for her fidelity. After she spurns his adulterous advance, Iachimo connives to win the wager by trickery: he will make it seem that he has slept with Imogen by stealing into her bedchamber (a plot device that Shakespeare lifted from Bocaccio's *Decameron*) and observing how it is furnished and decorated. Such intimate knowledge, he knows, will be taken as compelling proof of her infidelity.

Iachimo, putting his scheme into motion, asks Imogen to keep a trunk in her room overnight for safekeeping. She agrees, not realizing that he plans to stow himself inside it. In the middle of the night, as the rest of the house slumbers, he climbs, silently, out of the trunk. In the methodical manner of an inventory clerk, Iachimo looks around and names what he sees: 'But my design – / To note the chamber. I will write all down. / Such and such pictures, there the window; such / Th'adornment of her bed, the arras, figures, / Why; such and such, and the contents o'th' story' (2. 2. 23–7).

A true villain, Iachimo reduces the naked, sleeping Imogen to yet one more item in his inventory, an object to be handled, appraised and valued. Not just any object, but the most precious. It's one thing for him to convince Posthumus that his wife has been unfaithful by describing each piece of furniture in her bedroom. And yet, Iachimo ponders, his false claim would prove unassailable, beyond all doubt, if he observed 'some natural notes about her body'. He looks for, and finds, a tell-tale physical mark: 'On her left breast / A mole, cinque-spotted, like the crimson drops / I'th' bottom of a cowslip. Here's a voucher / Stronger than ever law could make' (2.2.37–40). In a final menacing touch, he removes from the sleeping Imogen's wrist the bracelet Posthumus had given to her.

Threat of rape hangs over the entire scene, though Iachimo never attempts it. He doesn't have to. Because now he can give witness to Imogen's supposed infidelity: he can describe her bedchamber, he can divulge the secrets of her body and he can produce the bracelet slipped off her wrist. Cruelly tricked, but not knowing it, Posthumus will instead believe that Iachimo has 'picked the lock and ta'en / The treasure of her honour' (2.2.41–2).

The Globe audience, familiar with probate inventories, would have grasped the broader point that Shakespeare was making. A society fixated on measuring, counting and valuing every last item in a dead person's home – a home in which grieving family members still lived – can end up treating people as mere chattel. Just like the violated, innocent Imogen, fast asleep in her bed. The mental act of reducing her to an object strips Imogen of her innate dignity, as much as would any overt act of sexual violence.

'Come, come, and sit you down'

After the performance at Elsinore of 'The Mousetrap', the play Hamlet uses to indirectly accuse Claudius of murdering his father, Gertrude summons her son to her closet. No sweet motherly invitation this, for she plans to rebuke him for offending his step-father and her husband.

In Shakespeare's time, a 'closet' referred to a variety of small spaces: a pantry, a prayer room, a study, a storehouse, a bedchamber or even, as with Gertrude, the most secluded, most inaccessible, part of a royal palace. What all these spaces have in common is their utmost privacy. A closet, whatever its nominal function, was, above all, a room that could be closed, locked if necessary and shut off from its surroundings and any intruders. The closet's power was its separateness from the life of the household; and therein lay its truthfulness. Only in rare seclusion can all pretences be dropped, all performances abandoned, all masks discarded.

When the audience at the Globe heard Rosencrantz tell Hamlet that his mother, the queen, 'desires to speak with you in her closet' (3.2.323), they expected not just a scene of charged intimacy – it was, they knew the castle's innermost room – but also one of honest terms and plain speaking. Gertrude's closet, in its cramped hiddenness, opposes the formal grandeur of the throne room or the castle's open battlements. It is the one room at Elsinore where truth beyond ceremony – beyond 'show', as Hamlet himself says – can finally be told, and told without guile.

Shakespeare delivers all that, and more, but with a twist. The closet belongs to Gertrude and so the scene is set up for *her* to confront Hamlet, whom she has invited into her private chamber. More, she has conspired to put him under surveillance. Polonius eavesdrops from behind the arras, so he can report to Claudius what Hamlet says. Gertrude, so she believes, wields total power in this particular space, the only one where she is sovereign.

But from the moment he enters Hamlet takes charge of the scene. Gertrude delivers just a single scolding line – 'thou hast thy father much offended' – before Hamlet immediately turns those words back on her – 'you have my father much offended' (3.4.10–11). Suddenly, power has shifted from mother to son. Rebukes and reproaches are now directed at her, and with shocking vehemence: Hamlets says he wishes she were not his mother. Seconds later, he stabs the hidden Polonius to death. Here, in the closet, home truths are certainly told, but not usually in so disrupted a way.

Alarmed, Gertrude tries to flee – flee from her own closet, the room where she should feel safest, but now feels most threatened. Hamlet blocks her exit. 'Come, come, and sit you down. You shall not budge' (3.4.19). In that simple, but, for the audience, aggressive bit of staging, Hamlet forces his mother into her chair, twice forbidding her – 'Peace! sit you down' (3.4.34) – to rise from it. He accuses her of moral cowardice, stripping her of royal dignity. Gertrude's authority is here overthrown in the very space that ought to signify and uphold her authority. A queen no longer, she is now but a minion or a prisoner under house arrest.

In all likelihood Gertrude's chair was the only object on the stage. Yet Shakespeare needed nothing else to make his point because the onstage chair symbolized authority, just as did the master's chair in the home of every person who watched this scene of domestic disarray. When the audience saw Gertrude trapped in her own chair, held hostage by her own son, they witnessed the natural order of things turned upside down. And they knew it. Like a wobbly chair in their own home, the times, in *Hamlet*, were out of joint.

'A Curtain Lecture'

As heads of the household, John and Mary Shakespeare likely slept in a large, four-poster bed with canopy and curtains. With its curtains drawn, their bed became a room within a room, offering warmth and privacy. Household inventories from the time reveal that some marital bedrooms also had smaller trundle or flock beds in them. If other people slept in the same room, and usually it was very young children, the couple had to whisper not to be overheard. But when its curtains were tightly closed, the marital bed was the one place in the house where Shakespeare's parents could be totally alone and so be totally themselves.

In 1598, the domestic conduct manual *A Godlie Form of Householde Government* warned potential husbands to 'take heed' in choosing a wife, because she 'must continually be conversant with thee, at thy table, in thy chamber, in bed, in thy secrets, and finally, in thy heart and breast'. Looking past the misogynistic cliché of the wife who talks her husband to death, this advice to would-be husbands tells us that Elizabethan couples experienced their homes as a sequence of smaller, and thus more intimate, spaces, into which they alone retreated. The hall, where they dined 'at table', was the household's most public room: everyone was there. The couple's bedchamber offered coveted privacy, but only in bed were they truly alone. Behind the curtains, the wife whispered secrets into her husband's ear. Last scene of all, no words were needed, for she lived in his loving heart.

Having sex was just the beginning of what Elizabethan couples did in bed. Wives, forbidden by the code of patriarchy to criticize their husbands in front of children and servants, could speak frankly to their spouses only when they shared a bed, the male ego being less threatened in darkened privacy. Only in bed could the wife speak her mind without fear of throwing the household into chaos. Few men welcomed such a 'curtain lecture', the chauvinistic term used in Shakespeare's time to describe a wife nagging, pestering, browbeating or otherwise scolding her husband in bed. It was pillow talk at its most one-sided.

The cover of Thomas Heywood's *A Curtaine Lecture*, printed in 1637, shows just such an imagined scene. Husband and wife, each dressed in nightcap and nightgown, lie awake in a canopied, four-poster bed. A side curtain is left open for us to witness this intimate moment. An hourglass and a candlestick are placed on a low, circular table with fringed covering. Also within easy reach are a cushion and a chamber pot. The wife sits bolt upright, her knees pulled up under the blanket, while her husband, annoyed at getting an earful, barely lifts his head from a stack of fluffy pillows. With clenched fist, he clings not to his dear wife, but to his heavy blanket. The sand that has fallen to the bottom of the hourglass tells us that this curtain lecture has been going on for quite some time. A crescent moon, glimpsed through the window, signals the late hour. Here, in the ultimate sanctuary of the marital bed, the norms of masculine dominance and feminine submission are reversed. Powerless, for once, the husband cannot stop his wife from speaking. He can only wait it out, hoping for a little sleep before the rooster crows at first light.

Other views of marital privacy were not so cynical. In *The Flower of Friendship*, Edmund Tilney singled out the martial bed as the 'place appointed for reconcilements and renewing of love and friendship'. In this space of absolute intimacy, the wife 'may lawfully pour out … all the thoughts and secrets of her loving heart'. The bed is not where wives harass their husbands, as the stereotype of the curtain lecture would have it, but where spouses confide in each other, heart speaking to loving heart.

Both images distort reality, one by hardening it and the other by softening. Somewhere in the middle lies the truth of Elizabethan home life: the marital bed was a privileged, even unique, space, the innermost sanctum for the mistress and the master. Words spoken there, late at night, or early in the morning, could not be uttered elsewhere in the house, and certainly not outside the house, for fear they might be overheard. Precisely because it was, symbolically, a world elsewhere, the spousal bed was the one place in the family home where, if only for a night's interval, the bonds of patriarchy could be slipped.

'My True and Honourable Wife'

The nearest Shakespeare came to writing a curtain lecture is the scene from *Julius Caesar* where Portia implores her husband, Brutus, to tell her what has upset and distracted him: 'You have some sick offence within your mind / Which by the right and virtue of my place / I ought to know of' (2.2.267–9). What she has a right to know, but does not yet know, is that Brutus has reluctantly agreed to conspire in Caesar's assassination at the Curia of Pompey. Complicity in political murder is the grave offence that sickens her husband's mind. Portia does not know this dark truth, but the audience does.

Shakespeare, with uncommon skill, writes this entire scene as topsy-turvy curtain lecture, its customary masculine and feminine roles reversed. To begin, the scene does not take place in bed. Tormented by his own thoughts, and not by any wifely scolding, the master of the house cannot sleep: 'Y'have ungently, Brutus, / Stole from my bed' (2.1.236–7). Portia, too, rises from their bed – it's now empty – and goes to comfort her husband, though he is not in a mood to be comforted. Instead of a wife unburdening herself to her husband, Shakespeare turns it around so that Portia entreats Brutus to share his sufferings with *her*: 'Dear my lord, / Make me acquainted with your cause of grief' (2.1.254–5).' He refuses, but she persists, declaring that it's not enough for her 'To keep with you at meals, comfort your bed, / And talk to you sometimes' (2.1.283–4). She will not just share a bed and a home with her husband, she will *know* him, in full, without 'sort or limitation' (2.1.282).

Overwhelmed by Portia's devotion, Brutus relents and assures his wife that soon he will confide in her: 'And by and by thy bosom shall partake / The secrets of my heart. / All my engagements I will construe to thee, / All the charactery of my sad brows' (2.1.304–8). And so, the scene ends conventionally, with one spouse promising to speak the truth to the other. Except that it's the husband who will pour out his pent-up, secret thoughts and the wife who will listen, lovingly, while he does.

'That Great Vow Did Make Us One'

Exactly how Shakespeare divided his time between Stratford and London is a question that has vexed biographers for centuries, partly because the answer is so elusive and partly because so much is at stake in that elusive answer. Did Shakespeare reinvent himself as a Londoner, keeping Stratford at arm's length, a place for family duties and the business of landowning? Or did he remain loyal to Stratford, there always in spirit, if not in body, with London commanding his time and creative energy but never the cares of his heart? Likely, we'll never know.

What we do know is that Shakespeare's marital bed was half-empty for a long, long time. All the intimacies customarily enacted there – curtain lectures, whispered secrets, apologies, reconciliations, outpourings of the heart, shared silences and, of course, erotic desires – were available to this couple only intermittently. Compared to his father, and most of his married friends, William Shakespeare was on the receiving end of many fewer curtain lectures simply because he wasn't around to hear them. And if Anne Shakespeare wanted to complain to someone, she could complain only to herself; if she wanted to open her heart, there was no one to open it to.

Except during the early years of their marriage, which might have been spent in the Henley Street house, Anne and William Shakespeare did not regularly share a bed. If the newly married couple did live with Shakespeare's parents, they must have found precious little privacy, for the best bed was not theirs to occupy. William and Anne came second place in the household's hierarchy, and so were expected to obey and defer to Shakespeare's parents.

Julius Caesar was written around 1599, not long after Shakespeare bought New Place, a grand family home where his wife and two daughters could live in envied comfort. Yet how often was he himself there? Is it possible that, at some inscrutable level, Portia's moving plea to Brutus – 'By all your vows of love, and that great vow / Which did incorporate and make us one, / That you unfold to me, your self, your half' (2.1.271–3) – is a transmuted echo of Anne's unfulfilled longing to have her husband right by her side, his warm bodily presence the surest sign of marital constancy. Did this Stratford wife also worry that she dwelled but in the suburbs of her husband's good pleasure? If so, she could not, as Portia did with Brutus, call him back to bed.

'The Entertaining of Honest Guests'

If the bed symbolized the deepest intimacies of married life, then hospitality was a household's public face. Hospitality in Shakespeare's time entailed much more than being a good host to your friends and relatives. An essentially moral concept, it was one of the religious works of charity and mercy, as Caleb Dalechamp, a minister at Cambridge University, explained in *Christian Hospitalitie* (1632). This inclusive social practice extended to 'the feasting of mean neighbours, the relieving of the poor, and the entertaining of honest guests and travelers of the same country'. Hospitality was, at its best, an ever-widening circle of courtesy.

Yet for all its kindness and generosity, hospitality was also a canny form of property insurance. If you are welcomed into someone else's home, if you are warmly received as a trusted guest, then you don't need to force your way in. That house is there for you whenever you need it because the owners are happy to share it with you. The reciprocal nature of hospitality – sometimes we are the host, other times the guest – protects every host's property while also satisfying every guest's need.

'See, see, our honoured hostess'

It was a scandal to violate the domestic virtue of hospitality. Far worse than a simple breach of etiquette, being a poor host was a major character defect. An inhospitable person was an immoral person. Just consider the Macbeths, who pretend to be good hosts even as they are plotting to murder in his sleep their honoured royal guest. King Duncan arrives at their castle in Inverness not knowing that he has just fallen into a deadly trap:

DUNCAN
This castle hath a pleasant seat, the air
Nimbly and sweetly recommends itself
Unto our gentle senses.

BANQUO
                        This guest of summer,
The temple-haunting martlet, does approve,
By his loved mansionry, that the heaven's breath
Smells wooingly here. No jutty frieze,
Buttress, nor coin of vantage, but this bird
Hath made his pendent bed, and procreant cradle:
Where they must breed and haunt, I have observed
The air is delicate

Enter LADY MACBETH

DUNCAN
                        See, see our honoured hostess . . .

LADY MACBETH
All our service,
In every point twice done, and then done double,
Were poor and single business, to contend
Against those honours deep and broad wherewith
Your majesty loads our house. [. . .]

DUNCAN
                        Fair and noble hostess,
We are your guest to-night.

                                            (1.6.1–24)

The tiny bird is the key to unlock this scene's meaning. Shakespeare uses the
archaic word 'mansionry' to convey that the martin's nest in the castle is a sort
of home within a home. As they approach Macbeth's castle, Duncan and
Banquo spot nests of martins everywhere: in a high corner ('coin'), near an
overhanging jutty or alongside the frieze on the wall. For them, it's an obviously
happy portent, because martins nest only where 'the air is delicate'. Remember,
the Elizabethans feared polluted air because they believed, mistakenly, that it
caused cholera and plague. The abundance of nesting martins at Inverness
really was a good omen. Far from being a stone-cold fortress, the castle feels
to Duncan like a warm and inviting home. A site of effusive hospitality. At
least that's the courteous impression he wants to give to his hosts.
    Too many productions of *Macbeth* miss this point entirely, opting for a
brutal and forbidding castle, a place where *no one* feels at home. Such a

dark atmosphere undercuts the scene's loaded irony, because Shakespeare builds up the image of an ideal home, a sanctuary of good health and warm hospitality, only to tear it down. Duncan and Banquo praise the castle's sweet and delicate air. Their hostess offers them an exaggerated welcome: 'All our service', Lady Macbeth over-promises, 'In every point twice done, and then done double.' Sweet extravagance everywhere. Yet all those niceties only conceal her foul intent to kill the king, the man to whom she owes not just charity, but fealty and obedience. Duncan will die within hours. The audience knows the awful truth that, despite the welcoming presence of the martin's nest, and despite Lady Macbeth's lavished courtesy, this castle's air is foul, its life diseased and its hosts of evil nature.

The Macbeths' regicidal plot, as the play goes on to reveal, carries devastating consequences for the kingdom of Scotland. Yet Shakespeare wrote this particular scene with a powerful sense of house and home, the smallest social unit. In doing so, he reminded us that a household truly was the bedrock of society, a little commonwealth that, if well run, would keep the commonwealth at large in proper order. It was the epitome of the whole world, as Henry Wotton put it. But if that bedrock weakened, or, worse, crumbled, the damage would spread, like an unstoppable infection. Once home life is corrupted, all of society will become corrupt. It's only a question of time. In the scene of Lady Macbeth greeting, with sinister hypocrisy, Duncan at the castle gate, Shakespeare was inviting his audience to ask themselves whether they, too, have violated the essential code of hospitality.

'Both baked in this pie'

Was William Shakespeare a good host? We don't know. In London, he lodged in other people's homes and so couldn't play the host, a role reserved for the master of the house. Back in Stratford, New Place was a grand residence for receiving visitors, but he was not always there. It must have been Anne, his wife, who played the chief host, extending hospitality to her guests. No doubt she was much better at it than Lady Macbeth.

But in the Scottish tragedy, just as in the curtain lecture between Portia and Brutus in *Julius Caesar*, Shakespeare turned on its head a domestic tradition that his own private life did not allow him to practice, at least not as much as other men. Nor was it just Lady Macbeth who was a bad host. The play's three witches throw ingredients into a caldron, something any housewife would do when cooking a meal over the fire. But the weird sisters aren't feeding their families; they're poisoning their enemies. In *The Taming of the Shrew*, Petruchio taunts Kate, his new and unruly wife, by presenting her with an array of sumptuous dishes that his servant snatches away before she can taste a single bite. Ariel, in *The Tempest*, conjures a disappearing banquet to trick Antonio, Sebastian and Alonso. And in Shakespeare's most macabre banquet scene, Titus Andronicus serves to Tamora a meat pie made from the flesh of her own sons: 'Why, there they are, both baked in this pie, / Whereof their mother daintily hath fed, / Eating the flesh that she herself hath bred' (5.3.59–61).

Shakespeare never wrote a play about an ordinary Elizabethan family living in an ordinary Elizabethan house. Indeed, he wrote fewer plays with a domestic setting than some of his contemporaries. Perhaps because his own household affairs were, for many years, so unusually arranged, he opted to write plays that inverted domestic norms. When you go to the theatre, you don't want to see a serving maid toss carrots and turnips into a pot simmering over the fire. You can do that at home. What you want to see, and what Shakespeare gladly gives you, is the amazement of home life turned upside down: intruders in bedchambers, sons disowning their mothers, spouses leaving marital beds empty and witches dropping into their bubbling hell-broth a newt's eye, a dog's tongue and a frog's toe.

PART TWO

The World and Shakespeare

5

Thy Stratford Monument

'The terms of our estate may not endure'
HAMLET (3.3.5)

In the mid-1840s, while living in Paris, the English pre-Raphaelite artist Ford Maddox Brown made sixteen drawings of scenes from *King Lear*, one of which became his watercolour painting 'Cordelia's Portion', now in the Lady Lever Art Gallery in Liverpool, England. In ochre, russet and muted browns, the painting depicts the climax of the tragedy's opening scene, when the old monarch, abdicating the throne, demands that his three daughters profess their love for him. Each sister is forced to compete against her siblings to win the greatest share of their father's kingdom. Cordelia, the youngest, unlike the scheming Goneril and Regan, refuses to speak, answering only that she loves her father 'according to my bond' (1.1.93). She means that her love is pure and not tied to hope of material gain. Her love cannot be bought with a bribe, not even a bribe as vast at the kingdom of Britain.

Her father's favourite, right up until this moment, Cordelia pays a sorrowful price for her silence. Already half-mad, Lear first disinherits her and then disowns her. Cordelia's 'portion', her share of the family estate, amounts to nothing. In Maddox Brown's painting, the now dowerless maiden all but collapses, held up by her future husband, the king of France. Meanwhile, Goneril and Regan, oblivious to their younger sister's suffering, exchange greedy looks, grasping after the crown that symbolizes their royal inheritance.

William Shakespeare wrote a play that begins with a patriarch dividing his estate among some of his children sometime around 1603 or 1605, not long after he had decided what to do with the house where he was born, having inherited it upon his father's death a few years earlier. Shakespeare didn't need the Henley Street residence because he already owned a much better one: New Place, an attractive mansion in the centre of Stratford, where his wife and daughters lived year-round and where he lived when he wasn't in London. Shakespeare's widowed mother, who lived until 1608, might have moved to New Place, or perhaps she remained in the house on

Henley Street, where she had dwelled since her marriage to John Shakespeare more than forty years earlier. Either way, the couple's eldest son, William, now owned the house; and he alone determined who could live there.

A loose parallel between *King Lear* and Shakespeare's private life doesn't make his tragedy even remotely autobiographical. But it does mean that the playwright was sharply aware how any family can be torn apart by greed, squabbles over real estate or emotional blackmail.

Fortunately, William Shakespeare's family was much better than King Lear's family at handling property, passing it on and not feuding over it. There's no record of family quarrels or legal infighting. Yet, like Lear, Shakespeare wanted his property to remain in his immediate family, handed down intact from one generation to the next. And so it was, for many years. But the story ended in a way that Shakespeare would not have predicted: the house where he was born ceased to be a private family home and became instead a public shrine dedicated to his memory.

That might never have happened. Shakespeare, after inheriting the Henley Street property, might have sold it, instead of allowing his sister Joan Hart and her three boys to live there, in the separate cottage, for a peppercorn rent. He might have written his will differently, not bequeathing the house to Susanna, his oldest child. His descendants might have lived there longer or not at all. The Birthplace might have burned down; it might have been torn down. If New Place, the house in Stratford that Shakespeare bought in 1597, had survived instead of being demolished, or if the original Globe on London's Bankside were still standing, those sites would have attracted all the tourists, leaving the Birthplace unprized and so forgotten. It wasn't inevitable that a plain house on a Stratford side street became a world-famous shrine to the Bard of Avon. But it happened. And it happened in the century and a half between Shakespeare's death in 1616 and the Stratford Jubilee, the world's first Shakespeare festival, dreamt up and led by the famed actor David Garrick in 1769.

How it happened – how the Birthplace *became* the Birthplace – is a roundabout tale of family fortunes, sheer chance, biographical curiosity, unembarrassed deceptions and a masterly publicity campaign conducted by an egotistical celebrity actor who realized that Shakespeare was his luckiest meal ticket.

The story begins with Shakespeare's death.

Shakespeare, Shakespere, Shake-speare, Shak-speare

In April 1616, when William Shakespeare of Stratford-upon-Avon, gentleman, died in his hometown, only eighteen of his plays, just under half, had been published. *Romeo and Juliet* (1597), *The Merchant of Venice*

(1600), *Hamlet* (1603) and *King Lear* (1608) were among those that had
been printed individually in small unbound versions called quartos. Unbound
because book owners at the time often combined several of them to make a
single, larger volume. They were about the size of a modern paperback, with
each sheet of printed paper folded twice to make four (hence, 'quarto')
leaves. *Richard III* was Shakespeare's most successful printed drama, going
through five editions between 1597 and 1612.

Yet his most frequently reprinted work was not a play but the long
narrative poem *Venus and Adonis*, first printed in 1593 and dedicated to his
young and handsome patron Henry Wriothesley, the Earl of Southampton.
Just a single copy of the first edition survives, now held in the Bodleian
Library at Oxford University. The most popular vernacular poem of its day,
Venus and Adonis gave Shakespeare his first taste of literary renown and
reputation. Capitalizing on its success, he published another classically
inspired poem, *The Rape of Lucrece*, the following year. He had plenty of
time to write, for an outbreak of plague had forced the closure of London
theatres for fourteen months. It wasn't Shakespeare's plays that initially
made him famous as a writer; it was his poetry.

In truth, there's no sign that Shakespeare took much care to get his plays
published. Other than the play's name, the only piece of information that
consistently appeared on quarto title pages was the name of the acting
company that first performed it. For Shakespeare, that usually meant the
Lord Chamberlain's Men, renamed the King's Men in 1603 after the newly
crowned James I became its patron, the company for which Shakespeare
was lead playwright, occasional actor and co-owner. 'As it hath been sundry
times publickley acted by . . .' was the standard form of words printed
beneath a play's title, an assurance to readers that the published text derived
from the actual script used in the theatre. Sometimes the playwright's name
appeared on the title page, but never spelled the same way: Shakespeare,
Shakespere, Shake-speare or even Shak-speare. Indeed, his name didn't
appear on the title page of *any* play until 1598, after seven of them had been
published, when he was finally identified in print as the author of *Love's
Labour's Lost*, *Richard II* and *Richard III*. Except for the delayed appearance
of his erratically spelled surname, William Shakespeare the author was
otherwise invisible in the first published versions of his plays.

How bizarre that the world's greatest dramatist wasn't always or even
regularly named as the author of his own works. It doesn't make sense.
'Shakespeare' is the name of all names, the one that attracts readers (and
book buyers) everywhere and forever. His name should dominate the page,
not disappear from it. It should appear *above* the title, printed in the largest
type size the page will accommodate.

Shakespeare and his contemporaries thought differently. For them, play
scripts belonged not to individual authors but to the acting ensembles that
staged them. In an age before copyright protection, theatre companies like
the Lord Chamberlain's Men hesitated to publish their scripts for fear of

giving ammunition to their unscrupulous rivals. And so, when they did publish a play text, they always branded it with the *company's* name, their business logo, as both advertisement to the public and warning – 'hands off our script' – to their competitors.

'Mr William Shakespeares Comedies, Histories & Tragedies'

All that changed forever in 1623, seven years after Shakespeare's death. His former playhouse colleagues John Heminges and Henry Condell – close friends, remembered in his will – collected the scripts of thirty-six plays by the late William Shakespeare, arranged them by genre, and published them as a single book. Fully half of them, including *Macbeth*, *Julius Caesar* and *The Tempest*, had not appeared in print before and so might otherwise have been forever lost. Each play was laboriously typeset in cramped double columns on quality French rag paper nearly a foot high. The title page, getting right down to business, names the entire work *Mr William Shakespeares Comedies, Histories & Tragedies. Published according to the True Originall Copies*. Posterity knows it simply as 'The First Folio', in recognition of the volume's imposing size and its inaugural place in the print history of Shakespearean drama.

Like the King James Bible, its near contemporary, the First Folio was expensive, prestigious, handsome and meant to last. Two hundred and thirty-two copies survive, a great number for a book printed nearly four centuries ago, and more than the extant copies of the famous English bible printed in 1611. Quarto texts, smaller and thinner, were prone to perish. The 1594 copy of *Titus Andronicus* now locked deep inside the vaults of the Folger Shakespeare Library in Washington, DC, is a unique copy of that edition, the only one remaining. Hefty and bulky, the nine-hundred-page First Folio impressed upon sight. Here was a book that shouted its own importance before you read a single word of it.

Beyond making twice as many of Shakespeare's plays available in print, the main difference between the First Folio and the quartos is the hyper-attention that the larger volume gives to Shakespeare himself. For the first time, his name appears consistently on the title page. His name *is* the title: *Mr William Shakespeares* . . . For the first time, we see Shakespeare's face. We can hardly miss it because this image takes up most of the title page. The woodcut of Martin Droeshout's copper engraving remains the world's best-known likeness of Shakespeare: a middle-aged man dressed in an expensive doublet and making no effort to hide a deeply receding hairline, the exposed forehead hinting at the author's massive brainpower. Next come pages of verses and eulogies to pore over, or skip over, depending on your tolerance for panegyric, each composed by a literary worthy of the day and each in praise of William

Shakespeare the man. And then, at last, the reader arrives at the first line in the first scene in the first of thirty-six plays, the basecamp at the foot of Mount Shakespeare. It's a stage direction from *The Tempest* – '*A tempestuous noise of Thunder and Lightning heard: Enter a Ship-master, and a Boteswaine.*'

All this apparatus, all this strange new fuss in word and image, tells us that this one particular book venerates its author as much as it gathers, preserves and celebrates what that author wrote. The First Folio is not just the proudest anthology of plays in the English language; it is the greatest monument to a writer the world has ever produced.

'Thy Stratford Moniment'

Building that monument was partly the task of the men who composed the First Folio's various prefaces. They knew that in Stratford-upon-Avon, another, more traditional, monument to Shakespeare already existed: the gravesite and the funerary statue sculpted by Gheerart Janssen in Holy Trinity Church. Yet the success of their bookish enterprise depended upon persuading the public, or, at least, the elite book-buying segment of it, that while brick-and-mortar memorials to Shakespeare would in time disappear, his printed works would last forever. It was an old idea, going back to the ancient Roman poet Horace, who declared that his writings would outlast bronze. That's what poet Leonard Digges had in mind when he penned his eulogy 'To the Memorie of the deceased Authour Maister W. Shakespeare', urging that the playwright's truest memorial was not found in cracked stone or dulled brass, but in a text freshly printed:

Shake-speare, *at length thy pious fellowes give*
The world thy Workes: *thy* Workes, *by which, out-live*
Thy Tombe, thy name must when that stone is rent,
And Time dissolves thy Stratford Moniment,
Here we alive shall view thee still. This Booke,
When Brasse and Marble fade, shall make thee looke
Fresh to all Ages

lines 1–7

The conceit here, and it's a familiar one, is that although Shakespeare the man is dead, Shakespeare the author lives on. The man rests in peace beneath his 'Stratford *Moniment*'. But it's only a matter of time before both the corpse and the tomb decay into dust, the common fate of all mortal things. What outlasts the corpse and what replaces the tomb is the book – '*thy Workes*' – the one site where Shakespeare the author survives and, in time's defiance, remains '*Fresh to all Ages*'. Ben Jonson shared that view in his more famous commendatory verse from the same volume, proposing that the late author would remain 'alive still' so long as his 'Booke doth live.'

The First Folio ignored Shakespeare's life so that it could obsess over his death. Or rather, so that it could redeem his death through a text that grants to him life everlasting. Shakespeare would have understood that idea perfectly because he had already expressed it himself. In a memorable meditation from Sonnet 18 on the power of language to reverse the ravages of time, the poet assures his beloved that 'Nor shall death brag thou wander'st in his shade / When in eternal lines to time thou grow'st' (lines 11–12). Beauty dies, but words never do.

In 1623, the crafty editors of the First Folio pushed the idea that an author, and this one author especially, lives on the page and nowhere else. Heminges and Condell killed William Shakespeare the man from Stratford a second time only to resurrect him as William Shakespeare the masterly author, perpetually alive through his undying words. If you seek Shakespeare's monument, don't bother travelling to Stratford-upon-Avon to visit his gravesite, because it may have already crumbled away. Buy the book instead.

'I Gyve Will bequeath & Devise'

With Shakespeare so imagined in the First Folio as pure spirit – 'Soule of the age', as his friend and rival poet Ben Jonson lastingly put it – how easy it must have been for readers at the time to ignore the pleasant Warwickshire market town where the first son of Mary Arden and John Shakespeare was born, baptized, schooled, grew up, fell in love, fathered three children, mourned the death of his only son, acquired land and tithes, bought one house and inherited another, lent money, made money, sued his debtors, retired, wrote his will and died.

Nowhere in its sundry prefaces does the First Folio mention either of the two houses in Stratford where William Shakespeare lived: New Place, the handsome residence with a large garden situated prominently on the corner of Chapel Street and Chapel Lane, which the thirty-three-year-old Shakespeare bought in 1597 and where nineteen years later he died; and on the north side of Henley Street, at the town's edge, the humbler dwelling where in 1564 he was born. The intertwined history of these houses explains why public attention eventually settled on the Birthplace, although it easily could have gone the other way, as the preferred destination of Shakespeare pilgrims the world over.

In 1623, when the First Folio was published, the Shakespeare family's claim upon both their houses was much more than a recent memory. It was a continuing fact of daily life in the town. When 'William Shackspeare of Stratford upon Avon' dictated his last will and testament, in March 1616, he instructed that his firstborn child, Susanna (1583–1649), by then married to the homeopathic physician John Hall, should inherit both properties: 'I Gyve Will bequeath & Devise unto my daughter Susanna Hall . . . All that Capitall Messuage or tenemente with thappurtenaunces in Stratford aforesaied Called the newe place wherein I nowe dwell & twoe messuages or tenementes with theappurtenaunces scituat lyeing & being in Henley streete within the borough of Stratford aforesaied.'

Susanna Hall and her husband took possession of New Place upon her father's death a month later. Shakespeare had further stipulated that his cash-strapped sister Joan Hart, his only surviving sibling, would be granted a life tenancy in the tiny cottage on Henley Street, 'wherein she dwelleth', for an annual peppercorn rent of twelve pence. Joan Hart outlived her famous brother by thirty years, before dying at the unusually advanced age of seventy-seven. All that long time, she lived in the two-room cottage next to the main house, in accordance with the terms of her brother's will. The larger eastern half of the house, the Maidenhead Inn, was then rented to one Lewis Hiccox, who probably acquired the lease directly from Shakespeare after he inherited the premises in 1601.

In Protestant theology, unchecked desire for worldly goods led to sinful acts, when a person really ought to be focused on the state of their immortal soul. How crucial, then, for someone on their deathbed – Shakespeare, say, in March 1616 – to make their last will and testament. A will took care of how a person's material possessions would be disposed, freeing them, in their last days on earth, to repent of their sins and pray for salvation. 'They whom the Lord hath endued with the goods of the world', as Thomas Becon advised in *The Sicke Mans Salve*, in 1561, 'should before their departure set a godly order . . . in their temporal possession.' It was the only way to get to heaven.

In Shakespeare's will, we see a dying man divesting himself of his amassed estate, but, unlike selfish King Lear, in a benevolent way. He even provides, in a final act of charity, for his widowed sister Joan and her three boys, who had fallen on hard times. As I was reading his will, I wondered whether Shakespeare would have been stunned by the far-reaching consequences of allowing his sister Joan to remain in Henley Street, a decision that, although charitable at the time, nearly led to the house's ruin two hundred years later.

'A neat Monument'

In December 1623, the Kentish baronet Sir Edward Dering recorded in his account book that he had paid two pounds – enough to buy eighty-eight loaves of bread – for two copies of the First Folio, thereby becoming the first documented owner of Shakespeare's collected plays. Sir Edward likely knew nothing about where the Shakespeare family lived in Stratford because there was no biography, not even a short one, to reveal such private and intimate details. There was no Shakespeare biography for a very good reason: there was no demand for it. Curiosity about Shakespeare's life had not yet developed among Shakespeare's readers.

Missing from seventeenth-century literary culture was a lively interest in what belletrists of the nineteenth century would call Shakespeare's 'homes and haunts': places he lived, places he knew intimately, places where his face was not just recognized but welcomed. Until such curiosity developed, where Shakespeare rested his head, whether in Stratford or in London, would not be thought important for understanding either the man or his works, let alone the relationship between them.

Indeed, public knowledge about Shakespeare the man was then little more than cursory. In 1634, a Lieutenant Hammond left his army camp in Norwich to join two friends as they toured the English countryside. Reaching Stratford, 130 miles to the west, they visited Holy Trinity Church, where they could not help but notice Shakespeare's funerary statue placed prominently on the chancel's north wall. Or, as you approach it, to the left. Hammond recorded in his diary exactly what he saw: 'A neat Monument of that famous English Poet, Mr. William Shakespeere, who was borne here.'

The playwright's reputation and family link to Stratford are here duly acknowledged, just as they were in the First Folio, printed a decade earlier; but still, the remark verges on the anecdotal. Hammond knew some barebones facts, yes, but he did not journey to Stratford in search of Shakespeare.

We can hardly accuse him of neglect when the town itself, increasingly a bastion of hardened Puritan sentiment, took little interest in honouring Shakespeare's memory. A mere six years after his death, the Stratford Corporation paid six shillings to the King's Men – his own company – so that they would *not* perform in the Guildhall, the very place where the young William Shakespeare likely saw his first play.

'One thing more'

Nor was seeking out Shakespeare the motive for the great historian Sir William Dugdale when he visited Stratford in the 1650s. He travelled there, and to many other sites in the county, to research his colossus of antiquarian labour, *The Antiquities of Warwickshire Illustrated*. Printed in 1656 in handsome folio and dedicated to 'My Honourable Friends The Gentrie of Warwickshire', this encyclopedia of local history was meant to last. Surely, a work written by a seventeenth-century Warwickshire man who esteemed relics and remains, and who had compiled his history as a '*Monumental Pillar*' erected to the memory of his worthy 'Ancestors', would devote a little attention to Shakespeare's life and where he lived. 'We might reasonably have expected [from Dugdale] some curious memorials of his illustrious countryman', reasoned the scholar Edmond Malone in his 1821 posthumously published biography of Shakespeare. 'But he has not given us a single particular of his private life; contenting himself with a very slight mention of him.'

Slight mention indeed. True, Dugdale describes and illustrates Shakespeare's grave, along with those, laid out alongside it, of Anne Shakespeare, Susanna Hall, her husband John Hall and Thomas Nash, the first husband of Susanna and John's daughter Elizabeth. He even transcribes the haunting inscription – 'Good friend for Jesus sake forbeare, / To dig the dust enclosed here . . .' – pleading for Shakespeare's bones to be left undisturbed. He had to step over the stone slab grave and then turn around to copy the inscription because its lettering faced away from the approach through the nave. Dugdale must have stood, as no visitor today is permitted, right on top of Shakespeare's grave. He meant no disrespect; it was just a good place from which to notice and describe some of the monuments, tombs and chapels in Holy Trinity Church.

The *Antiquities* makes no mention of the site where Shakespeare was born, even though his granddaughter Elizabeth owned it and his nephew Thomas Hart, son of Joan, lived in the cottage there as her tenant. The rest of the premises was still given over to the Maidenhead Inn, also rented out. Dugdale likely knew nothing about the Birthplace because he wasn't much interested in Shakespeare's life. So lowly a building was beneath the attention of so high-minded an antiquarian. In 1642, some Parliamentary troops, among those who fought against Charles I and the monarchy, stole provisions from the Maidenhead Inn where they were billeted. Clearly, nobody thought there was anything special about Shakespeare's house.

Historians in the seventeenth century studied public, not private, life. They grew obsessed with material remains of the past – old churches, old tombs, old castles, old coins, old statues and old bridges – which they collectively labelled 'antiquities'. And so, Dugdale compiled an illustrated history of official buildings and public places in the county of Warwickshire. Only incidentally did he write a history of Warwickshire people; and most of those he mentioned were earls and bishops, not poets and playwrights.

In the ten pages Dugdale allocated to Stratford, William Shakespeare the man figured, not prominently, but almost as an aside. After carefully describing 'a fair Bridg of stone over Avon, containing xiiii arches', Dugdale offered a final stray comment before moving on to the next locale: 'One thing more, in reference to this antient Town is observable, that it gave birth and sepulture to our late famous Poet Will Shakespere.' How oddly that reads. Today, anyone writing on the same topic would instinctively select Shakespeare as the dominant figure, not downgrade him to one more factoid.

But the biography that Dugdale wrote was of Stratford, not Shakespeare. In true antiquarian spirit, the town itself takes precedence over its inhabitants, however famous, with Shakespeare's life compressed to the point of invisibility between 'birth and sepulture', his arrival on earth and his departure from it. In the eyes of a renowned seventeenth-century historian, Shakespeare's life and times amounted merely to an afterthought.

'Remember to peruse Shakespear's plays'

In 1656, when Dugdale's *Antiquities* was first published, London theatres had been shut for over a decade, their closure forced by the ruling Puritans in 1642. They remained shut until the summer of 1660, when the English monarchy was restored under Charles II, son of the martyred Charles I. Shortly after ascending the throne, the young king granted his courtiers Thomas Killigrew and Sir William Davenant an exclusive licence to form acting companies and to open theatres in London.

Because theatres had been closed for a generation, new plays were hard to find. Killigrew and Davenant had no choice but to perform the 'old stock drama', as they called it, from before 1642. They resurrected dozens of plays written by Shakespeare and his contemporaries, especially Ben Jonson, Francis Beaumont and John Fletcher. Within a few years, Londoners could see productions of *Hamlet*, *Romeo and Juliet*, *Othello*, *Twelfth Night* and *A Midsummer Night's Dream*, plays still central to the classical repertoire.

Shakespeare's revival in the Restoration theatre – after nearly two decades of suppression, his plays were reaching audiences once more – inevitably sparked interest in Shakespeare the dramatist. Not the private man, but the public author. Visitors to Holy Trinity Church in the early 1660s asked so many questions about the playwright from Stratford that vicar John Ward had to brush up his Shakespeare, for fear of fumbling his answers. Yet as Ward's notebook reveals, the questions were about the plays, not the man who wrote them: 'Remember to peruse Shakespear's plays, and bee versed in them, yt I may not bee ignorant in yt matter.'

Ward's aide-memoire makes perfect sense. Shakespeare's plays were being acted for the first time in nearly two decades and so people were interested in them. They were the talk of the town. A new folio edition of the collected plays appeared in 1664, the first in thirty years. Mandatory it was for a Stratford clergyman to be well-versed in Shakespeare's plays; but being unversed in Shakespeare's life was nonetheless permissible – because nobody was yet asking questions about that.

6

Our Shakespeare's House

'Fore God, you have here goodly dwelling, and rich.'
2 HENRY IV (5.3.5–6)

Glimpses of Shakespeare biography first appear in the 1690s, when stories told in Stratford about the town's most famous inhabitant were finally put on paper, eight decades after Shakespeare's death. Consider the case of John Dowdall, a lawyer who visited Stratford in the early spring of 1693 and then recounted his trip in a twelve-page letter to his cousin, a Mr Southwell. This letter is carefully preserved in the Folger Shakespeare Library, where I read it. Like many fellow travellers, Dowdall paid his respects at the burial site – 'I saw the effigies of our English tragedian, Mr. Shakspeare' – and carefully copied both the gravesite epitaph and the inscription beneath Shakespeare's bust.

He learned a bit more about Shakespeare from the clergyman who escorted him on a tour of Holy Trinity Church:

> The clerk that showed me this church is above 80 years old. He says that this Shakespeare was formerly in this town bound apprentice to a butcher; but that he ran from his master to London, & there was received into the playhouse as a servitour, & by this means had an opportunity to be what he afterwards proved. He was the best of his family; but the male line is extinguished.

Fact, error and legend trip over each other in these few sentences. The 'clerk' was William Castle, the church sexton, then aged sixty-five, which for the time was a ripe old age. The young William Shakespeare might well have trained to become a butcher, although nobody knows for sure. His father, who needed all sorts of animal hides to make gloves, would certainly have known all the local butchers. No one has yet discovered precisely why Shakespeare left his hometown or exactly how he started in the theatre, although it stands to reason that he quickly worked his way up in London's burgeoning theatrical world. Without question, he became the most famous member of his family. The male line extinguished itself early on, when

Shakespeare's only son, Hamnet, died aged eleven in 1596. When Dowdall visited Stratford in 1693, Shakespeare's closest living descendants were the grandchildren of his sister Joan Hart.

Essential though it is to distinguish between fact and conjecture in stories about Shakespeare, there's another issue at stake here. Dowdall's letter reveals *how* Shakespeare biography emerged at the end of the seventeenth century. It emerged first as an oral tradition, Stratford locals telling stories to each other and to visitors, and then as a written one, with travellers keeping diaries or writing to friends about what they saw or heard during their trips. 'Now I proceed to inform you', as Dowdall announced in his letter, 'what Antiquities I have observed.' This antiquarian tradition of Shakespeare biography remained happily informal, even anecdotal. In the 1690s, no one gave talks about Shakespeare, no one wrote books about Shakespeare, no one studied Shakespeare in school and no one tracked down original documents to research his life story. All that lay in the future.

Moreover, Shakespeare's life didn't matter for its own sake. When scattered references to Shakespeare occur in either seventeenth-century travel narratives or antiquarian histories, like Dugdale's *Antiquities*, they're nearly always part of a larger and more important story. We need to remember that the first accounts of Shakespeare's life were penned not by Shakespeare enthusiasts, but by local history buffs, people who got excited by the material remains of the past, whether old coins, old bridges, old churches, old castles or old graves. When Dowdall visited Holy Trinity Church, the massive 'stately monument' to George Carew, Earl of Totnes, in the Clopton Chapel, impressed him far more than Shakespeare's plain gravesite. How could it be otherwise? Carew was a statesman, a man of public affairs, artillery master to King James I – a 'worthy', to use an epithet invoked at the time – while Shakespeare, although a lauded dramatist, was still essentially a private figure. Carew's elaborate raised tomb dwarfed Shakespeare's gravestone and funerary statue because Carew was then more deserving of posterity's regard.

Today, the reverse is true. Dowdall's remarks about Shakespeare as the apprentice butcher from Stratford who escaped to London stand out in bold relief. Indeed, the main reason we still know about this otherwise humdrum letter written more than three hundred years ago is because it refers to Shakespeare's youth, now a subject of enduring interest. But who remembers George Carew? Not the hundreds of thousands who year in and year out pass right by his monument in the Clopton Chapel as they make a beeline to Shakespeare's grave in the chancel.

How perceptions have changed. In the 1690s, William Shakespeare deserved a respectful nod or a lively anecdote, but not much more. For historians and tourists alike, Shakespeare was but a minor character in the history of Warwickshire and his life story barely amounted to a sub-plot in that broader and more consequential narrative. And his plain burial site was nothing compared to George Carew's elaborate carved effigy, complete with guns, powder kegs and cannons.

'Beyond any that have ever
been published'

It's not that seventeenth-century antiquarians like Dugdale and Dowdall willfully suppressed Shakespeare biography. They didn't conspire to downplay or sideline Shakespeare in favour of their preferred historical figures; rather, they never thought too deeply about his life story in the first place. For them, history was the narrative of noble personages and mighty events, whether for the kingdom of England, the county of Warwickshire or the town of Stratford-upon-Avon. In the grand pageant of history, the life of England's most famous dramatist didn't amount to much. Shakespeare biography had yet to rise above the level of a name check. Something in the wider culture had to change before Shakespeare's life story could progress from a topic of casual curiosity to a legitimate object of study and serious research.

What changed was how people thought about literature. In the final years of the seventeenth century, people began to think of 'English literature' as a distinct body of texts, a collective artistic achievement that spanned centuries and embraced the diverse genres of poetry, drama and epic. The corpus of English literature was valuable primarily because it expressed national identity. This work of creating a literary canon, England's triumphant homegrown answer to the classical laureates of Greece and Rome, began in the late seventeenth and early eighteenth centuries. At its core stood the plays and poems of William Shakespeare, the foremost literary source of national pride. It was Shakespeare, and Shakespeare alone, who embodied his homeland's artistic genius.

But even genius needs a little context to be appreciated. That useful context was nothing other than the author's own life, a point first made in works like Edward Phillips' *Theatrum Poetarum* (1675) and Gerard Langbaine's *An Account of the English Dramatick Poets* (1691), both biographical dictionaries of England's leading playwrights. These initial attempts at literary biography offered more praise than substance. Phillips, who rightly hailed Shakespeare as the 'Glory of the English Stage' – at the time he was writing, blockbuster revivals of *Macbeth* and *The Tempest* were drawing crowds to the new Dorset Garden Theatre in London – contented himself with repeating the platitude that Stratford claims the 'highest honour' of being Shakespeare's birthplace. Langbaine, who esteemed Shakespeare's works 'beyond any that have ever been published in our Language', supplemented his inventory of the plays with the few details he knew of their author's life, mainly his baptism and burial in Stratford. Factually, these works were decidedly skimpy, barely inching past Dugdale's pithy reference forty years earlier to Shakespeare's 'birth and sepulture'.

What these biographical dictionaries offered was not new knowledge but a new perspective, the 'life-work'. To understand an author's work, first you must understand that author's life, because the life generates the work.

Especially in Langbaine's dictionary of playwrights, an important line of thought emerges: Shakespeare's excellence as a dramatist astounds us even more once we learn that he was born in an ordinary town, where his education ended at the grammar school. The utter normality of his upbringing only deepens our admiration for him. The banal facts of Shakespeare's early life confirm the true extent of his natural or innate talent, a talent so prodigious that he required, as Langbaine put it, no 'Assistance of Art to polish it'.

'The Character of the Man is best seen in his Writings'

Once readers started thinking of Shakespeare's works as being rooted in the circumstances and events of his life, a view widely shared still today, they inevitably grew curious about that life. In 1709, the poet and playwright Nicholas Rowe invented Shakespeare biography when he prefaced his six-volume edition of the plays with 'Some Account of the Life, &c. of Mr. William Shakespear'. Although the dramatist had been dead for nearly a century, only four editions of his collected plays had been published, all in expensive folio versions. The last such edition, known as the Fourth Folio, appeared in 1685, a full generation earlier. Unlike the compilers of the four folios, Rowe commented on Shakespeare's text, modernized the spelling and punctuation and explained obscure or textually corrupt phrases. He set an enduring scholarly standard. Three centuries later, and Shakespeare editors still undertake those same tasks, although with a twenty-first-century readership in mind.

Rowe was also the first literary critic to investigate what he called Shakespeare's 'personal story' – how modern that phrase sounds – a dimension altogether lacking in the earlier folios, determined, as they were, to keep Shakespeare dead. Yet in attempting the world's first Shakespeare biography, Rowe didn't just record the sequential events of the playwright's life; he also appraised Shakespeare's achievements and evaluated his legacy. In short, he *interpreted* Shakespeare. Modern biographers like Stephen Greenblatt and Jonathan Bate take that obligation for granted. But in 1709, Nicholas Rowe was writing without precedent. John Aubrey had jotted down some random biographical notes a few decades earlier, but Rowe knew nothing of Aubrey's manuscript, which then lay undisturbed in Oxford's Ashmolean Museum. Rowe's 'personal story' about William Shakespeare ran to only thirty-five pages; but that was thirty-five pages more than anybody else had written.

With few sources to consult, Rowe gladly indulged in legend, error and apocrypha, many of these chestnuts still in circulation. Shakespeare left school to work alongside his father in the wool trade. Shakespeare poached deer in Charlecote Park and fled to London to escape arrest and prosecution.

Shakespeare played the Ghost in *Hamlet*. Shakespeare changed the character Sir John Oldcastle to Sir John Falstaff at Queen Elizabeth's command. Rowe made so many mistakes that, a century later, Edmond Malone, in his own life of Shakespeare, exposed every single instance where his predecessor had distorted the documentary record. 'There are not more than *eleven* facts mentioned', Malone judged harshly, 'and of these, on a critical examination, *eight* will be found false.'

Despite its compounded errors, Rowe's biography aspired to the new critical ambition of its time: to use Shakespeare's life to illuminate Shakespeare's plays. 'Knowledge of an Author', he explained, 'may sometimes conduce to the better understanding [of] his Book: And tho' the Works of Mr. *Shakespear* may seem to many not to want a Comment, yet I fancy some little Account of the Man himself may not be thought improper.' It's no accident, then, that in Rowe's edition the biography appears ahead of the plays; by reading it first, you will 'better understand' what follows.

Yet if the life explains the work, then the work explains the life, each shining a search light on the other. As Rowe affirmed, 'the Character of the Man is best seen in his Writings.' Thus began the still persistent belief that Shakespeare's dramatic characters reflect, if only indirectly, if only allusively, some trait or aspect of Shakespeare the man, and vice versa. To create a character like Macbeth, you must have a little bloodthirsty ambition lurking somewhere inside you. If you've felt the intoxicating danger of forbidden love, then you know what Juliet needs to say.

'Writ the Scene of the Ghost in *Hamlet* at his House'

Yet for all its accumulated detail, Rowe's biography overlooked *where* Shakespeare lived in his 'native Stratford'. We learn only that he 'had the good Fortune to gather an Estate equal to his Occasion, and, in that, to his Wish'. Correct as far as it goes, which isn't very far.

As I was reading Rowe's thirty-five pages, it dawned on me that he *did* know something more specific about Shakespeare at home. He knew a story about New Place, the grand timber and brick house that Shakespeare bought for his family and where he died nearly twenty years later. When Rowe referred to Shakespeare acquiring 'an Estate equal to his Occasion', it was New Place and its large working garden that he meant.

The story about New Place that Rowe chose not to tell had first appeared in Charles Gildon's *Lives and Characters of the English Dramatick Poets*. It was published in 1699, a full decade before Rowe's edition of the plays, and thus a work he would have consulted (there weren't many to choose from) in writing the biographical essay on Shakespeare included in his edition. Elevating folklore to the status of fact, Gildon asserted that Shakespeare 'writ the Scene of the Ghost in *Hamlet* at his House which bordered on the Charnel-House and Church-Yard'. The claim, though impressively precise, is untrue. Indeed, it's doubtful that Gildon, a hack biographer, ever walked the old streets of Stratford, because he totally muddled the town's geography. One side of New Place faced the medieval Guild Chapel, which lent something of a religious aspect to the immediate surroundings, but the charnel house and churchyard belonged to Holy Trinity Church, a few minutes' walk down Church Street and then toward the river Avon. In short, Gildon put Shakespeare's house in the wrong place.

Even so, this false image captivates. Shakespeare the working dramatist is found not at the Globe in London but in his grand Stratford home, feeling inspired by the world outside his lattice window. Chapel Lane, the street running between New Place and the Guild Chapel, was then commonly known as 'Dead Lane' and 'Walker Street'. With a little imagination we can see the author of *Hamlet* working away at his writing table, putting down his quill pen, gazing out his window, recalling the familiar street names and then realizing that what his tragedy really needed was a scene about a dead man walking. *That's* how Shakespeare wrote the ghost in *Hamlet*.

Why does this fascinating story, so exact in its detail and so consequential in its effect, not appear in Rowe's biography? It seems tailor-made for the occasion. The answer, I think, lies in how in Nicholas Rowe undertook his research on Shakespeare's 'personal story'.

Instead of journeying to Stratford himself, Rowe enlisted the veteran actor Thomas Betterton, the greatest Hamlet in living memory, to 'make a journey into *Warwickshire* . . . to gather up what Remains he could of a Name for which he had so great a Value'. To gather those remains, Betterton spoke to townspeople – that's the only way he could have learned about Anne Hathaway's family – and inspected old baptismal records in Holy Trinity Church. No antiquary, the aged Betterton made several mistakes in copying those records, mistakes then repeated, unknowingly, in Rowe's published text.

Betterton knew Gildon professionally, having staged his adaptation of *Measure for Measure* a few years earlier at the theatre in Lincoln's Inn Fields in London. So, if anything, he might have been inclined to take the story on faith. But the old actor would have seen with his own eyes that Gildon's vision of Shakespeare writing *Hamlet* from an upstairs room in his house was pure fantasy. The actual view from Shakespeare's window was not the one that Gildon had described. Shakespeare may well have written some or even all of *Hamlet* in New Place, who knows? But if so, he certainly didn't write it in the way that Gildon recounts.

Betterton would have known all that simply by standing in front of New Place and looking across the street. That's what I did when researching this book. Standing on the corner of Chapel Street and Chapel Lane, trying to see Shakespeare's neighbourhood with Shakespeare's eyes, it suddenly occurred to me why Rowe rejected this anecdote, enticing though it was, from his otherwise anecdote-stuffed biography of Shakespeare. He rejected it because he knew it was false. Not because any document disproved it – Rowe hadn't a clue that archival sources existed – but because experience contradicted it. What Gildon asserted was plainly impossible, as his Stratford emissary Thomas Betterton must have told him.

And yet, Rowe couldn't bring himself to ignore this story altogether. One part of Gildon's fictive account of Shakespeare writing *Hamlet* in New Place did resurface in Rowe's text, when he asserted that Shakespeare's best acting role, 'the top of his Performance', was 'the Ghost in his own *Hamlet*'. Though conjectural, this deeply powerful image, so powerful that Shakespeare's first biographer could not forsake it entirely, reveals how necessary it had become by the early eighteenth century to merge Shakespeare's life and works.

The need to believe that New Place and its atmospheric surroundings somehow led to Shakespeare inventing a character that he himself then portrayed on the stage must have been overwhelming – because no fact supported it. Not a shard of evidence proves that Shakespeare wrote a single line from a single play while living in Stratford, plausible though it is. And if a cast list survives from the first performance of *Hamlet* at the Globe in 1600 or 1601, its whereabouts are the world's best-kept secret. But a conceptual corner had been turned and turned decisively. Whatever was important in Shakespeare's plays, even if we can't quite put our finger on it, has something to do with where Shakespeare lived in Stratford.

'Our Shakespeare's House'

Shakespeare's next biographer, Lewis Theobald, adopted this new way of thinking in his seven-volume edition of the plays, first published in 1733. Theobald included Shakespeare's life story in his edition, just as Rowe had done a generation earlier, because he believed that if his readers learned about Shakespeare's life they would better apprehend 'the stronger Ideas of his extensive Genius'. One thing for readers to learn was where Shakespeare lived.

We must thank Lewis Theobald for including in a biography the first references to Shakespeare's house. This house, which is New Place, not the Birthplace, becomes a topic unto itself, a character with its own story. Here, extracted from Theobald's sixty-eight-page preface, are his several remarks on New Place:

> The Estate had now been sold out of the *Clopton* Family for above a Century, at the Time when *Shakespeare* became the Purchaser: who, having repair'd and modell'd it to his own Mind, chang'd the Name to *New-place*, which the Mansion-house, since erected upon the same Spot, at this day retains. The House and Lands, which attended it, continued in *Shakespeare*'s Descendants to the Time of the *Restoration*: when they were repurchased by the *Clopton* Family, and the Mansion now belongs to Sir *Hugh Clopton*, Knt.

In 1614, the greater part of the Town of *Stratford* was consumed by Fire; but our *Shakespeare*'s House, among some others, escap'd the Flames.

When the Civil War raged in *England*, and K. *Charles* the *First*'s Queen was driven by the Necessity of Affairs to make a Recess in *Warwickshire*, She kept her Court for three Weeks in *New-place*. We may reasonably suppose it then the best private House in the Town.

Far from being random, these details comprise a coherent micro-biography of 'our *Shakespeare*'s House'. Obviously, this narrative centres on Shakespeare, the house's most famous occupant, but it also both precedes and extends beyond him. Theobald, like most biographers, proceeds chronologically, starting with the Clopton family building New Place in the fifteenth century and then selling it, all of which occurred long before Shakespeare lived there. We then get the main account of New Place from the late 1590s, when Shakespeare's family first lived there, to the 1660s, when his last direct descendant died.

Theobald wants his readers to know that New Place still stands, although it was rebuilt first by Shakespeare and then by a later owner. (Theobald didn't know the backstory. The house was probably already in poor condition. In 1598, the year after Shakespeare bought it, he sold a load of stone to the Corporation of Stratford for ten pence. That was likely old stone that had been cleared from the building itself during the renovations.) Moreover, the house 'retains' the name that Shakespeare himself used for it. That's vital information for readers planning to visit Stratford, where they can see New Place for themselves. Next comes the teaser. The house survived a near-death experience, escaping the 'Flames' that destroyed much of Stratford in 1614, just two years before Shakespeare died. This, too, is valuable information, for it arouses our gratitude that the house remains intact, so easily could it have perished.

Yet a greater triumph still lay in store for the 'best private House in the Town'. In the summer of 1643, as civil war gripped England, Queen Henrietta Maria, the French-born consort of the embattled Charles I, broke her journey in Stratford as she travelled to meet the king in Oxford. She and her entourage stayed at New Place for three nights, which Theobald somehow misreported as three weeks. But three nights was plenty, because the queen's back-up forces included two thousand soldiers, a thousand horses and 100 wagonloads of goods and chattel. Royal house guests have always been high maintenance.

The burden of hospitality fell upon Shakespeare's daughter Susanna and her own daughter, Elizabeth, both of whom then lived in New Place. But Queen Henrietta Maria didn't spend three nights in Shakespeare's house to honour Shakespeare. She stayed there because royalty always stays in the best house in town. In Stratford, and in 1643, that meant New Place. Shakespeare's legacy had nothing to do with it.

'Modell'd it to his own Mind'

Theobald used an intriguing phrase – 'modell'd it to his own Mind' – to explain how Shakespeare refurbished New Place, which was already an old house when he bought it. The biographer's words create a subject who intends and then follows through. This is a Shakespeare possessed by a vision of what his new home should look like; what it should represent to those who dwelt there and to those he welcomed inside it. No slapdash renovations for him. The Shakespeare who rebuilds his house seems a lot like the Shakespeare who builds a play, knowing how to shape every character and how to craft each scene, all in the service of a larger structure.

Theobald's dynamic image conveys yet a broader truth, one that applies to us too. The truth is that the meaning of a house – Shakespeare's, yours, mine – isn't lodged inside it, waiting to be discovered, like a hidden ceiling beam or a boarded-up fireplace. Rather, meaning is what happens when we become attached to our homes. Real estate brokers insist that sellers remove photographs of themselves during viewings so that prospective buyers are free to project themselves into an open space, imagining what their life would be like if this house were theirs. Anyone who has ever moved into a new place, a roomy suburban home, a flashy loft apartment or a concrete-block dorm room, knows what it means to make your own dwelling an extension of your own self. To model it to your own mind.

Theobald insists that Shakespeare's house externalized the contents of Shakespeare's mind, his interior life, but then never tells us exactly what the renovated house made visible, other than its own status-symbol value. How frustrating that Shakespeare's final dwelling place fails to translate into what the editor himself termed a 'Method of Information', a biographical fact that will enhance our appreciation of the plays and poems. When it came to Shakespeare's house, Theobald opened a rhetorical door only to refuse to walk through it.

Even so, he clearly linked Shakespeare to his adult home in Stratford. That home boasted a singular history, a relationship to its most celebrated owner and a symbolic value understood and upheld by posterity. For all that insight, we are indebted to Lewis Theobald, the first biographer to give us some facts about Shakespeare's house.

Yet when I read his preface, I imagined how someone reading it back in 1733, someone who genuinely admired Shakespeare's plays and wanted to know more about the playwright himself, might have reacted. I was left with the disappointing impression that even so kindly inclined a reader would not have rushed to book a seat on the next carriage bound for Stratford. There didn't seem a compelling reason for anybody to visit 'our *Shakespeare*'s House'.

But all that changed in just a few years, thanks to a legend about a mulberry tree.

7

A Marvellous Convenient Place

The house that Shakespeare modelled to his own mind remained the property of his lineal descendants for just two generations. In the 1670s, after the death of Shakespeare's last heir, his granddaughter Elizabeth Barnard, New Place was sold to Sir Edward Walker, Garter King at Arms, whose daughter and heir, Barbara, married Sir John Clopton, thus bringing the house back into the possession of the distinguished Stratford family that first owned it.

Their son Hugh, who inherited New Place upon his father's death in 1719, ensured that the house became synonymous not with his family, but with Shakespeare's. For by then, it had become apparent that Stratford's future prosperity depended no longer on the Clopton family, but on William Shakespeare; or rather, on the emerging cult of Shakespeare worship that was gradually drawing visitors to the town of his birth. Sir Hugh became the first owner of New Place to treat it as a shrine to the Bard of Avon, a devotional act that Shakespeare's own daughter and granddaughter never undertook when they had lived there.

Like everybody in Stratford, Sir Hugh could recite in his sleep the legend that Shakespeare planted the mulberry tree that came to dominate the garden at the back of New Place. Though unproven, the story is fully plausible. In 1607, a decade after Shakespeare bought the house, James I encouraged the growing of mulberry trees imported from France to promote the silk industry in England, mulberry leaves being the food of choice for silkworms. Accurate or not, the story quickly passed into Stratford lore.

In the late 1780s, the Rev James Davenport, vicar of Holy Trinity Church, helped the literary historian Edmond Malone write the first full-length Shakespeare biography. Davenport told Malone about a living archive of Stratford history, the elderly Warwick alderman Hugh Taylor, who happened to be the father of his parish clerk. Born at the century's turn, Taylor boasted that, like his father and grandfather before him, he had grown up in the house next to New Place. More, he reported that 'the fact of Shakespeare planting the tree' had been handed down within his family, 'transmitted from father to son', ever since the time when Shakespeare lived at New Place. The old man fleshed the story out for Davenport, adding that as a boy he often ate mulberries grabbed from the long branches that reached into his own garden. For further corroboration, he advised, just ask a Clopton, because both families had 'preserved' the story of Shakespeare's tree.

What Taylor claimed as fact, we now call fiction, or at least tradition. Because it was nothing but a chain of hearsay. The scholar Edmond Malone in London heard from the clergyman James Davenport in Stratford, who had heard from his clerk's elderly father, who had heard from his father, who had likewise heard from his father, and so backward in time. The accumulated recollections stop – or rather, start – with the primal scene of William Shakespeare planting the roots of a mulberry sapling in the soil of his garden at New Place, entrusting it to the receiving earth with the very hands that had written of magical plants and enchanted woodlands in *A Midsummer Night's Dream*.

'Hospitably entertained'

On a spring day in 1742, three actors from Drury Lane Theatre in London – Charles Macklin, Denis Delane and the young David Garrick – climbed into a bouncy and cramped post-chaise headed for Stratford, a hundred and eight miles to the northwest. Likely they broke their journey in Oxford at the end of a long and confining first day, just as Shakespeare did on his trips back home, where they ordered a late supper and took rooms for the night at a coaching inn. Next morning, they secured a fresh pair of horses before getting back on the road for the final stretch to Stratford, where Sir Hugh Clopton awaited to entertain them under the shade and shelter of the legendary mulberry tree at New Place.

All three men owed their careers to Shakespeare. Macklin, although well into middle age, shot to stardom only the year before, when he abandoned the custom of playing Shylock for laughs and showed audiences instead a darkly menacing character. His performance so unnerved George II that he stayed awake all night at St James's Palace after seeing it. Alexander Pope, poet and Shakespeare editor, lauded Macklin's fresh, startling portrayal of Shylock as 'the Jew that Shakespeare drew'. The Irishman Delane had acted all the top roles in Shakespearean tragedy – Othello, Lear, Hamlet, Macbeth, Brutus, Antony – and then added Falstaff for a comic flourish. Destined to be the greatest of all, Garrick was then but a promising newcomer. The twenty-four-year-old from Lichfield made a splash in his London debut at Goodman's Fields a year earlier, playing Richard III. His mentor Charles Macklin had coached him in the role. Their shared love for Shakespeare had drawn these worshipful pilgrims to Stratford.

After a second day on the road their carriage finally approached the small town itself, crossing westwards over Clopton Bridge. Their first stop was the White Lion on Henley Street, Stratford's main coaching inn. Before railways, most out of towners arrived in Stratford via Henley Street, whose back gates opened onto the high road that stretched from London to Birmingham. The travellers rested at the White Lion, washed the sweat and dirt from their faces and put on the costume of every eighteenth-century English gentleman: open knee-length coat, buttoned waistcoat, linen shirt, knotted neckcloth, knee breeches and stockings.

Refreshed and suitably garbed for the occasion – their host was, after all, a knight of the realm, a man of wealth and pedigree – the trio walked the short distance down Chapel Street, stopping at the large brick house owned by Sir Hugh Clopton on the corner of Chapel Street and Chapel Lane. Plump, periwigged and likely sporting a sloppily tied cravat, known as a Steinkirk, whose fringed ends were tucked into a waistcoat buttonhole, the elderly Sir Hugh 'hospitably entertained' his London guests, as Macklin told Malone decades later, under the high spreading branches of Shakespeare's mulberry tree in the garden at New Place.

This merry meeting could hardly have been impromptu. Who would travel so uncomfortably for so many hours to arrive in Stratford with only a vague hope of stumbling upon Shakespeare? Better to have stayed in London, where they could act leading roles in his plays or discourse about them in the Grecian coffeehouse on the Strand, a favourite thespian hangout. No, the actors had journeyed to Stratford with strength of purpose. They knew that Shakespeare had lived in New Place. They knew that a house stood on that site. And they knew that the hospitable Sir Hugh Clopton lived there. They had learned all of that from reading Lewis Theobald's edition of Shakespeare's plays. On the off chance that they had never heard about the fabled mulberry tree, they were certainly educated about it and on the very spot, by Sir Hugh himself.

These three men were the first London actors to visit Stratford on a Shakespeare mission in over thirty years. Thomas Betterton, as we've seen, had journeyed there back in 1709 to check baptismal and burial records in Holy Trinity Church, doing a favour for friend Nicholas Rowe, then writing the first Shakespeare biography. But when Macklin, Delane and Garrick came to town in 1742, their intent was more ambitious still. Having learned about Shakespeare's life, they now wanted to experience it for themselves. And so, they headed straight to New Place, the site where Shakespeare the man came alive.

'A marvellous convenient place'

It's no coincidence that actors were among those who first performed the sacred rites of Shakespeare worship because the ancient alchemy of theatre is to transform a literal space into a figurative one, conjuring on a bare stage a succession of imagined, yet meaningful, worlds. In *A Midsummer Night's Dream*, the rude mechanicals, anxious about their upcoming performance of 'Pyramus and Thisbe' before Duke Theseus and his court, decide that a forest clearing will make 'a marvellous convenient place for our rehearsal' (3.1.2–3). As the amateur playwright Peter Quince decrees, 'this green plot shall be our stage' (3.1.3–4).

In that same transfiguring spirit, the green plot at New Place became itself a stage, the mulberry tree supplied the picturesque scenery, Sir Hugh acted the role of chief celebrant, while Macklin, Delane and Garrick rounded out the cast, filling the stage and voicing their lines. It was actors, not historians or literary critics, who helped to make Stratford an important site for commemorating Shakespeare because actors understood best of all the need for an established shrine where acolytes could perform their ceremonies of reverence. New Place was, truly, a marvellous convenient place.

Sanctioned by no fact, the ceremony of the mulberry tree nonetheless thrilled its partakers, who through it forged a living link to Shakespeare. The man himself was long dead, and New Place had been remade by the Cloptons into a modern brick townhouse; but that old tree lived on, just as Shakespeare's plays and poems lived on, rooted in the distant past but flowering afresh for each new generation of audiences and readers. The very antithesis of the gravesite in nearby Holy Trinity Church – a commemoration of the dead – the mulberry tree at New Place was the one place where Shakespeare himself, not his works, but his own actual self, still lived.

If the tree's authenticity could never be proven by documents, it could be fully felt by direct experience. Indeed, you had to be 'on the spot' – standing where Shakespeare stood, seeing what Shakespeare saw – for the tree to work its magic. Granted, the experience was mostly symbolic. Yet how else do authors connect with their readers or playwrights reach their audiences except through symbols? It mattered little whether the legend be fact or fiction; what mattered was that the legend had its effect. Ironically, it was actually preferable that New Place was not a fully reconstructed Shakespeare heritage site. The Romantic cult of the ruin, which prized crumbling Gothic arches and the debris of Greek temples, appealed so strongly precisely because it enabled visitors themselves to reverse the ruin, using their imagination to restore what had been lost, making the scattered fragments whole.

As Sir Hugh and his theatrical guests intuited, the mulberry tree *needed* visitors, because it was the visitors who made the tree complete by endowing it with the living presence of Shakespeare himself. No hoax can honestly ascend to true relic status, just as no true relic can degrade into a deceiving hoax. Those are objective conditions, immune from the competing pleas of partisans and sceptics. But that tree at New Place was neither true relic nor hoax. It stood, rather, somewhere in between, in that blurred boundary where history and mythology meet and shake hands. The mulberry tree was valid because it drew nourishment from the mixed soil of fact and fiction. No wonder even the fastidious Edmond Malone, in 1790, pronounced in his *Life of William Shakespeare* that the legend was 'as well authenticated as anything of that nature can be'.

'In Stratford Shakespeare had several houses'

When the three actors returned to their lodgings in the White Lion, after bidding farewell to Sir Hugh at New Place, they would have passed on Henley Street a line of Tudor half-timbered houses. It was a familiar sight in an old town like Stratford. So familiar that they may not have stopped to notice. Yet in one of those houses lived the seventy-five-year-old Shakespeare Hart. Fully entitled he was to bear that illustrious name for his great-grandmother was Shakespeare's sister Joan Hart, who was living in the small cottage at the Henley Street property when Shakespeare died and remained there for the rest of her life, thanks to a provision in her older brother's will. One hundred and thirty years after the playwright's death and his nearest relations were still living in that same house.

If only the actors had known. Soon enough they would learn all about the Birthplace, but at the time they were oblivious to its existence. Had they been aware that Stratford boasted *two* Shakespeare houses, then Macklin surely would have mentioned them both when he recounted his trip there to Malone. But he spoke only of New Place.

Why didn't they know about the Birthplace? Others certainly knew. A few years earlier, in October 1737, the engraver and antiquary George Vertue visited Stratford with Edward Harley, Earl of Oxford, another history buff. Nothing to do with the Oxfordian authorship controversy. After paying his respects at Shakespeare's gravesite in Holy Trinity Church, Vertue made his way to the house on Henley Street, where he spoke with none other than Shakespeare Hart. The old man must have told his visitor about the property's singular history because Vertue jotted down the key facts in his notebook:

> in Stratford Shakespeare had several houses. besides some Land – the Maiden head and Swann an Inn [now] did belong to him – and a house or two adjoining. These are actually in the possession of Shakespeare Hart. a glasier by profession, the remaining Heir of Elisabeth – only Sister to Wm. Shakespear. she Married to . . . Hart whose grandson George Hart. father of this present S. Hart living, about 70 years of age.

Except for getting wrong the name of Shakespeare's sister – Joan was the sister and Elizabeth was the granddaughter – Vertue's account holds up. Though he didn't refer to the Birthplace as such, he knew that Shakespeare had owned the property and that the Harts, his nearest descendants, now owned it and lived there. He knew that the original house had been divided into the Swan and Maidenhead Inn and an adjacent dwelling, the small cottage where the Harts lived. Vertue's travel notebook is the earliest written record to link Shakespeare with the Birthplace, a record whose impeccable source was none other than Shakespeare's great-grand-nephew.

Had the actors from London visited Shakespeare Hart, he would have shown them the prized possession that he had shown George Vertue five years earlier: a copy of Shakespeare's last will and testament. What he possessed was an undated, but wholly accurate, transcription of the original, not one of the several copies written and signed in March 1616. Still, it was rare enough. In the 1740s, Shakespeare Hart, a plumber and glazier by trade, was one of the few people in the world who knew the contents of Shakespeare's will. Local antiquarian and schoolmaster Joseph Greene made two more copies of the transcription, but it wasn't printed until 1752, when it was included in the posthumous third edition of Theobald's *Works of Shakespeare*. Macklin, Delane and Garrick, because they didn't stop to visit Shakespeare Hart, missed out on learning the secret story of Shakespeare's family. The story of how the direct line went rapidly extinct and how subsequent legal manoeuvres ensured that Shakespeare's nearest descendants continued to live in the Birthplace, first as tenants but, eventually, as its owners.

'The Inheritance of William Shakespeare, my grandfather'

That knotted history starts with Shakespeare stipulating in his will that his oldest child, Susanna Hall, would inherit the house on Henley Street, along with all his other property, but that his sister Joan Hart could keep on living in the small cottage there for a nominal rent. After Susanna died in 1649, the property passed to her only child, Elizabeth, widow of Thomas Nash, but who five weeks earlier had married John Barnard of Abington, Northamptonshire. When her second husband was knighted in 1661, shortly after the monarchy was restored under Charles II, Shakespeare's granddaughter Elizabeth became Lady Barnard. She died in 1670, having moved from Stratford to her husband's manor house in Abington a decade earlier, while Sir John lived on for another four years. All this long while, the Harts continued to live as tenants in the western side of the Henley Street property, just as they had done since Shakespeare's lifetime. The eastern side had for decades been leased out as the Swan and Maidenhead Inn.

Elizabeth Barnard was the last person who owned both New Place and the Birthplace. Under the terms of her will, the designated trustee would sell New Place, which had been rented out for some years, but only after Sir John's death if she predeceased him, which, as it transpired, she did. Most of the money generated by the sale would be distributed to her Hathaway cousins – their common kinswoman was Anne Hathaway, Shakespeare's wife – while ownership of the Birthplace would transfer to its then occupant Thomas Hart, her second cousin and Joan Hart's grandson. It does get all rather complicated, but when are property deals ever straightforward?

When I read Elizabeth Barnard's will, it struck me how much the memory of her maternal grandfather guided her bequests. I was not expecting that, because she barely knew him, being only eight when he died. Even so, she framed her entire Stratford estate in ancestral terms, labelling it 'heretofore the inheritance of William Shakespeare, gentleman, my grandfather'.

It was pointless for Lady Barnard to invoke Shakespeare's name in her will and yet also entirely to the point. Pointless because the genealogy carried no legal consequence. Elizabeth Barnard owned property in Stratford and was free to dispose of it however she wished. The identity of the previous owner was wholly irrelevant. Entirely to the point, however, because *how* she disposed of that property resulted from her pride in being Shakespeare's granddaughter. Her allegiance to the extended family – the Hathaways, descended from the siblings of Shakespeare's wife, and the Harts, descended from Shakespeare's sister Joan – determined the many bequests in her will.

Let's start with the Hathaways. Anne's cousin Thomas Hathaway, a carpenter, lived on Chapel Street in Stratford, a few doors down from New Place. He died around 1650, survived by five daughters. Four of them – Judith, Rose, Elizabeth and Susanna – were unmarried, which meant hard times after their father's death. Whatever income the women might earn on their own from sewing shirts or selling eggs and cheese wouldn't have amounted to much. Their sister Joan married Edward Kent, with whom she had a son, also named Edward.

Elizabeth Barnard instructed that most of the money raised from selling New Place should benefit her five Hathaway cousins. Judith would receive five pounds a year, half paid at Michaelmas in late September and half paid six months later on the Feast of the Annunciation. If Judith married, she could swap the annuity for a lump sum of forty pounds. The other unmarried cousins – Rose, Elizabeth and Susanna – would receive forty pounds each right away. The married Joan Kent was left fifty pounds. Her son, Edward, still a boy, was promised thirty pounds, but with the proviso that it must be spent on 'putting him out as an apprentice'. Elizabeth Barnard generously ensured her young cousin's future, giving him money to train as an apprentice, after which Edward Kent could make his own living as a trader or skilled craftsman. She understood the financial hardship that her unmarried female cousins faced and so provided for them, too. Moreover, it made sense to sell New Place. It was one of the most valuable properties in Stratford, she had no children to inherit it, the house was occupied by tenants, not family, and the Hathaways needed cash, not real estate.

The Harts presented a trickier problem because they needed cash *and* real estate. Elizabeth saw the obvious solution: she bequeathed to her 'kinsman' Thomas Hart, the grandson of Joan Hart, and thus her second cousin, both the cottage where he was living and the adjacent Swan and Maidenhead Inn. In other words, the entire site now known as the Birthplace. This way, the Harts could remain in their long-time family home, but instead of renting it from Shakespeare and his direct descendants they would, at last, own it.

More, they would become landlords themselves, earning income from leasing out the much larger Maidenhead Inn. It was the perfect legacy for a family that had been down at heel for decades.

When Thomas Hart died without issue, his inherited property passed to his younger brother George, a tailor, who by deed poll transferred it to his son Shakespeare Hart, the one who showed George Vertue his copy of Shakespeare's will and the one who *didn't* meet the actors Charles Macklin, Denis Delane and David Garrick.

'Our Shakespeare's house'

To my mind, the most consequential act in this long chain of events was Elizabeth Barnard's initial decision to leave the birthplace to the Harts. In so doing, she fulfilled a moral obligation to use her grandfather's landed estate to provide for his descendants and relatives. It was an intimate, personal decision. For her, William Shakespeare was first and foremost the head of her family; not a remote patriarch, but someone she knew and loved as a child, her grandfather William, who lived with her grandmother Anne in the big house around the corner. Elizabeth Barnard knew all about William Shakespeare the author, memorialized in the funerary monument at Holy Trinity Church but also living on in the folio editions of his collected plays. That man was a public figure, a writer whose reputation outlived him. The man whom she honoured in her will was a different person altogether, her treasured grandfather. So, when it came time for Shakespeare's granddaughter to dispose of Shakespeare's amassed wealth, she chose not to commemorate the poet and playwright but to provide for those who shared her kinship with William Shakespeare the gentleman landowner from Stratford-upon-Avon.

In 1670, half a century after Shakespeare's death, not even his sole surviving heir thought that the house on Henley Street was worth preserving because he had been born there. In fact, it wasn't necessarily worth preserving at all. It was one of two houses in the town that Shakespeare had owned and not the nice one. Absolutely no reason to single it out for special treatment.

Here's a turn of events worth pondering. If Elizabeth Barnard had bequeathed New Place, rather than the Birthplace, to her cousin Thomas Hart, then it might have been New Place that survived. Surely, the Harts would have kept on living in that grand residence for a long time. The Birthplace, a much less desirable property, would have been sold instead. A century would then pass before that now sacred site acquired anything like landmark status. In those risky intervening years, the house might have been demolished or altered beyond recognition by later owners, none of whom would have felt a duty to preserve the house where Shakespeare was born. The Birthplace as we know it today would likely not exist.

But the Birthplace does indeed still exist, mainly because it stayed in the extended family until the early nineteenth century and so was privately protected for nearly two centuries. By no means did Elizabeth Barnard intend to turn her grandfather's birthplace into the world's most popular site devoted to William Shakespeare. The mere idea of it would have made her laugh. Even so, she set in motion the long chain of events that made it possible when she bequeathed her second-best house to her second cousin.

Not that anyone outside the family paid much notice. Although continuously occupied by Shakespeare's close relatives, the Birthplace was for many years ignored by those drawn to the great national poet's hometown. For a Shakespeare enthusiast of the time, the Birthplace held little value. It was a jumble of a structure, a family dwelling on one side and a tavern on the other. Dismal in appearance, it belonged not to Shakespeare's lineal descendants, who quickly died out, but to those of his sister Joan. Shakespeare himself didn't live there much beyond his eighteenth year, when he married Anne Hathaway. Most regrettably of all, there was no mulberry tree in the garden to spark a visitor's imagination. All these considerations led *away* from Shakespeare, not toward him. Well into the eighteenth century, anyone curious about Shakespeare found in the Birthplace little to cherish, either in historical substance or imaginative possibility. One Shakespeare house in Stratford was enough and New Place was it.

'Gothick barbarity'

That changed forever in 1753, when the dyspeptic clergyman Francis Gastrell purchased New Place from Katherine Talbot, Sir Hugh Clopton's daughter. Gastrell, who hailed from Lichfield, claimed no link to Stratford, professed no interest in Shakespeare's life or legacy and had bought the house with his wife Jane's money as a second home. He could not have made a worse real estate decision. Word had spread that Shakespeare's mulberry tree still stood in the garden at New Place. Because the genial Sir Hugh had gladly welcomed visitors there the new owner was expected to offer the same hospitality. But Gastrell was no Sir Hugh. In fact, he strongly resented the parade of sightseers demanding access to his private garden so that they could stand on enchanted ground and gaze at the famous tree, forgetting that it was someone's private property. Especially in summertime, with the tree in full bloom, the clergyman bristled that so many selfish strangers knocked on his door and then, so it seemed to him, forced their way in.

For three years he endured such torments, until he could bear them no longer. The only guaranteed way to stop the onslaught of Shakespeare pilgrims, Gastrell determined, was to remove the object of their desire. He ordered his gardener, John Ange, to pick up an axe and cut the tree down, chopping it up for firewood. The quick-thinking clockmaker Thomas Sharp, who lived nearby, bought the entire dismembered tree, rescuing it from being set alight in sundry Stratford fireplaces, and then carved it up into snuffboxes, tankards, ink horns and other such trinkets. So began the manufacture and retail of Shakespeare souvenirs.

Yet that may not be the full story. Apart from the nuisance of tourists clamouring to see it, the mulberry tree had grown so large that it crowded the small back garden. Worse, the branches overshadowed the house, blocking any sunlight but causing moisture and damp. The tree, being so old, was likely already in decay. To order its destruction, as Gastrell did, was merely to accelerate nature's irreversible course. The Shakespeare tourist trade certainly annoyed the owner of New Place, who had bought it as a vacation home, but his annoyance may not have been the main motivation for getting rid of the mulberry tree.

Yet such was the growing cult of Shakespeare that Gastrell quickly became the necessary villain in a stock melodrama that pitted all true lovers of the poet against the vulgar new owner of New Place, the one man in town who dared to profane the hallowed ground. I do not exaggerate. Some local boys, according to Stratford legend, smashed his windows. No less an eminence than James Boswell, biographer of Samuel Johnson, branded the tree's destruction a 'Gothick barbarity'. At such a time, when neoclassicism reigned, the crude epithet 'Gothick' wounded deeply. In a letter printed in *The Gentleman's Magazine* in 1760, a few years after the fact, an anonymous 'Lady on a Journey at Stratford' grieved openly that Gastrell, possessed by some 'disgust', had killed her beloved Shakespeare a second time by cutting down 'a mulberry tree of his planting' and turning it into 'a stack of firewood'. She lamented Shakespeare's symbolic death more than his natural one, because it was so calculated, so violent and so absurdly gratuitous.

Before long, this tale of woe shifted from damning the perpetrator to sympathizing with the victims. Victimhood here was plural, starting with Shakespeare himself but soon extending to include all those forever prevented from seeing the mulberry tree. To be denied the experience was itself grounds for a grievance. In 1761, when stage impresario Benjamin Victor embellished the story for his *History of the Theatres of London and Dublin*, the whole event was remembered as a performance of mass mourning that turned into scapegoating:

> The alarm of this horrid deed soon spread throughout the town! . . . After the first moments of astonishment were over, a general fury seized them all, and vengeance was the word! – They gathered together, surrounded the house – reviewed with tears the fallen tree, and vowed to sacrifice the offender to the immortal memory of the planter.

The story's climax had yet to come because the parson's spite was not yet exhausted. Now, Gastrell found himself quarrelling with the Corporation of Stratford. While negotiating his intended purchase of some land running down Chapel Lane behind New Place, the area known today as the 'Great Garden', the Corporation discovered, so it claimed, that the lease for another plot of land Gastrell owned elsewhere in Stratford was null and void. He refused to forfeit the disputed land and the Corporation refused to back down. Three years of litigation ensued.

As if this protracted acrimony weren't enough, Gastrell and the Corporation found something more to fight over. Spending much of his time in Lichfield, where he was Canon Residentiary at the cathedral, Gastrell resented having to pay a tithe on New Place to aid the poor and indigent of Stratford. Because he did not live in the town for the entire year, Gastrell argued, he should not be held liable for the customary poor-rate. So much for Christian charity. The Corporation, still wrangling with him over other property leases, retorted that because some of Gastrell's servants resided at New Place year-round, he was indeed liable for the full tax. This was a rebuke too far. Fed up, Gastrell implemented the ultimate tax avoidance scheme by tearing New Place down, every brick and beam of it. No house, no tax. Only the barn and a few sheds remained, doubtless because they were not subject to tax.

This was not the unpardonable crime it might seem because it was not Shakespeare's house that Gastrell razed to the ground. That original sin had been committed decades earlier when Sir John Clopton, Hugh's father, demolished the expansive Tudor dwelling where Shakespeare had lived and erected in its place a townhouse in the popular Queen Anne style. New Place, built more than two centuries earlier, must then have seemed woefully antiquated. That Sir John's own ancestors had first built the house and that William Shakespeare later lived and died in the house were to him not sufficient reasons to preserve it. His need for a stylish modern residence trumped any regard for provenance or cultural heritage. And so, he levelled the entire structure right down to its stone foundations, as recent archaeological work on the site has confirmed. Shakespeare's cellar survived, but nothing else.

On top of this buried foundation was built a quintessentially Georgian mansion, a dwelling whose graceful neoclassical symmetry would have pleased Thomas Jefferson or Benjamin Franklin. Engravings from the time, although made after Gastrell's demolition job, depict a commanding two-storey brick house with rusticated stonework. The main entrance, on Chapel Street, was through a central door at the top of a small staircase and flanked by three tall windows on either side. Seven equally tall windows spanned the length of the floor above, with a small balcony off the central window. A dormer roof topped the house, complete with projecting cornice, two gabled windows on each side and, in the middle, a large projecting pediment on which was carved the Clopton family crest.

In his 1737 travel notebook, George Vertue, the man who visited Shakespeare Hart at the Birthplace, described the rebuilt New Place as a 'handsome brick house'. In the Folger Shakespeare Library, I came across a slightly later document that corroborates Vertue's account. The retired Stratford shoemaker Richard Grimmitt, in 1767, told the vicar of Welford, Joseph Greene, that as a child he had played in the courtyard of New Place, a 'Great House', he recalled, 'fronted with brick, with plain windows Consisting of Common panes of Glass'. That was precisely the sort of up-to-date residence that Vertue described, that the engravers drew and that William Shakespeare never saw. Sir John Clopton built it in the early eighteenth century and forty years later Francis Gastrell destroyed it.

'An established religion in poetry'

In 1700, when Sir John Clopton demolished the old house where William Shakespeare had lived and died, no one objected. In 1760, when Francis Gastrell demolished on the same site a modern house that had no architectural link to Shakespeare, everyone objected. Something had changed in people's minds, but what?

One change was the growing interest in Shakespeare's life, especially his domestic life in Stratford. In the early eighteenth century, Shakespeare was still mainly a literary figure, an entity detached from history. Indeed, he exceeded mere temporality in his writings of perennial relevance. This version of a Shakespeare *beyond* history, 'not of an age, but for all time,' to invoke Ben Jonson's prophecy, has never entirely gone away. But by the mid-eighteenth century, as poor Francis Gastrell learned the hard way, Shakespeare had orbited back into history, becoming once more a creature of flesh and blood, an actual man who lived in an actual house called New Place.

That this house no longer stood presented no quandary to anyone searching for Shakespeare because the search itself had become mostly symbolic. Just as it little mattered whether Shakespeare himself had planted the mulberry tree in the garden at New Place, it little mattered that a modern townhouse stood on the site where once he lived. What mattered was that Shakespeare pilgrims now regarded that site as holy ground, the final destination in their quest for the Bard of Avon, the vanishing point where history and mythology converge. This, I believe, was the most crucial change of all in how people thought about Shakespeare in the mid-eighteenth century. Francis Gastrell's offence was not that he destroyed Shakespeare's house – he didn't, Sir John Clopton did – but that he desecrated a hallowed site devoted to Shakespeare. That was the difference that made all the difference.

By shattering the idol, Gastrell ruined New Place as a privileged site for Shakespeare worship. Although if he hadn't torn it down, archaeologists might never have uncovered the stone foundations of Shakespeare's earlier house. Yet in the wake of Gastrell's vengeance, the site didn't look or feel like much of anything: no house, no host, no garden, no mulberry tree. Just a vacant corner plot with some old stones pushing up here and there through the soil. Even for those bewitched by picturesque ruins, so forlornly barren a site could not reach the status of a fitting memorial to William Shakespeare. Enchanted ground no more, New Place was, for Shakespeare's journeying pilgrims, off the map.

The timing was bad. By the mid-eighteenth century, Shakespeare was poised to become Britain's great national poet, far greater than in his lifetime. In 1741, Peter Scheemakers' life-size white marble statue of Shakespeare was unveiled in Poets' Corner in Westminster Abbey, belatedly atoning for the insult that the man himself was not interred there. 'After an hundred and thirty years' nap', Alexander Pope rejoiced in rhyme, 'Enter Shakespear, with a loud clap.' The collected plays, published in editions overseen by critical heavyweights like Pope and Samuel Johnson, supplied for general readers a model of native literary genius that owed nothing to imported French neoclassicism. At Covent Garden and Drury Lane, Shakespeare's plays became the standard against which theatrical fame was won or lost. In 1753, when Francis Gastrell mistakenly believed that New Place would make a tranquil holiday home, the English dramatist Arthur Murphy rebuked Voltaire's criticism of Shakespeare by boasting, without fear of contradiction, that 'with us islanders Shakespeare is a kind of established religion in poetry'. So he has been ever since.

Yet every religion needs a shrine. Where, in the absence of New Place, would it be?

8

Birth of the Birthplace

Enter, on cue, the Birthplace. With New Place pulled down, the house on Henley Street became Shakespeare's only surviving residence – not just in Stratford, but anywhere. Appealingly, it retained much of its Elizabethan character, inside and out. Exactly when the house on Henley Street first attracted visitors remains unknown, although George Vertue in 1737 was likely one of the earliest. It's revealing that the oldest reference to the house as the 'Birthplace' dates from the same year, 1759, that Francis Gastrell demolished New Place. In his 'Plan of Stratford', local schoolmaster Samuel Winter designated the property's western half as the 'Place where Shakespeare was born', one of twenty-seven sites marked on the town's official map.

In putting Shakespeare's birthplace on the map – literally, on the map – Winter was inviting locals and visitors alike to experience the town's Shakespeare geography in a new way. New Place was also identified on the map, as the site 'Where Died Shakespeare', even though it may already have been demolished. In this rivalry of two houses, the Birthplace now claimed primacy.

'Letter from the Place of Shakspear's Nativity'

In 1762, three years after Winter drew his map, the *British Magazine* printed a 'Letter from the Place of Shakspear's Nativity', in which, for the first time, the Birthplace eclipsed Holy Trinity Church as the preferred tourist attraction in the 'town which gave birth to the prince of dramatic poets'. New Place, of course, by then a vacant plot, didn't factor in. The unknown correspondent lodged for a few summer days in at the White Lion on Henley Street. The sightseer and his 'chearful landlord', while sharing their mutual devotion to Shakespeare, and also a good bottle of claret, decided to visit 'the house where the poet was born'. Happily, it was just three doors away. 'There I saw', the traveller recounted, 'a mulberry-tree of that great man's planting, a piece of which I brought away with me, to make a tobacco-stopper for our vicar. His monument in that noble old church likewise afforded me great satisfaction.'

A tree did stand on the grounds, but it was walnut, not mulberry. After being cut down a few years later, it, too, was transfigured into souvenirs, including a tiny replica of the marble Shakespeare statue in Westminster Abbey. Transplanting, as it were, the mulberry tree from New Place to the Birthplace was more than an out-of-towner's mistake. Rather, it reminded locals and travellers alike that for the Birthplace to stage an encounter with Shakespeare it needed to adopt the rituals once associated with the now demolished New Place, rituals that included chopping down trees of Shakespearean provenance and then carving them into saleable trinkets. Until it possessed an aura of its own, the Birthplace had to mimic the signs and symbols of a Shakespeare house that no longer existed.

George Hart, nephew of Shakespeare Hart, then owned and was living in the Birthplace. He received visitors there, just as his uncle had done a few decades earlier. But now the story reached a much wider public, starting with the *British Magazine*'s nearly fifteen thousand subscribers. Carvings from the walnut tree spurred a brisk trade in reputed relics, the enterprise abetted by the timely intercession of a genial neighbouring publican eager to capitalize on his proximity to a unique tourist attraction. The Birthplace created, at least for this one visitor, more vivid and more lasting memories than did Shakespeare's gravesite and funerary monument, which for over a century had been the preferred Shakespeare memorial in Stratford. The competition for tourists had begun.

'There is a certain degree of pleasure'

A problem stood in the way of the Birthplace's claim for supremacy, the problem of its own miserable appearance. In July 1769, the first published image of William Shakespeare's birthplace appeared in *Gentleman's Magazine*. Based on a watercolour drawing made seven years earlier by the antiquary Richard Greene, it depicted a detached, three-gabled building with dormer windows. The caption underneath read, 'A House in Stratford upon Avon, in which the famous Poet Shakspear was born'. An impressive abode, especially for the family of a town glovemaker like John Shakespeare.

But it wasn't altogether real. The Birthplace appears isolated in an open field, when actually it stood in a row of shops, inns and other houses. The drawing combines the eastern and western halves of the property to form a large single dwelling, when, in fact, the premises had long been divided into a private family residence and a public tavern, the Swan and Maidenhead Inn. The exterior looks clean and fresh, even though the house, then inhabited by the descendants of Shakespeare's sister Joan Hart, was falling into disrepair. It was an eighteenth-century version of Photoshopping.

Granted, illustrators back then often modified details in architectural or topographical drawings to achieve picturesque effects, as Greene did by having puffs of smoke billow pleasingly from one of the house's five chimneys. But something more than decorative detail must have been at stake. After all, the drawing misrepresents where the birthplace was and what it looked like. Hardly a cosmetic retouching.

To understand why Shakespeare's birthplace was so falsely depicted, we need to remember that the image was published on the eve of the Stratford Jubilee, the world's first Shakespeare festival, dreamt up and led in September 1769 by the celebrated actor David Garrick. The magazine engraving was part of the Jubilee's advance publicity campaign. Although it was a much-mocked fiasco in the short term, the Jubilee transformed the town of Stratford-upon-Avon into a gigantic Shakespeare tourist site. Such it has been ever since. In Shakespeare's hometown, what site could be more compelling than the house where he was born?

Alas, the house looked too ordinary. Its humdrum appearance could never beguile or enchant any onlooker. And yet now, in the wake of the Jubilee, and with New Place demolished, the birthplace had become a tourist attraction in its own right. No longer a private family home, as it had been for centuries, it had suddenly risen to the status of a public monument to Shakespeare. A monument that looked better on paper than in three-dimensional real life, but the printed image would suffice to give the needed false impression. Shakespeare's house, to be appealing to the public, had to be rendered untrue to life.

And so, the artist went to work, replacing the banal with the colossal and the drab with the fantastical. This ideal version of Shakespeare's birthplace obscured the humble truth – and it was meant to. In 1769, what looked authentic to a Shakespeare devotee was not the squat house on Henley Street but its mass-produced likeness that was, by design, no likeness at all.

In the pages of the *Gentleman's Magazine*, everyone could see for themselves the house that William Shakespeare *should* have been born in but wasn't. And they didn't have to travel to Stratford to do it. Posterity gifted to Shakespeare the birthplace he deserved but never had: a grand dwelling, set apart, approached from all directions, a landmark unto itself. A house that made you stop and stare. A house that was worthy of the immortal Bard of Avon.

Tension between the Birthplace as it is and the Birthplace as it ought to be, the same tension concealed in Greene's fanciful drawing, surfaces in the description that accompanies it, written by one 'T.B.' of Lichfield:

There is a certain degree of pleasure, better felt than described, excited in the mind, upon visiting ... the places of nativity of extraordinary personages deceased ... I do not know whether the apartment where the incomparable Shakespeare first drew his breath, can, at this day, be ascertained, or not; but the house of his nativity (according to undoubted tradition) is now remaining. My worthy friend Mr Greene, of this place, hath favoured me with an exact drawing of it.

T.B. was either a liar or a fool. Greene's rendering of the Birthplace was the very opposite of 'exact'. Still, he was confident that visiting 'places of nativity' should be a pleasurable experience that fuelled the visitor's imagination. With great authors like Shakespeare, such places could enhance 'the impressions and improvements we have received from their writings'. Such a conviction rings true in the literal, but hardly trivial, sense that although we cannot all be famous writers we have all lived somewhere. We may not share much with William Shakespeare, but we do share this: we, too, were born and grew up in a particular place. Like him, we've lived under a certain roof. Home life is our point of contact and connection with Shakespeare the man, a shared dimension of daily human experience.

But a deeper assumption is also working here. Curiosity about an author's home depends upon believing that what holds true for ordinary people holds true equally, or even more so, for great writers: namely, that the *real* person – unbuttoned, shoes kicked off, hair let down – can be found only at home. Public life requires a crafted performance, a rehearsed charade. But in 'domestic privacies', as Samuel Johnson put it, all such 'exterior appendages are cast aside'. Only home life grants us the freedom to be who we truly are, what Johnson, whose own redbrick townhouse at 17 Gough Street, London, survives as a museum, called our 'private and familiar character'. The hope that the Birthplace would reveal Shakespeare's true character, a hope first articulated in the mid-eighteenth century, explains the undimmed allure of visiting it.

'An ode without poetry, music without melody'

In 1769, the Birthplace became something of a tourist attraction during the Stratford Jubilee, the three-day Shakespeare extravaganza devised and overseen by David Garrick, one of the three actors who, a quarter-century earlier, had raised a glass to Shakespeare under the shade of the mulberry tree at New Place. Then a mere beginner, Garrick had long since risen to the top of his profession. Not only did he manage Drury Lane Theatre, but he reigned supreme as England's greatest interpreter of Shakespeare's dramatic characters, showing audiences everything from Hamlet's frozen terror upon seeing his father's ghost to Macbeth's deranged ambition, and from Romeo's sweet ardour to Richard III's evil cunning. James Boswell wept openly at the poignant frailty of the actor's King Lear, an experience so oddly pleasurable that he returned for more.

Even so, Garrick's lasting legacy was his belief that Shakespeare epitomized the greatness of English culture. Shakespeare the great national poet had by now became his country's triumphant answer to Homer and Virgil, rivalling those laureates of classical antiquity to express his homeland's global economic and colonial power. He had become a synonym for Englishness itself, the very substance and image of national identity. All this, David Garrick believed and professed. More than any other figure of his time, he codified for a mass audience the public rites and rituals of worshipping William Shakespeare.

The founding worshipful event was the Stratford Jubilee, for which Garrick served as architect, steward and high priest. Though the celebrations were held in Shakespeare's hometown, the target audience was neither the people of Stratford nor the local gentry, which may explain why the town council declined to subsidize the Jubilee. Rather, Garrick sought to attract high society for the prestige they would bring to the festivities and London theatregoers for the money they would spend. In this endeavour, he succeeded. Heavily trailed in the popular press, and just as heavily mocked by the actor's enemies, the Jubilee featured performances, masquerades, orations, concerts, breakfasts and banquets, all to celebrate and commemorate Shakespeare in his hometown. Held in the first week of September, it also featured spoiling torrential rain. Wet fireworks fizzled, the parade of two hundred Shakespeare characters was cancelled – it was meant to pass in front of the Birthplace – and the octagonal amphitheatre, newly built on the banks of the Avon, and which boasted a chandelier with eight hundred candles, soon flooded. By the Jubilee's third day, rain-soaked visitors from London called it quits and headed back home. Only they couldn't, because their coaches departing from the White Lion got mired in mud that refused to dry.

Samuel Foote, manager of the Haymarket Theatre in London, travelled to Stratford not to praise the Jubilee but to bury it under ridicule. Later, he quipped that the much-heralded event put together by his theatrical rival amounted to 'an ode without poetry, music without melody, dinners without victuals, and lodgings without beds'. The entire occasion proved, literally, a washout.

This fiasco left Garrick saddled with debts totalling £2,000, an immense sum that he nonetheless quickly recouped with proceeds from his play *The Jubilee*, an indoor version of the rained-out pageant of Shakespeare characters that was supposed to have wound its way around Stratford. Burned by the Jubilee's failure, he refused to organize another celebration in Shakespeare's hometown. Spurning a request from the Corporation of Stratford, Garrick offered this caustic advice: 'Let your streets be well paved and kept clean, do something to the delightful meadow, allure everybody to visit the Holy-land, let it be well lighted and clean underfoot, and let it not be said ... that the town which gave birth to the first genius since the creation is the most dirty, unseemly, ill-paved wretched looking place in all Britain.' Despite all its embarrassing failures, the Jubilee established Stratford not just as a town-sized shrine to the Bard, but as a culture factory that has successfully engaged in the lucrative Shakespeare trade ever since.

'The very small old house'

So successfully did the Jubilee deify Shakespeare – "'Tis he! 'Tis he! / "The god of our idolatry"', as Garrick exclaimed in his quasi-operatic ode that he recited while gazing upon the poet's sculpted likeness – that any object associated with the Bard would be gratefully revered. If a mere cup reputedly carved from that legendary mulberry tree was endowed with talismanic powers, as Jubilee folklore had it, then Shakespeare's actual birthplace merited veneration on a public scale.

Although more Jubilee visitors journeyed to Shakespeare's gravesite than to the Birthplace, the 'very small old house', as Garrick's first biographer described it, was for the first time celebrated in a formal way. Recognizing, perhaps, that the ordinary old house lacked the glamour needed for his grand celebration, Garrick gave the Birthplace a touch of theatrical glitz when he commissioned Drury Lane's fencing master, Domenico Angelo, to install over its front windows a painting of the sun emerging from behind thick clouds. An apt symbol, Garrick decided, for Shakespeare's ascent from humble origins to the 'Glory of his Country'. Signor Angelo set candle lamps behind the canvas, so that when the lamps were lit at night they shone through the painting. Other buildings across Stratford were similarly decorated with coloured lanterns, giving the whole townscape a festive appearance. Irradiated from within, the entire front of the Birthplace dazzled with colour against the stern night sky. Like a blazing Broadway marquee, the lighting effect demanded you attention. You could no longer walk by the Birthplace and ignore it.

'A good deal of money'

Throughout the Jubilee, entry to the Birthplace was regulated in a gentler, more amateurish, version of how museums today herd patrons along prescribed routes through galleries and exhibition halls. As Boswell sardonically noted in *The London Magazine*, Garrick stationed his literary agent, Thomas Beckett, inside the upstairs birthroom, where he hawked official Jubilee publications, notably Garrick's 'Ode on Dedicating a Building and Erecting a Statue to Shakespeare'. The building was the Stratford Town Hall, in whose central niche was placed a statue of William Shakespeare. (This statue was magnificently restored in 2022, with funds raised in a marathon Shakespeare play reading organized by Paul Edmondson.) Might one also, in the Birthplace, buy a copy of *Othello* or *Much Ado about Nothing*? Alas, no. Only works by David Garrick were available for purchase.

Beckett was not the sole merchant in the temple. We know that because of a naval surgeon turned belletrist named James Solas Dodd, whose literary career had sprung into life in 1752 with his 'Essay Towards a Natural History of the Herring'. Dodd's eyewitness account of visiting the Birthplace – 'A Detail of the Whole Diversions of the Jubilee at Stratford Upon Avon', published in 1770 – deserves to be much better known. In this travelogue, he relates his surprise at discovering that the 'mistress' of the house was named 'Shakespeare' (no, she definitely wasn't) and that she earned 'a good deal of money by shewing the room where he was born, and the chair in which he used to sit when he wrote' (yes, she probably did). We must imagine this woman gleefully running a lucrative sideline under Beckett's snobbish nose, welcoming into *her* abode, and out of the miserable rain, many of those tourists who had descended upon Stratford only to have their enthusiasm quickly chilled. How genial a scene. In the ensuing tussle for customers, she probably claimed victory. After all, Beckett sold words that only honoured Shakespeare; the mistress of the house sold Shakespeare himself.

As much as I was enjoying Dodd's account of the Birthplace, I began to see how much he got wrong. Not a little off the mark, but wildly so. He misreported the woman's last name, or was misled about it, because Shakespeare had no surviving male heirs to carry his name. The direct line ended with him. At the time of the Jubilee, the Birthplace belonged to the elderly widower George Hart. The woman that Dodd encountered could have been one of Hart's older daughters or daughters-in-law. We don't know. But whoever she was, she must have surmised that her takings would increase exponentially if she borrowed, for three days only, the surname of the Hart family's distant but famous uncle.

Just as her name was an imposture, so, too, was the hallowed chair, to say nothing of the preposterous claim that Shakespeare wrote anything of note in his childhood home. To these compounded errors we may add Dodd's equally fantastic declaration that the hostess's fourteen-year-old daughter 'has many features which resemble the best painting we have of Shakespear'. More nonsense. She wasn't descended from Shakespeare. Nor is there any such thing as a 'best painting', not even the Chandos portrait now in the National Gallery in London, probably the only image of Shakespeare made in his lifetime, because there is no objective standard by which anyone could judge such a painting to be good, better or best. Naïve or mischievous, this jolly story was spun out of half-truths.

'Awake your faith'

I've been guilty of reading James Solas Dodd the wrong way. How pointless it has been for me to verify, or rather, falsify, a narrative that wishes only to offer pleasure and delight, not rigid accuracy. Like the legend of the mulberry tree, stories about the Birthplace captivate us most when they are told from the vague, imprecise boundary between the genuine and the sham. Getting the mixture right was everything. Too much credibility dulled the tale; too much flimflam insulted the reader. But when held in perfect equipoise, the result was an exhilarating time-travel game that you somehow forgot was a game.

The lesson of the Stratford Jubilee is that historical authenticity was *never* what visitors experienced or wanted to experience at Shakespeare heritage sites. It was not true of New Place, which had been altered beyond recognition by one later owner and then demolished by another. It was not true of the chopped-down mulberry tree, for which no hard evidence whatsoever confirmed that Shakespeare had planted it. Nor was it true of the subsequent trade in relics, for which a mulberry tree of infinite abundance was required.

Least of all was it true of the Birthplace. Nothing proved that Shakespeare had been born in the upstairs chamber that Garrick peremptorily declared to be the birthroom. It's just as likely that he was born in the downstairs parlour because in Elizabethan times the best pieces of furniture, such as a four-poster marriage bed, were displayed in the main rooms to make houseguests envious. The tour guides, if they were indeed descended from Shakespeare's sister Joan Hart, stretched the truth by claiming the great author's surname as their own. And the one person who never sat in that fireside chair was Shakespeare the working dramatist. Though authentic on the outside, for the house largely retained its original Tudor character, the Birthplace on the inside was a site of rank imposture. Fake rooms, fake furniture, fake stories, fake people.

Yet these compounded deceptions only enhanced, not diminished, the Birthplace's stature as a privileged site for honouring Shakespeare. It was never a matter of unscrupulous tour guides defrauding gullible visitors. Rather, the whole experience hinged on the visitor's tacit complicity with the half-truths, conjectures and outright lies peddled there. Like any holy shrine, the Birthplace depended upon the pilgrim's heartfelt intercession, without which the charm failed to work. Enchantment is always a two-way street. Or, as Paulina, in *The Winter's Tale*, instructed the disbelieving court of Leontes when unveiling the statue of Hermione that came suddenly to life, 'It is required / You do awake your faith' (5.3.94–5).

'I have not the faith to believe'

It can be hard to awaken your faith. Just ask Samuel Vince, a bookish plasterer's son from the Suffolk village of Fressingfield. When I was researching the Birthplace at the Folger Shakespeare Library, I discovered an eighteenth-century notebook, long unread, in which was recorded one of the earliest and most revealing accounts of a visit to the Birthplace. It belonged to the aforementioned Samuel Vince, then aged twenty-seven.

In the summer of 1777, Vince and one of his fellow Cambridge classmates made a tour of England and north Wales, during which they spent a day in Stratford. Throughout the entire trip Vince kept a travel diary, filling thirty-eight pages in his notebook. After his death, in 1821, the diary passed to his Cambridge colleague F.J.H. Wollaston. It was acquired later in the century by the Shakespeare scholar and collector James Orchard Halliwell-Phillipps, the one who bought the New Place plot and undertook the first archaeological works there. Oddly, he purchased Vince's diary only to ignore it, never citing this unique source in any of his numerous books and essays on Shakespeare. After Halliwell-Phillipps died, in 1889, the manuscript was next purchased by the American collector Marsden J. Perry and eventually acquired by the Folger Shakespeare Library, where I read it.

To me, this manuscript was a prized discovery, because it came as close as I could get to time travel. Although I cannot interview Samuel Vince, I already know his answers to some of the questions I would ask him. There, in his own careful handwriting, is a rare testimony of someone who visited the Birthplace in the first few years after it gained public attention.

In his diary, Vince appears to be an enthusiastic, open-minded and inquisitive young man. Granted, no one is quite the same on the page as in real life; but it's all the evidence we have. An ideal travel companion, he appreciated pretty much everything, from scrutinizing a detail in the oak wainscotting at a Tudor manor house to savouring the view from high atop a medieval castle. But he didn't worship Shakespeare. In fact, he mentions Shakespeare only when recounting his few hours in Stratford, while everywhere in the diary he pays tribute to David Garrick, his favourite actor. Garrick, as we know, had been Shakespeare's promoter-in-chief during the Stratford Jubilee a decade earlier, which makes his young fan Samuel Vince, someone *not* invested in the playwright's reputation, the perfect test case to find out whether there was any merit in all that Jubilee hoopla. It was Vince's admiration for Garrick that led him to Shakespeare, the playwright who gave the actor some of his best roles.

Here, published for the first time in a book, is what Vince wrote about his visit to Shakespeare's house:

> The Country from thence to Stratford is very beautiful & rich, a Place justly famous for giving Birth to Shakespear. The House, where he was born, is still standing. It is a small cottage, & in one of the Rooms below stairs, there is still remaining an old chair, fixed in one of the chimnies, in which the Poet used to sit. The Woman of the House informed us that Mr. Garrick & many other Gentlemen had sung many a good Song in that Chair. We found that most, who visited this Place, had cut off a small Piece from the Leg of the Chair, to preserve in Honour of Shakespear, and as we were not wanting in curiosity, each took a small Piece, though I have not the Faith to believe I shall find any Inspiration from it. This is the only piece of his Furniture now remaining. We also visited the Room in which he was born, and found that the floor had suffered much, as the Chair below had done. We also paid our respects to his Tomb and Monument, which are in the Chancel, belonging to the Church.

A mere six sentences, but they reveal a good deal about Vince's experience of the Birthplace. The first thing we might detect is that his visit followed the pattern that James Solas Dodd had outlined during the Jubilee: the 'Woman of the House' conducted a tour whose highlights were the display of Shakespeare's chair, now placed in the back kitchen hearth, and a wander around the upstairs birthroom. That famous chair and, apparently, the sliced-away floorboards in the birthroom, had all gained all the efficacy of a holy relic. The faithful were ever anxious to obtain the merest sliver of that most precious wood, believing that Shakespeare was fully present in it, just as medieval pilgrims had believed that a saint was fully present in a blackened tooth or shard of knee bone wrapped in silk and housed in a gemstone-studded reliquary. Eternally regenerative, Shakespeare's chair remained miraculously whole no matter how much of it was sliced off.

Should relics prove insufficient, the reluctant, the doubtful and the wavering could bolster their faith through stories of illustrious visitors, something akin to hearing the lives of the saints. While there is no record of Garrick having led a chorus during a pilgrimage to Henley Street, this charming anecdote served, undeniably, a seriously valuable purpose. It offered tourists like Vince a guarantee that if they paid the price of admission an equally memorable encounter awaited them.

A curious tactic, pushing the average visitor into better appreciating their own experience by reciting to them a roll call of superior personages. If the famous David Garrick enjoyed his visit here, and most assuredly he did, then so will an ordinary person like *you*. But the use of this tactic, which is rather more strong-arming than at first I thought, tells me that the people running the house were, in fact, expecting that visitors would feel ambivalent about the Birthplace. Samuel Vince certainly did.

'We were not wanting in curiosity'

Then still a student, Vince went on to become an expert on logarithms and imaginary numbers, Plumian Professor of Astronomy and Experimental Philosophy at Cambridge and author of the *Complete System of Astronomy*, whose three volumes were published between 1797 and 1808. True to his lifelong calling, Vince approached the Birthplace not as a diehard Shakespeare fan but as a scientist; he came to scrutinize Shakespeare, not to worship him.

Given how infrequently Vince mentioned Shakespeare in his travel diary, I had assumed that he would be an impartial judge of the Birthplace, agnostic toward all things Shakespearean. I was wrong. He was, in fact, an enemy of Shakespeare myths and rituals, someone guided always by logic and reason and never by false nostalgia, cheap sentiment or unquestioned reverence. What a wonderful specimen he turned out to be. Because if the Birthplace could convert Samuel Vince, astronomer-in-training, then it could convert anybody.

With a scientist's curiosity, he pocketed a 'small Piece' of the fireside chair. With a scientist's scepticism, he felt it unlikely that this memento, prized so highly by others, would bring to him any 'inspiration'. Importing further data, as it were, into his experiment, he could not help but observe that when compared to the 'most beautiful' countryside, the elegance of the Earl of Warwick's castle and the 'handsome' Stratford town hall – he had just visited all those sites – the 'small cottage' on Henley Street left him unenthused.

Yet here's the twist: Vince felt that he *ought* to have been enthused. The spell ought to have worked on him. His faith should have been awakened. Indeed, he wished that it had been. How else to explain why the Birthplace, a site to him of myth and magic, received more attention in this budding scientist's diary than the rock-solid factuality of the 'Tomb and Monument' in Holy Trinity Church, which he accorded but a passing remark? No doubt Vince's esteem for Garrick inclined him, if not to share, then at least to regard seriously, the great actor's devotion to Shakespearean 'idolatry'. Granted, the Cambridge scientist played the game of the Birthplace less passionately, and less proficiently, than had visitors like James Solas Dodd. Yet Vince, too, understood, and understood in spite of himself, that you had to play up and play the game. No sitting on the sidelines. You just had to take a 'small Piece' of the chair home with you. Whether or not you dared to admit it to yourself, that's exactly what you came to the Birthplace for.

Slowly, then all at once. Before the 1750s, the house on Henley Street seems to have escaped attention altogether. Yet when the stars and planets aligned – biographical interest in Shakespeare, lack of alternative sites in Stratford, the rise of Shakespeare worship, the consequent emergence of a tourist trade, a sympathetic popular press – it took but a single decade for the Birthplace to become the site most closely associated with William Shakespeare in the popular imagination. At last, the ghostly author of the First Folio was vanquished. Shakespeare, it turned out, was not dead after all. He was alive and well and always glad to have company at home.

9

Cottage of Humility

'From the four corners of the earth they come / To kiss this shrine.'
THE MERCHANT OF VENICE (2.7.39–40)

In July 1777, the month when Samuel Vince visited the Birthplace, so did the historian and cartographer George Augustus Walpole, who wrote about his trip in *The New and Complete British Traveller*, published in 1784. Much of Walpole's account matches the one written by Vince, notably its observation that many visitors had sliced off parts of Shakespeare's chair to take home with them as a souvenir or collectible. Yet with an antiquarian's eye for local colour, he added a telling comment about the house's inhabitants: 'The people who live in the house say they are his [Shakespeare's] next relations; they are poor.'

What Walpole reported was correct. The Harts were indeed Shakespeare's closest surviving relatives, and they were chronically poor. So poor that when the Birthplace, their long-time home, was firmly established as a tourist site during the Shakespeare Jubilee in 1769, it was in a parlous state. Successive generations of the family mortgaged, and then re-mortgaged, the property, releasing cash for themselves but never setting aside anything for the upkeep, let alone improvement, of the house. Nor did they give much thought to how they would pay off their accumulated debts. The Harts were so persistently short of cash that every so often they sold bits of land adjacent to the Birthplace to generate some quick money. Shakespeare Hart received seven pounds from John Payton in 1746 for part of the backyard between Hart's garden and the Maidenhead Inn. A few decades later, Thomas Hart earned £140 by selling yet more land, including the site of a barn at the far north end of the plot behind the Birthplace. We can scarcely blame the Harts for turning their land into cash because Shakespeare's own father had done the same when he had fallen on hard times, selling to his neighbour George Badger, in 1597, a small strip of land along the western boundary of his property.

At the time of the Jubilee, the entire property was owned by the elderly George Hart, upon whose death, in 1778, it passed to his son Thomas, a local woodworker. After his death, in 1793, the Maidenhead Inn passed to his son John, a chair-marker in London and, soon afterwards, in the Gloucestershire market town of Tewkesbury. The remainder of the premises, including the cottage traditionally known as the Birthplace, was inherited by his other son, Thomas, a Stratford butcher.

Sadly, within a year, Thomas Hart lost his wife and infant daughter, after which he decided to leave Stratford. The grieving widower was the last blood relative of William Shakespeare to live in Shakespeare's birthplace, thus ending a family tradition that had endured for more than one hundred and seventy years. On 20 May 1794, he leased 'all that messuage or tenement, shop, backside, and premises in the Henley-street' to Thomas Hornby, another town butcher, and a relation by marriage, for an annual rent of seven pounds. Although Thomas Hart didn't rent the Birthplace because of its connection to Shakespeare, his tenants were fully aware of the house's unique pedigree. Not long after settling into their new home, Mary and Thomas Hornby had a son, whom they named William Shakespeare. He died in December 1803, aged eight years and seven months. Though we must leave Mary Hornby for now, we will come back to her, for she plays a colourful and decisive role in the Birthplace's history.

Just two years after becoming the Hornby's landlord, Thomas Hart sold his share of the property to his brother John, who then became owner of the entire premises – cottage, butcher's shop and the Maidenhead Inn – all of which he leased to tenants. But the rental income proved insufficient to cover his mounting debts, including the sum still owed on the heavily mortgaged property itself. The Harts grew poorer and poorer while the neglected Birthplace sank into an ever-deepening decrepitude, even as the Hornbys ran it as their own private tourist attraction. After John Hart's death in 1800, his widow, Mary, and their three children – William Shakespeare, John and Sarah – determined that to escape financial ruin they must sell the entire Henley Street property and at a good price. Only then could the family get free of their accumulated debts. That was what they told Robert Wheler, their Stratford lawyer.

'2 hundred and Ninty pounds'

At this point in the story, the archival record leaps into life. Carefully preserved in the vaults of the Folger Shakespeare Library is an unusual batch of letters exchanged between the Harts and Robert Wheler from 1793 to 1808. Wheler's own son, the antiquarian Robert Bell Wheler, wrote the first history of the Birthplace, published as a pamphlet in 1824. These letters poignantly document the family's dire financial plight. Because they could not afford to pay even the interest on their outstanding loans, the Harts insisted on an exorbitant asking price for the Birthplace. They had to make a killing from the sale. But with the price set so high, potential buyers stayed away. And yet the mortgage repayments kept coming due. Simply as a rough and tumble narrative of the property market, the letters tell the sad tale of a family in steady decline. For the Harts, it must have felt like there was no way out.

On 10 November 1804, John Hart, acting on his mother's behalf, instructed Wheler to sell the house for at least £290 and promised to send him a copy of his late father's will, confirming that Mary Hart was now the house's legal owner. Here is the unaltered transcription of John Hart's letter, which he no doubt wrote himself, rather than dictating to a scribe or secretary:

> I should be glad if you will advertise it to be sold by privet contrack in the paper wich you munched and I will send you my late farthers Copey of is will in a day or to is will was left . . . for to be Aqualy to be devided at my mother's deth and whe are all Agreeable to sine ower and to sell it should not wish to sell it fore less 2 hundred and Ninty pounds from your humble servent.

When I first read these letters on a lovely summer's day at the Folger, an institution faithfully devoted to celebrating Shakespeare's life and works, it struck me that their saddest and deepest irony was not that the Harts risked poverty, though that was misery enough, but that they were barely literate. Two hundred years after Shakespeare's death and *Hamlet* was out of reach for his closest surviving relatives, a text too difficult for them to master. Certainly, they took pride in their illustrious ancestor and, at times, sought to capitalize on the family connection. But could they experience for themselves the joy of reading his immortal verse? The gift seems to have been lost.

'A ruinous State'

It was a tough sell. The house had fallen into extreme disrepair and yet the price remained inflated. Inflated, not because of the property's direct link to Shakespeare – curiously, his name featured not once in the sale advertisements – but because of the Hart family's debts. To us, today, any price seems impossibly low, for Shakespeare's Birthplace is literally priceless. A unique heritage asset, not a commodity to be bought and sold. That's our point of view, heirs as we are to the global cult of Shakespeare worship. But in 1800 it wasn't anyone's point of view, and certainly not that of the Hart family. If we find it incredible that Shakespeare's house was once put on the property market, and without any reverential nod to Shakespeare himself, it's because we are attributing to the Birthplace a protected cultural status that it did not then possess.

The Harts were not obsessed with Shakespeare heritage, but they were obsessed with money. Mary Hart's initial asking price, set in 1800, was

£300. 'Under that money', she told her lawyer, 'I do not intend to Sell.' An ideal buyer came forward: their own tenant, Joseph Jobson, proprietor of the Swan and Maidenhead Inn, which was included in the sale. Alas, he was put off by how derelict the whole property had become. 'Some parts of the Buildings are in such a ruinous State', Wheler explained to his clients, 'that unless something is done to them before winter it will be impossible to inhabit them and he [Jobson] hopes that either some of the family will come up to Stratford or otherwise give Directions for the necessary Repairs'. Jobson was not exaggerating. The house had run to ramshackle, while what was left of the yard, after the Harts had sold off bits and pieces of it, was all but obliterated by stables, slaughterhouses and sundry outbuildings. A far cry from the gently landscaped 'Shakespeare garden' that visitors enjoy today. The Harts refused to make the necessary repairs and so Jobson walked away from the deal.

By 1803, the Harts had fallen eight months behind in their mortgage payments, with a total debt of £140. There was no buyer in sight. Another year passed. Still, no sale. In the winter of 1804, the family lowered the price by a negligible ten pounds (this was the '2 hundred and Ninty pounds' that John Hart stipulated in his letter to Robert Wheler). Predictably, this miniscule price drop failed to generate any interest in the property. Yet, as the patient lawyer kept reminding his stubborn clients, the house declined further in value with each passing day. Shakespeare's Birthplace was a depreciating asset.

The Harts kept trying for a sale. On 26 November 1804, the *Birmingham Gazette* featured an advertisement for 'Two Freehold Houses with the Stables, Outbuildings, and Yards belonging to the same eligibly situated in Henley Street in the Borough of Stratford upon Avon'. But that wasn't the whole description. Now, for the first time, the house's illustrious pedigree – its unique selling point, in modern business parlance – was publicized: '[I]n the House . . . our Immortal Bard Shakespeare was born about the middle of the 16th century, since which time they have continued in the possession of the Hart Family the present proprietor being the seventh Descendant in direct line from Joan, the eldest Sister of the Poet.'

Astonishingly, no buyer appeared. Shakespeare genealogy took centre stage in this new marketing campaign, but it made no difference. The market shrugged. Three months later, the Harts changed tactics and agreed to a public auction, held at the nearby White Lion Inn on the afternoon of Thursday, 7 March 1805. Another announcement was placed in the *Birmingham Gazette*, but this time the paragraph trumpeting Shakespeare was deleted entirely. Still, no buyer for the house.

It seems odd that the reference in the newspaper advertisement to Shakespeare and his descendants had no effect. After all, that's the reason why the house has become famous the world over. Yet perhaps the Shakespeare allusion made no difference to the property's resale value because it was so plainly redundant. Visitors had been finding their way to the Birthplace for more than thirty years, ever since the Jubilee in 1769, when the earliest illustrations of the house had appeared in the popular press. Over the past decade, Mary Hornby had been taking money from the tourists she escorted around the Birthplace, just as the Hart family had done in previous decades. If you were the type of buyer who could be swayed by the house's link to Shakespeare, then you already knew about that link. If you were unlikely to be swayed, then such information was superfluous. Indeed, so gratuitous were reminders that Shakespeare was born in the house that not once in their lengthy correspondence, stretching across fifteen years, did either the Harts or Robert Wheler refer to it.

'Have they risen or fallen in the world?'

Although everyone in Stratford knew about the Harts and their house on Henley Street, few people elsewhere knew about this family, their connection to Shakespeare and their continuing ownership of the Birthplace. Edmond Malone, the first scholar to undertake careful archival research in Stratford, sent a letter in 1788 to the town vicar, Rev James Davenport, seeking information about the Harts. 'I see by the [parish] Register that Shakspeare's Brother in law, Wm. Hart. Was a Hatter', he wrote. 'Pray have they risen or fallen in the world; and in what situation of life are his descendants at present?' Malone, the person who knew more about Shakespeare biography than anyone else in the world, knew nothing about Shakespeare's closest surviving relatives. Today, any twelve-year-old with an internet connection can find that same information on Wikipedia or through a Google search within minutes.

It saddened Malone when Davenport replied that 'a remote descendant of our great poet's sister' lived in Stratford in 'distressed circumstances'. Out of pity, he sent old Thomas Hart ten pounds, about what he paid his London housemaid over an entire year, hoping that it would be useful 'to the poor man'. A few decades later, in 1829, the poet Robert Southey, shocked that 'the descendants of Shakespeare are living in poverty, and in the lowest condition of life', proposed that a perpetual copyright be established for Shakespeare's works, with all the royalties paid to the Harts as their 'proper inheritance'. For him, it was a matter of natural justice that the Harts should live in 'respectability and comfort'. Southey's idea went nowhere. Yet a perpetual copyright, had it been granted, would have made the Harts and their descendants so rich that even J.K. Rowling would seem petty bourgeois in comparison.

But the Harts were the opposite of rich; and it was precisely the family's 'distressed circumstances' that forced them to sell the Birthplace. The auction in 1805 had failed to attract a buyer because the lowered reserve price still was too high. A month later, the exasperated Robert Wheler was ready to call it quits: '[I] cannot meet with any person that will offer more than £210

& in the bad state of Repairs they are in I do not expect any person will give more than that Sum. As things are circumstanced I am at a loss how to advise you.' Relenting, at last, the Harts further reduced the price to £210, even though William Shakespeare Hart, the eldest son, grumbled that 'at that prise . . . is all most Give Away'.

Give away or not, the price was finally right. In early July 1806, and after a few false starts, Thomas Court, proprietor of the nearby Garrick Inn (still serving customers, it's reputed to be Stratford's oldest pub) paid the full asking price of £210 for the entire property. With Robert Wheler acting as solicitor for both buyer and seller, the deal was sealed on Clopton Bridge at four o'clock on a July morning. A new day indeed was about to dawn.

After paying off their long-deferred debts, the Harts returned to Tewkesbury with a modest profit of twenty-one pounds. The house on Henley Street had been owned for the past 250 years by John Shakespeare and eight generations of his lineal descendants. Now, it passed forever outside the family. Granted, the Courts had been known in Stratford for as long as the Shakespeares. One of Thomas Court's ancestors succeeded John Shakespeare as a town alderman, while another one drew up the legal documents when he sold a strip of land to George Badger. A later ancestor, Richard Court, was a Stratford apothecary who worked with Shakespeare's son-in-law, the physician John Hall. The Courts kept the house for a much shorter time, just forty years. They were the last private individuals to own Shakespeare's Birthplace.

'Reliques of Shakespeare'

In taking ownership of the house, the Courts also took on the sitting tenants Mary and Thomas Hornby. The Hornbys lived in one side of the house and used the other side as the husband's workplace, just as John and Mary Shakespeare had done more than two centuries before. While Thomas Hornby was busy running his butcher's shop, his wife kept several rooms open to the public, which she advertised as Shakespeare's birthplace, and so continued the hospitable practice begun by the Harts a few decades earlier. Mary Hornby gained notoriety as an energetic tour guide who, once her visitors had paid the entrance fee, showed them fake Shakespeare relics and told them equally dubious stories. If only it were true that Restoration actor Charles Hart, who taught Nell Gwyn how to act, was the grandson of Shakespeare's sister Joan Hart.

In the late 1790s, early in her tenancy, Mary Hornby had purchased from Thomas Hart, her original landlord, sundry 'Reliques of Shakespeare'. Curiously, these relics had not hitherto been displayed in the birthplace. When Samuel Vince visited in the late 1770s, when the Harts still lived there, he noted that Shakespeare's chair, itself of highly doubtful provenance, was 'the only piece of his furniture now remaining'. Yet two decades later,

Thomas Hart suddenly found himself encumbered with prized artefacts – two dozen of them – including a gold-embroidered black velvet tablecloth that Elizabeth I gave to Shakespeare, the matchlock that the young Shakespeare used to shoot deer in Charlecote Park, a goblet said to be carved from the mulberry tree at New Place and decorated with the Shakespeare family coat of arms, Shakespeare's own pencil case and his wife Anne's shoe. In a textbook case of supply meeting demand, Thomas Hart sold every last relic to the entrepreneurial Mary Hornby.

For the details of this intimate inventory, we are forever indebted to Miss Laetitia Matilda Hawkins, whose three-volume *Anecdotes, Biographical Sketches and Memoirs* includes an account of her visit to the Birthplace in 1819. Her recollection of Mrs Hornby was sympathetic, noting how politely she guided her guest around the Birthplace – 'Lady, can I show you', 'Lady, if you will please to look' – pointing out to Miss Hawkins all the various relics.

Where had this ton of antique treasure been hiding? Nowhere, because it wasn't treasure and it wasn't antique. Every last object was a fake. Not that the truth of it was a secret. For as one of Thomas Hart's neighbours cynically remarked, he never hesitated 'to attach a reliquary reputation to any article by which a penny could be turned'. But no matter: because most of Mary Hornby's guests happily joined in the game of Shakespeare worship, a game whose cardinal rule was that you must never inquire too deeply about the authenticity of any item displayed in the 'Shakespeare Museum'. As the *Gentleman's Magazine* later observed, and with unusual insight, the 'sentiment' felt by a visitor to the Birthplace mattered far more than the legitimacy of any relic exhibited there.

By this time, the Birthplace had become a living museum; a place not just for passive looking, but for hands-on experience, an immediate tactile encounter with Shakespeare's remains. The Irish printer and bookseller John Ferrar visited the Birthplace in the summer of 1795, accompanied by his clerk, Henry. Recounting the trip in his travelogue *A Tour from Dublin to London*, published the following year, Ferrar told his readers little about the house itself. Instead, he focused on what he and Henry did there. They enjoyed 'the supreme satisfaction of handling the old painting box and pencils of our immortal bard' and took with them a sliver 'of his mulberry tree'. Henry, an aspiring author, 'sat down' in Shakespeare's chair and 'received such inspiration, that we know not what will be the consequence, for he has been writing on every opportunity since'.

Despite his jocular tone, Ferrar gets at a serious and paradoxical truth: the most important person in the Birthplace is not the absent Shakespeare but the flesh-and-blood visitor. True, Shakespeare lingers in the house; but only as deficit or lack – the empty chair in the hearth, the pencil with no hand to guide it across the page, the window with no one to look through it. Shakespeare is gone, never to return. But *we* are there, fully ready to take his place. As Ferrar intuits, Shakespeare's disappearance is precisely what creates a space for us, a space for tangible action. We sit in his otherwise empty chair, we grasp his otherwise untouched pencil and we look through his otherwise neglected window. The true value, then, of the Birthplace is not historical, whatever we might learn there about Shakespeare, a figure from the past, but contemporary: the inspiration we derive on the spot, the house's effect on us, the spark it ignites. Henry, the printer's clerk, knew this truth first-hand, because sitting just once in Shakespeare's vacant chair drove him to a burst of writing.

None of this would have surprised Mary Hornby, who knew perfectly well that her guests needed to take centre stage. Occasionally she granted a visitor's request to spend a night in the hallowed birthroom itself, no doubt pocketing a hefty fee for her consent. More routinely, though, she stood calmly by as emotionally wrought pilgrims, some having journeyed from afar, burst into tears, fell prayerfully to their knees and kissed the bare floorboards. 'Such fits of enthusiasm' struck Mrs Hornby, according to the American writer Washington Irving, who observed her at close range during his three visits, as 'ordinary matters, scarcely worth her noticing'.

Yet the hostess herself was not immune to the motivational powers of the Birthplace. Like John Ferrar's clerk, she, too, was stimulated to put words on paper. For her, however, literary inspiration came only at night (she suffered from insomnia) and from being 'in the same room which gave birth to my great Predecessor, the immortal Shakespeare'. Never one to underestimate herself, Mary Hornby, self-designated successor to the Bard of Avon, privately published two of her dramatic works, *The Broken Vow* and *The Battle of Waterloo*. They quickly sank into well-merited oblivion. Still, she offered copies for sale in the Birthplace, along with a collection of 'extemporary verses' composed by some of her visitors. A folio notebook was kept nearby to capture any lyrical outpouring at the very moment of its creation. Mrs Hornby herself, and solely for the encouragement of others, penned the collection's opening verse, 'Invitation to Shakspeare's Spring', which begins: 'Come drink of the fountain where Shakspeare was born, / Like me shed a tear, that from earth he was torn; / Yet his name will out-live all the tyrants on earth, / All princes and heroes that ever had birth' (lines 1–4).

'A garrulous old lady, in a frosty red face'

Mary Hornby, despite her lack of poetic genius, lives on through the intercession of a more renowned nineteenth-century author, Washington Irving, the one who admired her composure as ecstatic visitors to the Birthplace fell to pieces. In September 1820, while living in England, Irving published a fictionalized account of his 'poetical pilgrimage' to Stratford in his popular series of essays and stories known as *The Sketch Book of Geoffrey Crayon*. He is now best remembered for two other stories in that collection, 'Rip Van Winkle' and 'The Legend of Sleepy Hollow'. For my money, his eyewitness account of Mrs Hornby in action rivals the vivacity of his fictional Connecticut schoolmaster, Ichabod Crane:

> The house is shown by a garrulous old lady, in a frosty red face, lighted up by a cold blue anxious eye, and garnished with artificial locks of flaxen hair, curling from under an exceedingly dirty cap. She was peculiarly assiduous in exhibiting the relics with which this, like all other celebrated shrines, abounds. There was the shattered stock of the very matchlock with which Shakspeare shot the deer, on his poaching exploit. There, too, was his tobacco-box; which proves that he was a rival smoker of Sir Walter Raleigh; the sword also with which he played Hamlet; and the identical lantern with which Friar Laurence discovered Romeo and Juliet at the tomb! There was an ample supply also of Shakspeare's mulberry-tree, which seems to have as extraordinary powers of self-multiplication as the wood of the true Cross.

These 'relics' were the very ones that Mrs Hornby had purchased from Thomas Hart a quarter-century earlier. When displaying them to visitors, she evidently provided colourful commentary on each item's provenance – how else could Irving have learned so many details? – thus earning her chatterbox reputation. But in such matters it is always better to say too much than too little.

Sceptics will ask how an imaginary character like Friar Laurence in *Romeo and Juliet* came to possess an actual lantern; or how Shakespeare came to play Hamlet, a role that does require a sword, when all the evidence indicates that the part then belonged to the great tragedian Richard Burbage. They likewise will inquire how that fabled mulberry tree came to enjoy its 'extraordinary powers of self-multiplication'. Such questions, although fully valid according to the norms of logic and reason, failed to trouble the conscience of Washington Irving, at least when he wrote in the voice of his story's ostensible narrator, Geoffrey Crayon. Far from being a curmudgeonly naysayer, Crayon freely confessed that he was 'always of easy faith in such matters', 'a ready believer in relics' and 'ever willing to be deceived, where the deceit is pleasant, and costs nothing'. Nothing, that is, beyond the coinage placed in the upturned waiting palm of Mary Hornby's hand.

'Mary Hornby respectfully informs the Nobility and Gentry'

It was shortly after Irving's visit that Mary Hornby and her landlady, Ann Court, became lifelong enemies. For thirteen years, from 1793 to 1806, the Harts had charged the Hornbys a reasonable rent of seven pounds a year. We know this because, amazingly, the original receipts have survived, now part of the Folger's collection. The new landlords, the Courts, upped the rent. It's not clear whether they wanted to force the Hornbys out or to get more money from them, knowing that their tenants were profiting from a steady tourist trade. Either way, they raised the rent; and kept on raising it. Within a decade, by which time Mary Hornby was widowed, her rent increased from seven to twenty pounds a year, nearly three times as much. Worse was yet to come. On 3 October 1820, Ann Court, now herself a widow, sent legal notice to her longstanding tenant that the rent would double, rocketing from twenty to forty pounds a year, on the 'Tenement or Dwelling House Building & Yard and premises with the Appurtenances which you rent of or hold under me situate in the Henley Street Stratford upon Avon'.

Things now turned ugly. Mary Hornby, unable to cope with the exorbitant increase in rent, left the house where she had resided for more than twenty-five years, outliving both her husband and her son. This seems to be exactly what Ann Court wanted because she promptly announced that she would install herself as the Birthplace's new custodian. Outraged at being denied her livelihood, the wrathful Mary Hornby waited until her last night in the house to take her revenge. She whitewashed the low ceiling and plastered walls in the birthroom, the very places where famed visitors like Lord Byron, actress Dorothy Jordan, the Duke of Wellington and the Prince Regent himself, along with many of the not so famous, had inscribed their names and the occasional impromptu verse in praise of Shakespeare. This living record of the house's popularity had become its own tourist attraction. Yet overnight, it was gone, hidden beneath a pasty veneer of water and calcium carbonate. Some of the whitewash was later removed, but lasting damage had been done.

Ann Court, when apologizing to visitors for the many obliterated signatures, mocked her predecessor as a 'silly capricious woman'. What else could she say? But she knew perfectly well that Mary Hornby was actually a shrewd competitor. Evicted from the birthplace, she had packed up her roomful of relics and carted them off to her new home across the street. In a defiant rebuff to her former landlady, Mary Hornby created a rival Shakespeare shrine directly opposite the birthplace. She no longer had the house; but she did have the relics. And it was the relics, she gambled, that would lure visitors away from the Birthplace and into her own 'museum'. Mary Hornby's long tenure at the Birthplace taught her that visitors needed tactile objects to immerse themselves in the whole experience. Without those objects – things to hold, to handle, even to caress – the house risked becoming barren and sterile

'How I wish the Relics were again in this room', lamented one John Harper when he visited the Birthplace after Mrs Hornby had removed them. 'Then there would be a chair for visitors to sit down upon, – and we might stay & meditate for an hour – while now you seem to have no wish to make a long stay.' To satisfy that desire, John Harper had only to walk across the street, sit down in the legendary Shakespeare chair and stay comfortably there, lost in reverie, for however long he wished.

Bolstering her claim to offer a superior 'visitor experience', as we would now say, Mrs Hornby procured a dubious certificate of authenticity for those sundry Shakespeare relics. It was signed by old Thomas Kite of Gloucestershire, father of Thomas Hart's late wife, Mary. On 9 May 1822 he swore that the 'articles and things' that Mary Hornby had obtained in 1795 from his former son-in-law 'had been in the Hart's family ever since the death of Joan Hart, own sister of William Shakspeare'. Having acquired her certificate of authenticity, the proprietor of the 'house opposite his Birthplace' promptly issued this advertisement:

> Mary Hornby, respectfully informs the Nobility and Gentry who visit Stratford, that she and her late husband occupied the house where Shakspeare was born, for 14 years before it was sold out of the Hart's family, his lineal [sic] descendants, from whom they purchased the various Articles they possessed that originally belonged to the Immortal Bard. These HIGHLY VALUABLE RELIQUES are now shewn by her at a house opposite his Birthplace, where she was obliged to remove them in consequence of her rent having been risen, at different times from 7l. to 40l. per annum . . . A Copy of Shakspeare's Will and many other curious Manuscripts, are likewise in her possession. – Every visitor will be most thankfully received as she has no other means of support.

Ann Court, no pushover, disputed Mary Hornby's claim for the legitimacy of the Shakespeare relics by obtaining the testimony of a more credible witness. Somehow, she persuaded William Shakespeare Hart of Tewkesbury to swear in writing, a mere eight days after Thomas Kite's declaration to the contrary, that when his family had sold the Birthplace to the Courts in 1806, it contained no genuine objects whatsoever (apart from the fireside chair, which everyone ludicrously insisted was the real thing):

> there neither was, at the period of such Sale, nor for many years previous thereto, any relic or point of property of the great Poet remaining there, which could, with any degree of certainty, or even traditionally, be considered as having ever belonged to him . . . And I further certify my positive belief that any thing advertized or shewn there, or in the neighbourhood, at present, as such, must be spurious and deceptive.

Roused in self-defence, Mrs Hornby enlisted the support of her own expert witness, Jane Iliff of Leamington, who was Thomas Hart's only surviving daughter and thus William Shakespeare Hart's aunt. It was now a cross-generational family feud. Contradicting her own nephew, Jane Iliff signed with her mark, not her signature, a document declaring that the relics now owned by Mary Hornby were indeed genuine:

Thomas Hornby, late husband of Mary Hornby, first rented the house called Shakespeare's birth-place, in 1793, and purchased all the articles, by valuation, then in possession of the said Thomas Hart, which had, from time immemorial, been shewn as reliques of the Great Poet, by the Hart family; . . . I also declare, that I have frequently heard my father [Thomas Hart] say he had the same articles from his father [George Hart], and I have often heard my grandfather, (who was a very old man when he died,) and my father say, the whole of those articles had been in their family ever since the death of the Poet.

But it wasn't enough for Mrs Hornby merely to have the authenticity of her relics affirmed a second time. She had to do something more decisive, something to discredit Ann Court once and for all. So, at Mary Hornby's likely urging, Jane Iliff launched a smear campaign against a family member:

William Shakespeare Hart of Tewkesbury, was at that time a little boy, and never was in the house many times while my father was living, or before the reliques came into the possession of Thomas Hornby; and . . . he cannot know any thing, or very little, even 'traditionally,' and of course 'with no degree of certainty', about the reliques, as the sale of the house to the present occupier [Ann Court], in 1806, had nothing whatever to do with the articles which had, thirteen years before, been purchased by Mr. and Mrs. Hornby . . . I further certify and declare, that any thing said to the contrary, by any person whomsoever, is false and 'deceptive'.

Assurances given by William Shakespeare Hart were undermined with forensic precision: he was then a boy, he never spent much time at the Birthplace, and his later involvement in selling the house to the Courts had nothing to do with the relics. Not a man to be trusted. In a crowning touch – for which, surely, we must credit Mary Hornby – the man's words are turned against him, transformed from his sworn oath into weapons of his destruction. Each word or phrase that appears in quotation marks in Jane Iliff's accusation – 'no degree of certainty', 'deceptive' – is taken directly from William Shakespeare Hart's statement and then twisted to mean the opposite. It's not the relics that are deceptive, it's my nephew.

Quite an achievement, sowing division within Shakespeare's extended family and goading his closest surviving relatives into bickering in public over what remained, or not, of his earthly possessions. Contested will, indeed.

'Ye brawling blowses!'

Sparring within the Hart family was but a carefully orchestrated proxy war between Mary Hornby and Ann Court. On the north side of Henley Street stood the actual house where William Shakespeare was born, but it contained no objects associated with the immortal genius himself. On the south side, directly opposite, were assembled various objects purportedly belonging to Shakespeare, but displayed in a setting that lacked authenticity.

And so, the battle raged, but now much more openly. Each dowager tried to deter visitors from setting foot and spending money in the other one's property. Their favourite tactic was to stand on their respective doorsteps at the same time and shout abuse at each other. These impromptu street performances led by the Widow Hornby and the Widow Court provided, rather than merriment for passing tourists, strong incentive to head elsewhere. One disgruntled traveller penned a few verses on the spot: 'What – Birthplace here! – and relics there? / Abuse from each! ye brawling blowses! / Each picks my pocket, – 'tis not fair, – / A stranger's "Curse on both your houses!"'

So much for the assurance of Miss Laetitia Matilda Hawkins that 'no predominant vulgarity' was detectable in Mary Hornby's speech. Gentle though she may have been with her guests, she fiercely challenged her foes. The same went for Ann Court. Their accursed brawling went on for three full years, until Mrs Hornby decamped with her relics to nearby Wood Street, leaving the now much quieter Henley Street to Mrs Court. Their endless shouting matches seem to have discouraged visitors from entering either property. These two worthy opponents, each as conniving as the other, achieved the remarkable result of ending up both on the losing side.

'The worst house in the town'

Not that the house itself seemed worth fighting over. One reliable guide for how the Birthplace looked in the late eighteenth century, when the entire property was still divided into a cottage, a butcher's shop and the Swan and Maidenhead Inn, is the engraver and author Samuel Ireland. He made several drawings of the Birthplace when he visited in October 1792 while preparing his *Picturesque Views on the Upper, or Warwickshire Avon*, which was published three years later. For Ireland, history was an essentially pictorial genre, a story best told not in words, but in sketches and scenic views. Thus, he considered his 'primary duty' to be the strict 'delineation of truth' in visual aspect.

When Samuel Ireland stood in Henley Street and looked at the birthplace, he did not see the dormer windows, gables, porch and large bay window that featured so charmingly in Richard Greene's well-known drawing that had been reprinted in *Gentleman's Magazine* to mark the 1769 Shakespeare Jubilee. Those features were nowhere to be seen because, as we know, they were of Greene's invention entirely. With a gentle swipe at images that sacrificed truth for exaggerated pictorial effect, and thus falsified the historical record, Ireland promised that he would disown the 'fanciful, adventitious ornaments' indulged by other artists. And so, his sketch of the

Birthplace's façade, although it makes the ramshackle house look at bit more upright than it actually was, shows us, nonetheless, not an imaginary house (as Greene had done) but an actual one.

After Ireland's more honest depiction of the Birthplace, other visitors felt free to share their regret that the house had become so rundown. We turn once more to our Miss Hawkins, who visited in August 1819 and compiled the detailed inventory of Mrs Hornby's relics. She felt obliged to inform her readers that 'Shakespeare's house is a little old butcher's shop, of the lowest description', made worse by a 'miserable' kitchen and a 'very bad staircase'. In his *Historical Account of the Birth-Place of Shakespeare*, printed in 1824, the local antiquarian Robert Bell Wheler also observed that the house disappointed him. Why? Mainly because its previous owners had let it fall into disrepair: 'the want of sufficient repairs to these houses whilst in the possession of the Harts of the last and present centuries, who were burthened with a heavy mortgage, and in humble circumstances, have tended in a great degree to their gradual neglect and decay'. Wheler made no idle claim, for his father, Robert Wheler, was the lawyer who repeatedly urged the Harts to refurbish and maintain the house, advice they repeatedly ignored.

Visiting the 'small, mean-looking edifice', as Washington Irving tersely described it, was, in those years, nothing like visiting it today. Back then, decades before the house was acquired for the nation and subsequently restored, the 'Birthplace' amounted to no more than a few grubby rooms – butcher's shop, back kitchen, birthroom – made open to the public in an otherwise private building. The 'wretchedness' of the house's exterior was surpassed only, as the *Illustrated London News* informed its many readers, by the 'squalid forlornness' of the rooms within. The antiquary Joseph Hunter put it this way after visiting Stratford in 1824, writing even in his diary with a Yorkshireman's expected bluntness: it was 'the worst house in the town'.

A thick scrapbook assembled by the Victorian scholar James Orchard Halliwell-Phillipps contains a stinging description of what it felt like to tour the Birthplace before it was transformed into an official monument to Shakespeare:

The front has no glazed casement, but is protected from the rain and sun by a drooping shed, like a flap to a table. Above that is a kind of signboard formed by two slips of wood, jutting out and uniting at an angular point on which is inscribed 'The immortal Shakespeare was born in this house'. Above is a window in four compartments with small cottage-like panes of glass not diamond fashion as formerly, that lights the chamber of the poet's nativity. You enter the shop, which is only guarded by a rustic half-door (the other half pinned back to the wall) and you find yourself in the world's belief on sacred ground. The shop is of the size of a small parlour, at the back of which is a kitchen still smaller with a large fireplace wherein you are told the poet, as a boy, was supposed to have sat. The kitchen is lighted by a small window looking into the backyards of the neighbouring tenements, and out of which we may suppose the poet may have looked ... [Y]ou feel eager to ascend the tottering staircase and find yourself in the chamber where the idol of your admiration is stated and believed to have been first ushered into the world.

As this anonymous scribe correctly observed, a rudely painted signboard protruded from the façade directly above the butcher's shop. Now preserved in the museum adjacent to the Birthplace, it read 'WILLIAM SHAKSPEARE WAS BORN IN THIS HOUSE. N.B. – A horse and taxed cart to let'. Visitors noticed the sign because they entered the house directly from Henley Street, as Shakespeare himself had done. Pushing opening the hatched door and crossing over the threshold, they found themselves immediately in what had been the butcher's shop, with an unevenly paved stone floor and an old kitchen visible behind it. The walls were plastered and the ancient oak beams rested on the stone foundation. The legendary Shakespeare chair was placed, invitingly, in the roomy kitchen hearth, as noted by the many guests who thrilled to sit there. The disused butcher's shop was likely located in what had originally been the hall. The back kitchen was a later addition, not part of the house when Shakespeare lived there.

The high point came when visitors climbed the teetering back stairs, also built after Shakespeare's time, and turned left into the low-ceilinged birthroom. Here, the most prominent feature was not a fake relic but some genuine artefacts: the many pencilled, inked and, thanks to the popularity of pocketknives, etched signatures that covered every surface, including the windows, spreading line by line in all directions, like a spiderweb. Not even Mary Hornby's vengeful whitewashing had fully obliterated them; and in the years since, even more signatures had been added. 'Look up, look down, inside and outside, the door, round the fireplace, and up the chimney!' – so Ann Court encouraged her visitors – 'Didst ever see such an autographed Museum, never I truly think!'

Set against the obvious, but still enjoyable, fakery, the genuine autographs must have felt like the most compelling part of a visitor's experience, abundant direct testimony of how much Shakespeare has meant, and continues to mean, to people of all ranks and all stations from around the world. More, it was a living document, one to which they could affix their own corroborating signatures. As one visitor with immortal longings put it: 'E'en on thy walls to scrawl my humble name / May well be deemed for me some share of fame.' Though now detached from the window frames and placed within protective cases, the glass panes with crowded etched signatures still fascinate visitors to the Birthplace.

That was it. The little cottage to the left was still a private home, occupied first by the Harts, followed by the Hornbys and then the Courts, while on the right stood the Swan and Maidenhead Inn. The Birthplace that resulted from the architectural restorations carried out in the 1850s – that is, the fully remodelled site we visit today – is a larger and more unified space than the cramped gloomy premises once visited by John Adams, Thomas Jefferson, Nathaniel Hawthorne, Charles Dickens and thousands of more ordinary travellers.

'It only brought human nature closer to him'

Nathaniel Hawthorne conveyed particularly well the shock of discovering how mean and lowly the birthplace really was, a shock felt all the more sharply because he had, in his thoughts, enthroned the immortal Shakespeare in a grand palace. Surely, so Hawthorne had assumed, the greatness of Shakespeare's poetry would be mirrored in the greatness of the house where he was born. As it turned out, surely not:

> I found my way to Shakspeare's birthplace, which is almost a smaller and humbler house than any description can prepare the visitor to expect; so inevitably does an august inhabitant make his abode palatial to our imaginations, receiving his guests, indeed, in a castle in the air, until we unwisely insist on meeting him among the sordid lanes and alleys of lower earth.

Still, Hawthorne wasn't going to let 'grimy actualities' besmirch his admiration for the world's greatest playwright. Indeed, to his surprise, he was glad to be dragged down from his 'castle in the air' to be set amidst the 'sordid lanes and alleyways of lower earth'. It was only by admitting how small and humble the Birthplace actually was; how it opposed, in its plainness, every exalted revelry, that Hawthorne came to appreciate that 'Shakespeare's genius' was a 'hardy plant'. So hardy, in fact, that 'it could not be blighted in such an atmosphere'. Overturning his earlier verdict, Hawthorne now rejoiced that Shakespeare had been born in so depressing a place, because 'it only brought human nature closer to him'.

Nathaniel Hawthorne's new regard for the ordinariness of Shakespeare's birthplace was not a sentiment unique to him. His feeling was, rather, an expression of the Romantic myth of natural genius, a myth in which Shakespeare owed his rare talent to none but himself. For he was Nature's own true child, untutored, yes, but unequalled in glory and achievement. It was precisely because Shakespeare wrote from pure inspiration, as the Romantics would have it, that his birthplace needed no pomp or grandeur. Indeed, it was preferable that Shakespeare 'proceeded from the cottage of humility', as the antiquary J. Norris Brewster explained in his *Histrionic Topography* (1818), because the poet's humble origins rendered his mature accomplishments even more praiseworthy. For Shakespeare to have been born elsewhere – a grand Tudor manor house, say, like Charlecote Park –

would have been wasteful and ridiculous, no more necessary than gilding refined gold or painting the lily.

This poignant lesson was lost in the decades that followed, when the Birthplace was transformed from a private residence into a public monument and when its official custodians remodelled the house to turn it into something it never was. But before any of that could happen, the house had to be put up for sale.

10

This House for Sale

Ann Court, under the terms of her husband's will, held a life interest in the entire Henley Street property, including the Swan and Maidenhead Inn and the adjacent cottage shown to visitors as Shakespeare's birthplace. After evicting her quarrelsome tenant, she played the overlapping roles of tapster and tour guide until her death, in 1846. The entire premises was then put up for sale at a public auction by the estate's trustees, with the proceeds to benefit the Court's four surviving children and grandchildren.

The Harts, who for years had struggled to find a buyer for the Birthplace, were relieved when Thomas Court finally offered £210, even though it was considerably less than what the family wanted. But times had changed. The Birthplace had come up in the world, aided by the Victorian cult of Shakespeare worship, also called 'Bardolatry', a term coined at the start of the twentieth century by the Anglo-Irish playwright George Bernard Shaw. He meant it somewhat pejoratively, for he considered Shakespeare a 'pilferer of other men's stories and ideas'. Yet this cult was all-pervasive, embracing not just the professional London theatre and its audience, but schools, social clubs, popular journalism, lectures, public readings and private theatricals across the land.

The unrestrainable abundance of books and pamphlets written about Shakespeare and the Birthplace threatened, by the 1840s, to overwhelm tourists as they embarked on their pilgrimage to Stratford. Should they read Charles Knight's *Pictorial Shakespeare* or William Howitt's *Homes and Haunts of the Most Eminent British Poets*? How to decide between Washington Irving's *Sketchbook* and Robert Bell Wheler's *Historical Account of the Birth-Place of Shakespeare*? So many books that so imaginatively combined travel-writing with literary biography, turning the map of Stratford into a map of Shakespeare himself.

Best to pack them all and read them on the train. Gone was the rough overnight journey by horse and carriage. In the first decades of the railway age, the trip from London to Stratford was shortened to just over four hours. It's not significantly quicker today. Yet the consequence of this 'railroad rate of traveling', so *Fraser's Magazine* warned, was that visitors might 'see too much, and ask inwardly too little'. By mid-century it had become so easy to

get to Stratford from any urban hub that some tourists allowed themselves
a brief hour to see all the sites and then sit down to a hot meal before getting
back on the train. Day trippers raced from the 'poking little hole of a place
where he was born' at the northern edge of the town down to the 'poet's
grave' in the church at the southern edge of the town, and then hurried to
an inn, probably right in the town centre, 'for fear the fish should be
overdressed'. Whether done fast or slowly, it was all done out of reverence
for Shakespeare.

So revered had Shakespeare become – glorified by most, quoted by many,
betrayed by few or none – that Matthew Arnold could without fear of
contradiction laud him in a sonnet for 'out-topping knowledge'. The fiery
Scottish historian Thomas Carlyle, more accustomed to critiquing political
orthodoxies, hailed, nonetheless, 'King Shakespeare', whom 'no time or
chance, no Parliament or combination of Parliaments, can dethrone'.
Shakespeare, as Henry Crawford blithely summed it up in Jane Austen's
Mansfield Park, was simply 'part of an Englishman's constitution'.

With the Elizabethan poet reigning so loftily supreme in British culture,
and with the railroad putting the poet's hometown within reach of all
Britain, the Birthplace became more widely recognized than it had been at
the start of the nineteenth century. For the Harts, it had been a virtually
unsellable property, a dud. But now, a mere four decades later, it had become
Shakespeare's anchor-site on earth, the solid material expression of his
transcendent genius. If Shakespeare belonged to the people of Britain, then
so did his house. Where else would his votaries congregate to make their
ritual obeisance than at the site of his birth? To put this particular house, the
house of all houses, on the auction block was wildly heretical, a scandalous
blasphemy against the Shakespeare religion professed throughout the land.
The auction mart was where a farmer sold livestock and grain or where an
executor disposed of a dead man's furniture. It was not, and must not ever
be, where Shakespeare was bought and sold.

'Traded upon as a common show'

Yet nothing could prevent Shakespeare's house from being, as one journalist
lamented, 'haggled for like any common pile of bricks and mortar'. In the
weeks and months before the sale, daily newspapers and high-brow literary
magazine alike insisted that the Birthplace was so precious to the nation that
it must not fall into private hands. Downplaying the inconvenient fact that
the house had always been privately owned, the press summarily declared
that it now belonged solely to 'the people' – and with the people it must
remain. 'If the house be transferred out of the hands of its present proprietary
by a private bargain', *The Times* gravely warned, 'it will be traded upon as
a common show'. William Hepworth Dixon, writing in the *Athenaeum*,
echoed the fear that, unless the house were rescued, it would end up no

better than a flashy circus attraction. A property 'sanctified' by its direct link to Shakespeare must, he urged, and no matter the cost, be saved 'from the vulgarity of showmanship and the commonplaces of commercial speculation'. That Shakespeare himself was a showman who made his money as a shareholder in a commercial theatre company was just one more awkward fact for the press to overlook.

A month before the auction, the *Athenaeum* declared that no right-thinking Briton would advocate letting the Birthplace be owned by anyone other than Britain itself. Would anyone dream of putting Westminster Abbey or the Tower of London on the auction block? Merely to think it was unpatriotic. So, too, with Shakespeare's house:

> of all the heart-stirring relics which this old country boasts, there is not one so deeply interesting as this – there is not one which we would less willingly suffer to disappear – there is not one on the removal of which by the sacrilegious hand of modern avarice or utilitarianism would inflict a more lasting reproach upon the nation; and yet, the house is to be sold by auction; and may be carried away piece-meal and cut into tobacco-stoppers.

This panicked imagining hints at two equally deplorable outcomes. The mere presence of the Birthplace on the auction block would render it worthless as a heritage site, reducing it from a venerable relic to mere goods and chattel. Once the sacred destination of Shakespeare pilgrims, the house would, henceforth, be not so different (except in size and scale only) from all those tobacco-stoppers, snuffboxes, clothes pegs and other trinkets carved, allegedly, from the mulberry tree at New Place. The house would be just one more shoddy hoax. A terrible prospect, yes; but at least the house would remain intact. More awful was the risk that some 'clownish purchaser' would burn it to the ground and leave not a trace behind, valuing the plot of land more than what had stood on it since Shakespeare's time. Worst of all, and much too terrible to contemplate, was that the birthplace would be dismantled – beam by beam, stone by stone, window by window – and shipped overseas, disappearing forever from its homeland. As with Macbeth, present fears were less than horrible imaginings.

'Doomed to mutilation'

If the house must be sold then it should be bought by some person or entity fully committed to honouring and preserving it. The Royal Shakespearean Club in Stratford, which had helped to restore Shakespeare's burial site and the chancel in Holy Trinity Church, was immediately interested in securing the Birthplace for posterity, true to its mission to 'preserve everything connected with his mortal remains from further disrespect'. They had the motive but lacked the means. Short on cash, the Club turned to Parliament for help. They appealed to Viscount Morpeth, First Commissioner of the Department of Woods and Forests, the closest thing the government had to a historic buildings and monuments commission, urging that they buy the Birthplace on the nation's behalf. Morpeth might well have been their ally. No philistine, he had once exchanged sonnets with William Wordsworth and advocated that same year, 1847, for a monument in honour of William Caxton, the first printer of books in England.

But it was an era when laissez-faire ruled culture as well as the economy – in all matters, let the market decide – and so the state refused to intervene in what it considered a purely private affair. 'Members of the Government', his lordship explained in a politely roundabout way, 'are disposed to think that the acquisition of so interesting a property pertains still more to the people of England than to the Government'. In short, if you want the birthplace so badly, then find the money yourself. Such was the cold, fixed logic of supply and demand. *The People's Journal* denounced 'the continued apathy' of a government that proudly, but hypocritically, called itself 'the friend and disciple of progress and illumination', while the *Spectator* wondered why 'Royal authority' protected swans but not the Sweet Swan of Avon himself.

The government's hands-off policy forced the responsibility to buy the house back onto the world of private philanthropy. And so, the Royal Shakespearean Club launched a subscription drive, hoping to raise enough money from individuals to purchase the Birthplace. At the same time, a high-profile steering committee – no worthy Victorian cause was complete without a committee – was formed in London under the leadership of Charles Dickens, with Prince Albert as royal patron. The German-born prince, eager to demonstrate his acquired Englishness, promptly pledged a generous £250. Queen Adelaide, widow of William IV, gave £100. Lord Morpeth, though he had refused to involve the government, was personally sympathetic to the cause: he offered fifty pounds and agreed to serve as the London committee's president. The Earl of Ellesmere donated £100, but judged the whole endeavour misguided: 'A single copy of Shakespeare in the backwoods of America was a more enduring monument to the genius of our immortal dramatist than any structure of marble could possibly be.' His lordship, appointed to be the London committee's vice-president, rehearsed the old argument that Shakespeare's plays were his true monument – that's what the First Folio, in 1623, had insisted – but added the twist of classic English snobbery.

Other prominent figures lined up to pledge sums large and small, from £100 given by the Corporation of Stratford to twelve pounds and twelve shillings from the actor William Charles Macready, whose long theatrical career had been devoted to high-minded productions of Shakespeare, five pounds each from Dickens and the historian Thomas Babington Macaulay and four pounds and ten shillings raised from a public reading of *Othello*. Each week, the *Athenaeum* published a list of new donors, flattering the most recent benefactors and, so they hoped, inspiring still others to open their wallets. The published lists did not include the names of those who donated less than one pound each because the additional advertising space needed would have cost more than the sum of all those small donations.

But the donations weren't coming in fast enough. Alarmed by the prospect of imminent failure, the London committee began to meet every Tuesday and Friday evening at 18 Abingdon Street, opposite the Houses of Parliament, to plan its strategy in the final weeks before the auction. In early September 1847, with one week to go, and with not nearly enough money raised, they turned their sights on the people who owed their success, or even fame, to Shakespeare: actors and theatre managers. 'The Committee earnestly requests the co-operation of . . . those connected with the drama . . . in London and the provincial cities'. If anybody was going to help, then surely it would be the people whose livelihood depended upon Shakespeare. A promising approach but it lacked smooth execution. Because the London committee's idea of progress was to set up yet *another* committee somewhere else.

Such, frustratingly, was the Victorian way. Every worthy cause was somehow turned into either petty bureaucratic infighting or a staid gentleman's club. Absorbed by their own flattering self-image – valiant knights all, rushing to the aid of the distressed damsel named William Shakespeare – the committee's leaders forgot to win over the people whose money they urgently needed.

'Chopkins, late Shakespeare'

The Irish-born playwright J. Stirling Coyne – his real name, not a punning pseudonym – lost no time in mocking the whole affair. *This House to be Sold*, a musical comedy extravaganza first performed at London's Adelphi Theatre in early September 1847, imagines the fate of Shakespeare's birthplace after it has been sold at auction. In Coyne's satiric foretelling, the 'dilapidated, but interesting premises', a phrase he lifted directly from Robert Bell Wheler's 1824 history of the birthplace, is acquired not by the Royal Shakespeare Club of Stratford, but by a mysterious out-of-towner, who buys the house sight unseen. He is one Chatterton Chopkins, a small-time Cockney shopkeeper from London's East End. When he eventually arrives in Stratford, his first act is to hang a new signboard – 'Chopkins, Late Shakespeare' – above the entrance to his new place of business. So much for respecting the Bard's mortal remains.

In the figure of Chatterton Chopkins, the son of a hog-butcher, *This House for Sale* realizes the 'profanation most horrible' that William Hepworth Dixon had darkly predicted in *The People's Journal*: the birthplace falls into the hands of a philistine who has enough money to acquire, and then deface, the symbolic heart of English culture. 'Like any other goods and chattels', Dixon warned, Shakespeare's house would go to the highest bidder, 'whether he be a Jew or a Gentile, the agent of a Yankee speculator or the deputy of a reverent people'.

Or a parvenu from London's East End who fancies himself a gentleman and yet knows nothing about Shakespeare's plays, has never before been to Stratford, asks the house's caretaker, in the year 1847, if she herself had nursed the infant Shakespeare and then fails to recognize Shakespeare's ghost when it rouses him from sleep on his first night in the Birthplace. All Chatterton Chopkins knows, and it's plenty enough for him, is that he can get away with charging five shillings for each visitor and thus monetize Shakespeare to achieve his 'ambition above hogs'. Five shillings was more than twice the price of admission to the pit in a West End theatre. Like any good utilitarian, even one of petty bourgeois interests, Chopkins appreciates Shakespeare only for his economic use-value.

'You will all of you give your pennies'

Shining a spotlight on the butcher's son who presents himself as 'the legitimate successor to the Bard of Avon', Coyne's theatrical fantasia mocks the snobbish insularity of the Stratford and London Shakespeare committees, those twin assemblages of the great and the good that preoccupied themselves, above all, with keeping impeccable records of their many meetings. The populist antidote to the genteel Shakespeare bureaucracy arrived in the iconoclastic figure of Harriet Martineau. A lifelong social activist, she made her living in a traditionally masculine way, by publishing essays on serious topics like politics, finance and abolishing the slave trade. Martineau claimed in her autobiography that being a writer granted her the freedom to 'truly live instead of vegetate'. A surprise best-seller, her *Illustrations of Political Economy*, first published in 1832, earned her an invitation to Queen Victoria's coronation. In later years, she argued that women should have the right to vote and prostitution should be legalized. Harriet Martineau was a person well ahead of her times.

To someone so unafraid of being controversial, the fate of a simple house in the English midlands must have seemed beneath her interest. Yet she heartily championed the cause of Shakespeare's birthplace, beginning with her rousing 'letter to the people', printed on 28 July 1847 in the working-class newspaper *The People's Journal* and soon afterwards in local newspapers nationwide. Here is part of what Miss Martineau told 'the whole people of this country':

> Shakspeare's house is to be sold. If not bought by the nation, it will be lost to the nation forever. A committee is formed in Stratford, and another is forming in London, to collect the money, and manage the purchase.
>
> Now, it may be or it may not be, that the rich men of our country will contribute money enough. Shall we put the matter to this risk? The

necessary sum might presently be raised by penny subscription. Shall not the whole people of this country have the pleasure and the honour of securing Shakspeare's house as the property of the nation forever? Shall not every child of future generations who may visit the abode where Shakspeare's mind grew to what it was, have the privilege of saying that his ancestor helped to make this house national property! Let the rich do their part: but shall not we who are not rich claim our part also? Let those who wish for the honour set to work at once.

In every town and neighbourhood set on foot a penny subscription. Speak of the matter, all of you, wherever you go. You will all of you give your pennies . . .

By all the noble thoughts that Shakspeare has aroused in you, I appeal to you to honour him now. By all *his* noble thoughts – by the philosophy of Brutus and the mirth of Rosalind, by the remorse of Macbeth and the innocence of Desdemona, by the dreams of Hamlet and the fidelity of Imogen, by the misery of Othello and the patience of Cordelia – I appeal to you to honour Shakspeare now. And according to your love and reverence of him, be quick and diligent in your work.

Good sentences and well pronounced, as Portia would say. Banished was the sluggish prose ('the Committee earnestly requests . . .') of the Stratford and London worthies. The muse of fire had arrived; and with fiery disdain she doubted whether 'the rich men of our country' could make good on their lofty promises. We must not put our trust in princes, peers and men of letters, she urged, for they cannot save us. Rather, we must believe only in *ourselves*, trusting in our shared 'love and reverence' for Shakespeare. If enough of the common people – Shakespeare's own people, for he, too, was born of the common stock – will give just one penny each, then money enough can be raised to buy the Birthplace and preserve it for the nation. When honour is at the stake, Shakespeare's people must do the honourable thing.

Although this anti-elitist rallying cry was addressed to the people of Britain, its leader did not come forth from their midst. Harriet Martineau, although not born into great wealth or high rank, enjoyed, nonetheless, a privileged life. Much more privileged, in fact, than the mass of readers to whom she preached her now condescending brand of cultural patriotism. Something of the Victorian schoolmistress comes through in her finger-wagging decree, 'You will all of you give your pennies.' Easy for her to say, for she had pennies in abundance. Still, Harriet Martineau used her privilege to advance a common goal, even if she reserved to herself the right to define it: 'the pleasure and the honour of securing Shakspeare's house as the property of the nation forever'. This task, too momentous to be entrusted to the rich and mighty alone, properly belonged to the masses; and so, the masses shall play their proper part. The working class, doing what it does best, will *work* for Shakespeare.

Some high-minded men dismissed Martineau's grassroots campaign as a waste of time and effort. William Hepworth Dixon, writing again in the *Athenaeum*, applauded the democratic appeal of neighbourhood fundraisers and acknowledged the '*universality* of right and interest' in securing Shakespeare's birthplace for the nation. Yet that shared mission, the twenty-five-year-old critic asserted, could be achieved only by one part of the nation, that part which measured its largesse, not in pennies, but in pounds and guineas. Dixon believed there was zero chance that a penny subscription would succeed in raising the money required to purchase the Birthplace.

A cold calculus, but fair. Despite Harriet Martineau's clarion call for pennies to ring in coffers throughout the land, the labouring class never made a significant contribution to the Shakespeare cause. Who can blame them? 1847 was a year of hardship, with factory closures, poor harvests, higher prices for imported good and losses in railway speculation all conspiring to create a full-blown financial crisis. It's hard to raise money during an economic downturn because money is precisely what's in short supply. Everybody has less of it. Most of all the working class, who spent whatever they did have on food, clothing and shelter, not on grand causes that made little difference in their daily lives.

And so, the struggle to preserve Shakespeare's birthplace, and to amass the wherewithal to do it, remained mostly an elite concern. The most generous donors, apart from a few noble lords, were leading figures in the arts and media, from the historian Henry Hallam to the playwright Douglas Jerrold, and from the poet-politician Richard Monckton Milnes to the actor Charles Kemble. Having to bear the Shakespearean burden only flattered their self-image as saviours of English culture. But who were they saving it for? Not for themselves, but for the poor unfortunate others who, in their uninvited judgement, lacked culture but needed it the most. By preserving Shakespeare's house for the benefit of the entire nation, they could 'inspire the uneducated mechanic with aspirations beyond those . . . of the humbler classes of society'. It was the familiar Victorian cult of bourgeois respectability in yet another guise, with the higher orders telling the lower orders that Shakespeare was good for them, a paternalistic stance that has not entirely disappeared in the twenty-first century. With the magic of his poetic powers, Shakespeare might inspire an 'uneducated mechanic' to rise above his humble origins. Chatterton Chopkins has something to say about that.

'This large and liberal offer'

On the afternoon of Thursday, 16 September 1847, when auctioneer Edmund Robins stepped up to the rostrum in the crowded upstairs room at the Auction Mart in Covent Garden, in the heart of London's theatre district, his task was to sell an unusual object in the presence of an unusual audience. The 'truly heart-stirring relic of a most glorious period' available for purchase that day, to invoke the floridly optimistic description in the sale catalogue, was Shakespeare's birthplace in Stratford-upon-Avon. The audience gathered to witness the sale of this 'singular domicile' included men who owed their prominence mostly to Shakespeare, among them the American actor George Jones, the Shakespeare editor and biographer Charles Knight, the artist George Cruikshank and scholars John Payne Collier and James Orchard Halliwell-Philipps.

These eminent figures had not come to bid on the property. They had come, rather, because they cared about the Birthplace, their own careers being intertwined with Shakespeare's popular appeal. And so, they supported the charitable committees from London and Stratford who were hoping to place the winning bid. For the Shakespeare acolytes who crowded into the upstairs auction room, the one below proving too small, the stakes were high.

Yet on that long-anticipated day there was no showdown. The whole matter was settled within minutes. After some quickly dispatched preliminaries – 'Was the house really the one where Shakespeare was born?' – no definitive proof, but the weight of tradition and circumstantial evidence was overwhelming – 'Was the title to the property valid?' – relevant legal documents were reproduced in the sale catalogue – the bidding commenced. The fast first bid was for £1,575. Mr Butler of Upper Clapton, in east London, whoever he was, raised it to £2,000. His bid was marginally bettered by an offer of £2,100. And then, before things could really accelerate, everything came to a halt. A clerk handed a letter to Mr Robins. That was not customary practice at the London Auction Mart, where sales proceeded briskly and without interruption. Hesitantly, the auctioneer took the letter, scrutinized it in silence and then read it aloud:

> We the undersigned, deputed by the united Committees of Stratford and London for raising subscriptions for the purchase of Shakspere's House, hereby offer a bidding of £3000. The Committees having purchased another property, which really constitutes an integral portion of Shakspere's house, have expended a considerable part of the amount already raised by public contribution; but, looking at the duty imposed upon them in undertaking to represent the feeling of the nation, they have come to the resolution of making this large and liberal offer for the property now on sale, without regard to the funds which they at present command, in the confidence that the justice of the public will eventually discharge the Committees from the individual responsibility which they thus incur.

Robins asked if anyone wished to bid higher. No one spoke. Minutes passed. Still, no one spoke. The silence was then broken by the decisive sound of the auctioneer's hammer. At a quarter to two on that mid-September afternoon, Robins declared that Shakespeare's birthplace was duly sold to

the London and Stratford committees for £3,000. Whereupon a great cheer
rang throughout the packed upper room, many of those in the crowd having
hoped for just that result.

Historical currency comparisons are never exact; but still, the sale price
does seem impossibly low. After all, the London and Stratford committees
acquired not just the house on Henley Street but the entire compound,
including the adjacent Swan and Maidenhead Inn, a brew house, four stables
and two brick piggeries. Today, the equivalent sum spent in Stratford-upon-
Avon would not buy you a charmless Victorian terraced house where no one
famous ever dwelled. Such a thought must have occurred to the crowds that
gathered outside the Birthplace on 17 September 1997 to witness a re-
enactment of the auction that had taken place exactly 170 years earlier.

Mr Butler, the losing bidder, returned home to Upper Clapton with the
consolation prize of five visitors' books from the Birthplace, each filled with
the signatures of thousands who had toured the house. In 1812, the wealthy
Boston merchant Thomas Perkins had initiated the custom of visitors
recording their name, hometown and date of visit when he gave Mary
Hornby a blank quarto notebook titled 'Tribute of Respect to the Bard of
Avon'. The first signature inscribed belonged to the donor himself, 'T.H.
Perkins, Boston, United States of America'. Butler paid seventy-three pounds
and ten shillings for the record books. He must have rejoiced in outbidding
the London and Stratford committees, who had offered just fifty pounds for
the lot.

11

Snatched from Quick Decay

The game had been rigged from the start. Committee members from London and Stratford had taken their places in the auction room knowing full well that their bid would be no better than a promissory note because they didn't have the cash on hand. Hyped, though it was, in the popular press, their subscription drive had nonetheless failed to raise all the money required. Moreover, they had already spent £820 to buy from Elizabeth Izod four cottages on Henley Street adjacent to the birthplace. Their supreme goal of acquiring the birthplace itself now seemed out of reach; because even if the committees spent all their remaining funds, it still wouldn't be enough. Undeterred by the brutal facts of monetary life, they decided to bid for the house anyway. And so, their winning bid of £3,000 was a pledge without substance, a hopeful resolve only masquerading as actual wherewithal.

Not that their ruse deceived anyone. In fact, they freely conceded, in their open letter to the auctioneer, that they placed their bid 'without regard to the funds which they at present command'. That was a polite way of admitting that they couldn't put their money where their mouth was. But it didn't matter, because both the auctioneer and the trustees of the late Thomas Court, the only people empowered to accept or reject bids, were in on the scheme from the outset. They had all previously agreed that the London and Stratford committees *must* win the auction, no matter what it took, because it was intolerable that Shakespeare's birthplace should remain in private hands. What it took was letting them buy the house with money they didn't have.

For all the suspense that the media attributed to it, the auction was not, in the end, a cliff-hanging moment when Shakespeare was either rescued or lost forever. Indeed, there was no genuine drama whatsoever, for the outcome had been determined in advance. Ironically, the only Shakespearean touch in the auction was its crafted theatricality, the whole event being a carefully stage-managed performance of false expectancy.

Yet what other option was there? The cause had by then become so well-known that it would have been a national disgrace for Shakespeare's house to end up in the money-grubbing hands of a speculator, especially a notorious American one who (as we will shortly see) boasted that he would dismantle the Birthplace and ship it to New York City. Everyone agreed, something must be done. But no one wanted to do it. Lord John Russell and his ministers decided that because Shakespeare's house belonged to the 'people' it was up to them to pay for it – if they wanted to. Agnostic about the house's future, the government refused to get involved. Harriet Martineau believed that a grassroots movement could raise enough money to buy the birthplace. She was wrong. Not nearly enough hard-earned pennies were contributed to the cause. William Hepworth Dixon and his literary brethren believed that the wealthy would step up and save the day. They, too, were wrong. A few, like Prince Albert, offered generously; but many in the metropolitan elite offered nothing. The British people in 1847 wanted desperately to preserve Shakespeare's house, to judge from the spirited rhetoric of all those speeches, songs, letters, placards and petitions. It's just that they wanted someone else to find the money. Yet no matter in which direction you looked, there was no someone else appearing on the horizon. Rhetoric and reality didn't align.

Fudging the whole issue was the only way forward. Let the committees buy the birthplace with money they did not have, let that outcome be loudly celebrated and let the true reckoning be put off until another day. And so, the committees promptly secured a bank loan for the shortfall of £1,400, which then enabled them to pay the sale price and close the deal. The new owners took possession of the house on 11 November 1847, eight weeks after the auction. *The People's Journal* rejoiced that the 'House is now the people's – it has been purchased in their name, and will be secured to them and their posterity for ever.'

The financial problems were not solved but only deferred; and, worse, they were compounded, because now the committees had to pay five per cent interest on top of the principal. No amount of collective rejoicing could stop the bill from eventually coming due. Nor could it be paid in the cheap journalistic currency of taffeta phrases and silken words precise. 'The purchase-money is not yet complete', the *Athenaeum* whispered in warning soon after the auction. Yet instead of grappling with the facts, the press defaulted once more to hollow patriotic bombast: 'To suffer this house to pass away is, as it were, a national denying of Shakspeare – and that is *not* possible in England.'

And yet the denial of Shakespeare was all too possible. William Howitt, author of *Homes and Haunts of the Most Eminent British Poets* (1847), measured the moment with greater honesty:

The Shakspeare House Committee has bought the house of the poet's reputed birth-place for the nation, and all England cannot pay for it. It is one of the most remarkable things of modern times, that the nation is so poor just now, that there cannot be found in it *just one hundred individuals who have fourteen pounds a-piece* to bestow on the completion of this national purpose . . . The enthusiasm of the nation has been tested, and found wanting ... We are not yet far enough emerged from our barbarism. We are yet only capable of endowing warriors, and ennobling bloodshed; it will remain for some future and more intellectual race to honour poets and the descendants of poets ... A confiding committee with the old house on their hands, and no money *in* their hands to pay for it. A fourteen hundred pounds overestimate of the national intellectuality.

If all England cannot summon the modest funds needed to preserve Shakespeare's birthplace, then all England does not deserve it. They have been betrayed by their own fecklessness. If the nation cannot achieve this high purpose, then let it achieve what little it can; let it rank soldiers above poets, bloodshed above art. Because when barbarism triumphs over thought and imagination, hope vanishes.

'England's heart now beats at Shakespeare's call'

Theatres in London had contributed little to the cause, apart from occasional donations by actors William Charles Macready and Charles Kemble, both well-known for performing Shakespeare. Oddly, no one had thought of appealing to theatre *audiences*, who were, in fact, already paying for Shakespeare by buying theatre tickets. That changed when Frederick Beale, manager of Covent Garden, one of London's oldest, largest and most famous theatres (now the Royal Opera House), volunteered to host a benefit performance. Leading actors from nine theatre companies across the city would appear together for one night only, each company to perform a scene from a Shakespeare play in its repertoire. The idea was genius, because it gave spectators a chance to see their favourite actors share the stage, an ensemble that would otherwise never form because those actors belonged to rival theatre companies. But for this one night, fraternity reigned. The actors would lend their services so that all the proceeds could help to pay off the accumulating debt. This charity performance was needed, as the *Athenaeum* tartly put it, to 'arous[e] the sluggish sympathies of the nation'.

The rousing 'Shakespeare Night' took place at a packed-out Covent Garden Theatre on the night of Tuesday, 7 December 1847. First to take the stage was Samuel Phelps, manager of the popular Sadler's Wells theatre, in suburban Islington, who recited an overwrought poem written for the occasion by the Shakespeare biographer Charles Knight. It was, fittingly, composed mainly in iambic pentameter, the ten-syllable metric line with alternating stress (de-DUM de-DUM de-DUM ...) that was the core rhythm of Shakespeare's own dramatic verse. Lest the audience, now hailed as 'th'assembled Nation', needed reminding, its vital task was to rescue Shakespeare from 'quick decay':

For here th'assembled Nation stands to say
Our Shakspeare's home is snatched from quick decay;
Is the work finished – or but yet begun?
Complete! Maintain! Do all that needs be done!
Yes! England's heart now beats at Shakspeare's call –
The Muses' bower is saved – yours is the pledge of all.

Not that anyone heard Samuel Phelps declaim these lines. A noisy tussle for seats broke out during his recitation, as too many people tried to squeeze onto the benches near the orchestra. Three times the actor attempted to deliver the prologue over the clamour and three times he failed. Mistaking the commotion for heckling, Phelps fled the stage in embarrassment, leaving most of Knight's prologue unspoken. On balance, perhaps not such a bad thing. To calm everything down, the theatre's manager broke his own rules and allowed the overflow spectators to stand at the back of the auditorium. Anyone curious as to how the prologue ended had only to wait until morning, when *The Times* printed the verses in full.

Once the noise in the audience subsided, the Shakespeare extravaganza resumed. The nine scenes performed included Macready as the dying Henry IV, Phelps (summoning his courage to return to the stage) as the wizard Prospero and Priscilla Horton as the sprite Ariel in the second scene from *The Tempest*, Fanny Kemble as Queen Katharine in *Henry VIII*, Helen Faucit and Julia Glover as Juliet and her Nurse and Mary Warner as the wronged queen Hermione in the famous statue scene from *The Winter's Tale*. This jumbling of moments from different plays – Prospero on his enchanted island runs into Juliet from fair Verona, while Katherine the shrew collides with Katharine of Aragon – lent a holiday spirit to the occasion, the whole performance likened by one journalist to 'a masque – a great procession of the Shakespeare creations'.

The prologue had beseeched the audience to 'do all that needs be done', but such pleading was redundant. The audience had already met its obligation by purchasing tickets at inflated prices. The most expensive private box sold for five guineas while the cheapest seat in the nosebleed third gallery, long known as 'the gods', cost two shillings (twenty-four pence), much more than Harriet Martineau had appealed for in her 'penny subscription' So successful was the Covent Garden event that it raised £900 in a single night, slashing by nearly two-thirds the amount owed by the London and Stratford committees.

'The royal patrons stayed away'

The capacity audience that night at Covent Garden was attracted not just by the distinguished acting ensemble but also by a performance of a different sort: the promised appearance of Queen Victoria and Prince Albert. Their patronage, though never taken for granted, was not a complete surprise either, given that Albert had made an early and substantial donation to the charitable cause of buying Shakespeare's birthplace. Moreover, both Victoria and her consort were passionate, even indiscriminate, theatregoers, sometimes occupying the royal box at Covent Garden or Drury Lane two or three times in a single week.

The queen's early views on Shakespeare were shaped by Lord Melbourne, her first prime minister, with whom she conversed frequently about the plays and how they were acted. She never much liked the tragedian William Charles Macready, especially after he stared directly at her while acting in *King Lear*. In private, she branded the play 'horrid', no doubt because the title character was a mentally ill monarch. Victoria always had a soft spot for the actor-manager Charles Kean, later inviting him and his company from the Princess's Theatre on Oxford Street to perform *Macbeth*, *The Merchant of Venice* and *Richard II* at Windsor Castle. Yet far from limiting herself to Shakespeare and grand opera, she shamelessly delighted in gory melodramas, historical romances, pantomimes, farces and circus acts. After watching the lion tamer Isaac Van Amburgh at Drury Lane, the young queen went backstage to see the lions up close. She knew better than most what it was like to be either kept in a (gilded) cage or put on public display. Victoria loved all kinds of theatre and Prince Albert loved a worthy cause; it made perfect sense for them to be the royal patrons of the 'Shakespeare Night'.

In vain did the public rejoice at the prospect of the 'queen drinking enjoyment at the sweet Shakespeare fountain'. Because on that night, the night of all nights, the royal box at Covent Garden remained empty. The couple's absence could not be hidden because the royal box was placed at the side of the auditorium, right next to the stage, so that everyone in the audience could see whoever sat there. Occupying a theatre's royal box was no less a public performance – witnessed, scrutinized, judged – than what the actors did on the stage. But on this night, the scheduled royal performance was cancelled without explanation at the last minute.

Victoria and Albert weren't just absent from the theatre, they weren't anywhere near it. They could not be found at Buckingham Palace, a carriage ride away. No, they were in Osborne House on the Isle of Wight, a hundred miles and a train and boat ride away. The royal patrons, it seems, never had any intention of showing up at Covent Garden. The comic magazine *Punch* reported, facetiously, that 'Her Majesty and Prince Albert' spent the evening playing cribbage. So little did the 'Shakespeare Night' matter to Victoria that she never mentioned it in her otherwise meticulous diary, the whole event wiped from her memory.

The press, however, refused to let such desertion go unchallenged. A few days later, the *Athenaeum* declared there was something 'painful in the sight of their vacant box. It was more than empty – it looked *foreign*.' That was a direct swipe at Victoria's love for French and Italian opera and her marriage to a son of the House of Saxe-Coburg and Gotha. The queen's failure to show proper reverence to Shakespeare was, as journalists would have it, a shameful forfeiture of national identity, a surrendering of her own Englishness. After all, the least one can expect of a monarch is that she knows over which country she reigns.

In a uniquely scandalous way, the royal no-show exposed the central hypocrisy of the Victorian cult of Shakespeare. Devotion to England's greatest dramatist was mostly a matter of 'seeming', as Hamlet himself would say, and not of doing. It was enough to declare the right intentions and to mouth the right words. But never was it necessary to suit your actions to your words. In 1847, many long and eloquent tributes were paid to Shakespeare. But when the time for action came, Victoria and Albert stayed away, the great and the good failed to find the money, the penny campaign never got off the ground and the government washed it hands of the whole affair.

'Chaps from Yankee land'

The most fascinating aspect of how Shakespeare's birthplace was sold wasn't the auction itself, which was, despite all its surrounding hype, a lacklustre affair, but rather the media narrative that shaped the public's perceptions of events as they unfolded. This narrative featured homegrown heroes, stock villains and an apocalyptic outcome averted just before the final curtain. It was, in short, a heart-warming English melodrama. Heart-warming, that is, for the English.

In this melodrama, guardian angels of English culture fought dollar-crazed Yankee devils. On one side, a valiant band of Shakespeare's countrymen, drawn from all segments of society and motivated by the purest national pride, fought to preserve the birthplace in perpetuity for the nation. On the other, money-grubbing American speculators plotted openly to turn Shakespeare's house into a lucrative tourist trap. If necessary, they would dismantle the house and ship it across the Atlantic. In the contested middle stood the Birthplace itself, alone and vulnerable. The high stakes were clear to everyone. Either Shakespeare belonged to all people and for all time, occupying the high ground of culture and heritage, or he was just another commodity in the marketplace, more prestigious than turnips or teapots, obviously, but something to be sized up and haggled over just the same.

The indefatigable William Hepworth Dixon, who penned weekly editorials in the weeks before the auction, conjured up for the readers of *The People's Journal* the nightmarish spectre of two wealthy Americans, each as loathsome as the other, bidding for Shakespeare's birthplace,

> Yankees . . . would immediately detach [the Birthplace] from the sacred soil on which it stands, separate it from the kindred holy places in the neighbourhood, set it on a truck, carry it out of the country, and hawk it

about the States as an exhibition – profanation most horrible! . . . The Americans are, as yet, the highest bidders in the field. The showman has offered 1200*l*. for it, and, if we may believe the owners, another American – a private gentleman, who wishes to have the precious relic to adorn his villa . . . has offered a still larger sum . . . Surely it cannot be that England is already declined to the condition in which she can no longer retain her national treasures!

This warning had its intended effect: word of the calamity that must at all costs be avoided was picked up and passed on by other messengers. Frederick W. Fairholt's *The Home of Shakespeare*, originally published in 1845, was reissued before the auction (complete with thirty-three engravings) and became a best-seller. The *Illustrated London News*, which sold eighty thousand copies a week, devoted an entire issue to the sale of the birthplace. Lyrics to the mawkish parlour song 'Thou Art Gone from my Gaze', which profess a love that survives the beloved's death, were rewritten to incite fears of American cultural invasion, an imminent search-and-seizure mission that would culminate in 'chaps from Yankee land' returning home with their new plunder:

And is it true this house is coming down
To be put on wheels and dragged about the town?
Can such things be, can it be so!
What, make this classic pile a traveling show?
Tis true, tis pity chaps from Yankee land
Are coming over with the cash in hand.

In framing events in such emotive, even xenophobic, terms, the media succeeded where the London and Stratford committees had failed: it reshaped public feeling and made the Birthplace an object of national pride and nostalgic affection. But it did so through blatant scapegoating. Instead of admitting a collective national failure to protect Shakespeare's house in the first place, a fault so grievous and so embarrassing that it must be denied at all costs, they projected the blame onto some Americans who had not, in fact, done anything blameworthy. No American had purchased the house, let alone turned it into a circus sideshow or shipped it across the Atlantic. No American had desecrated the birthplace. No American had profited from it. It was all fake news. But the very thought of those catastrophic eventualities distracted England from the guilt she refused to feel, the guilt that Shakespeare's own people left him alone and undefended, subjected to the cruel whims of the marketplace. If you cannot bear to reproach yourself then your only option is to point an accusatory finger at someone else and so displace the psychic pain onto them. Better to accuse Americans, especially the flashy hucksters and the millionaire rubes, than to admit the unpalatable truth.

'I've a notion that I'd ship every crumb of it'

The main target of those denunciations was none other than Phineas T. Barnum, the blustering American 'showman' to whom William Hepworth Dixon had darkly alluded in his warning that Shakespeare's birthplace was vulnerable to a hostile takeover. Thomas Court's trustees were required to sell the Henley Street property to the highest bidder, whoever that was, be that person native or foreign, refined or vulgar. All that mattered was the money. Barnum had a big mouth and bigger pockets. If his were the winning bid then nothing could stop him from dismantling the Birthplace – beam by beam, stone by stone, brick by brick – shipping it across the Atlantic and displaying it in his five-storey museum of curiosities in New York City. Come see Jumbo the elephant. Come see Captain Costentenus, the tattooed Greek prince. Come see the Fiji mermaid. Come see Shakespeare's house.

Such was the fear that the English press whipped up to frenzied new heights in their smear campaign against Barnum. *The Times* warned, extravagantly, that the birthplace would soon be 'trundled about on wheels like a caravan of wild beasts ... through the United States of America'. Barnum was just a hillbilly with money, *Punch* explained, when it imagined the letter that he had written to the mayor of Stratford-upon-Avon on behalf of all 'free Americans': 'Jist say the number of dollars that your Stratford critters want for the immortal location, and I'll consign 'em slick ... And as for gittin the house over here, I've a notion that I'd ship every crumb of it.'

Yet contrary to all such lampooning, Barnum was no bumbling hayseed. He was actually a hard-nosed businessman from the city of Bridgeport, Connecticut. Nor was he a stranger to England, for he lived there in the mid-1840s, when he made 'General' Tom Thumb – born Charles Stratton, also from Bridgeport – a must-see attraction in London's West End. At his peak, in the spring and summer of 1844, Tom Thumb was bringing in a phenomenal £500 a day at the Egyptian Hall in Piccadilly Circus.

So famous had the American impresario and his diminutive protégé become that before long a soldier from the Household Cavalry was dispatched to their mansion in Bond Street, bearing an invitation to a private audience with Queen Victoria at Buckingham Palace. The date was set for the evening of Saturday, 23 March. Eager to meet Tom Thumb, Victoria cut short the official period of mourning after the death of Prince Albert's father, Duke Ernst of Saxe-Coburg and Gotha. Outfitted in the traditional court costume of velvet coat, knee breeches, white stocking and buckled shoes, and brandishing a tiny ceremonial sword, Tom Thumb climbed the palace's marble staircase and walked straight into the royal picture gallery, where he found the queen, Prince Albert and the Duke of Wellington all waiting for him. Undaunted in the presence of royalty and military heroism, he sang 'Yankee Doodle Dandy', anthem of the American Revolution, to the granddaughter of George III. She laughed and then invited him to come back a week later.

As Barnum had hoped, Tom Thumb's 'visits to the Queen' were box-office gold. After a few weeks more of counting ticket receipts, he took a break from theatre management and set out on a tour of the English countryside. Inevitably, he made his way to Stratford-upon-Avon, where, like so many American pilgrims over the years, including John Adams and his travelling companion Thomas Jefferson, he was dismayed to learn just how badly Shakespeare was neglected in the town of his birth. We know this because the London journalist Albert Smith, who accompanied Barnum, wrote a comic account of their visit to Stratford for *Bentley's Miscellany*, his article published under the jocular title, 'A Go-a-Head Day with Barnum'. At six o'clock on the morning of Thursday, 5 September 1844, a coach and driver met the pair outside the Hen and Chickens tavern on New Street in Birmingham. Getting an unusually early start, Barnum and Smith climbed into the carriage and headed for Stratford at the unhurried pace of twelve miles an hour. Upon entering the town, they rode by carriage to the Red Horse Hotel, where they alighted and ordered breakfast. While waiting for their meal, they asked for a local guidebook. The waiter brought them the well-thumbed copy of Washington Irving's *Sketchbook* kept in the hotel's parlour for just such an educative purpose. It didn't take Barnum long to realize that twenty-four years earlier his fellow American had lodged in the same hotel.

One droll anecdote stands out in Smith's travelogue. Barnum offered to send to the house's 'old lady' custodian, who must have been the elderly Ann Court, a portrait of Tom Thumb to hang alongside that of Shakespeare in the upstairs birthroom. It never happened, of course; and Barnum knew that his offer would be rejected. Yet he also knew that his absurd proposal was not, in fact, absurd at all – because it hinted at something true. This truth, which neither alarmed nor embarrassed Barnum, was that the Victorian cult of Shakespeare was a specialty brand of humbug, a fakery not so different from his own museum of curiosities. It was laughable and yet somehow logical, too, that a likeness of Tom Thumb should adorn Shakespeare's birthplace, because both the man and the house were engaged in the business of fooling the public. Except that one did it more openly than the other.

Barnum must have felt entirely at home in the Birthplace, sensing that it was, like his own establishment, a site where gullible customers ('suckers', he called them) could be hoodwinked and then be glad for the swindle. 'A man has quite a right to take in the public if he can', he confided to Smith as they left Stratford for nearby Warwick. 'It's the greatest credit to him if he whops 'em, for they are long odds.' Before departing, Barnum made sure to leave in the Birthplace a stack of calling cards advertising Tom Thumb's forthcoming appearance at Dee's Hotel in Birmingham, just twenty short miles away. It was a shrewd marketing tactic. He and Shakespeare were, after all, competing for the same clientele.

'I'll put a glass case around it'

It's a verified fact that Barnum went to Shakespeare's birthplace for his signature appears in the visitors' book, dated 5 September 1844. It's not nearly so clear, however, when he seized upon the idea to buy it and what he planned to do with the house once he had bought it. His first autobiography, *The Life of P.T. Barnum*, published in 1855, seven years after the auction, makes no mention of a failed, earlier scheme to purchase the birthplace, let alone to transport it across the Atlantic Ocean. Not until 1869, in *Struggles and Triumphs*, his revised and self-adulatory memoir, did Barnum finally make public his original plan:

> During my first visit to England I obtained verbally, through a friend, the refusal of the house in which Shakespeare was born, designing to remove it in sections to my Museum in New York; but the project leaked out, British pride was touched, and several English gentlemen interfered and purchased the premises for a Shakespearian Association. Had they slept a few days longer, I should have made a rare speculation, for I was subsequently assured that the British people, rather than suffering that house to be removed to America, would have bought me off with twenty thousand pounds.

Though stated with bravado, this account of events doesn't hold up. The house wasn't for sale when he and Albert Smith visited it because Ann Court, who held a life interest in the property, was still residing there. Barnum was correct that a 'Shakespearian Association' eventually bought the birthplace, but that wasn't until 1847, three years later. £20,000 was an impossibly large sum given that the London and Stratford committees couldn't manage to raise a mere £3,000. And at the time of Barnum's trip to Stratford, nobody much cared who owned Shakespeare's birthplace.

Despite his erratic chronology, Barnum was steadfast in his claim that he wanted to take the birthplace home with him – literally, pack it up and put it on the next ship bound for New York – and make it the lead attraction in his 'American Museum' on lower Broadway. The great American humourist Mark Twain, in his travelogue *Following the Equator: A Journey Around the World*, reported a conversation that had taken place decades earlier between Barnum and Charles Jamrach, who supplied the impresario with rare and exotic circus animals. In a tiny space behind cages of snakes and monkeys, all part of Jamrach's menagerie on the Ratcliffe Highway in east London, Barnum boasted that he planned to

> buy Shakespeare's house. I'll set it up in my Museum in New York and put a glass case around it and make a sacred thing of it; and you'll see all America flock there to worship; yes, and pilgrims from the whole earth; and I'll make them take their hats off, too. In America we know how to value anything that Shakespeare's touch has made holy. You'll see.

The American was no profane despoiler, at least as Twain would have it, but a true acolyte, for he had 'roused into its present vigorous life England's dead interest in her Shakespearean remains'. So greatly did Barnum revere the Bard of Avon that he would preserve the poet's ramshackle birthplace by enclosing it behind glass, as if set within a gigantic display case. Such a barrier would fulfil a dual purpose: it simultaneously protected the house and focused the viewer's attention, framing the entire structure as valuable ('look over here') and thus needing protection ('but don't get too close'). From an imposed safe distance, pilgrims from all continents could pay their respects to Shakespeare. Should a man forget to remove his hat, just as he would at a Sunday morning church service, Barnum was on hand to enforce the rules. He was ahead of his time. Anyone visiting Chawton Cottage today will see Jane Austen's writing table set behind a transparent plastic screen.

Barnum agreed with many English people that Shakespeare's house was a sacred site; he just thought it was in the wrong place. 'Americans appreciate the immortal Bard of Avon as keenly as do their brethren in the Mother Country', he insisted, 'and I greatly desired to honour the New World by erecting this invaluable relic in its commercial metropolis.' If the English couldn't save the birthplace from ruin, then why shouldn't a Yankee speculator jump in to finish the job? Who cares if he makes a few dollars out of it? After all, Barnum was no ransacking looter; he was the house's saviour.

It's tongue-in-cheek, of course, but the American wins his point. The English, for all their spouted Shakespearean pieties, failed to muster the wherewithal to preserve the house. Had they done so, Barnum would not have emerged as a threat, real or concocted, to the Shakespeare establishment. The great showman knew humbug when he heard it. 'You talk a good deal about your Shakespeare being the pride of England', he told Albert Smith; 'but I can see nobody knew or cared a cent about him while he was alive, or else you'd have known more of him now'. And so, Barnum rewrote the narrative, exposing the smug hypocrisy of London cultural elites whose fixed habit was to heap blame on everyone but themselves. The truth, he urged – though what is truth in the dark arts of fake news and media warping – was that Shakespeare needed to be rescued from the English, his own people, the ones who abandoned him in his hour of greatest need. And it would be the Americans who came to his rescue. Oh, the irony.

12

Restoring Shakespeare

Buying the Birthplace solved one problem only to create another. True, the house had been bought on the nation's behalf and so never again would it risk falling into private, or worse, foreign, hands. Its future was secure. But the site itself didn't live up to its new formal status. The house was too dismal in appearance, too irregular in its structure.

What the joint London and Stratford committees had acquired in September 1847 on behalf of a less-than-grateful nation was not one building, but three: a tiny gloomy cottage on one side, an ugly brick-fronted pub called The Swan and Maidenhead on the other side and a former butcher's shop in the middle. Albert Smith, Barnum's travelling companion in Stratford, was not impressed by the disjointed, down-at-heel property:

> The tenement in Henley Street is a humble-looking place enough, with a public-house on the right hand, and a small abode with a shed on the left. It is inlaid with rough beams, black with age; and there is a rickety tumble-down board over the door, very like an inn-sign, which might be taken down with advantage. The room into which you pass from the street was a butcher's shop; the fittings up still remain, but the business is not carried on. It has also a small shed before the window, and the floor is paved with irregularly-shaped stones.

The nine members of the London and Stratford committees who became the Birthplace's trustees, and therefore its new legal owners, spent the next few years sprucing up and safeguarding the property. Every house in Henley Street was built partly of wood, which meant that fire could quickly spread from one house to the next, the flames engulfing an entire row of them. What a tragedy it would be if Shakespeare's birthplace were saved from desecration by private speculators only to be consumed shortly afterwards by fire, the very means of destruction it had escaped for two and a half centuries. And so, the new owners tore down a stable and a shed in the back garden to lower the risk of fire reaching the main house itself. The street in front of the Birthplace was paved over, giving visitors a more dignified experience upon their arrival. No more slipping and sliding in the mud, no more stepping into wheel-rut puddles, no more dust whipped up by the wind on a hot summer's day. Yet more dignity was acquired when the Swan and Maidenhead Inn was lent to a publican who, astonishingly, promised never to serve alcohol and so brought a quintessentially Victorian sobriety to the premises.

The trustees could afford no other changes to the Birthplace because most of the money they had left was earmarked for paying off the loan from when they had purchased the house at the 1847 auction. No money was left over to renovate it; and yet renovations were urgently needed.

'Desirous of honouring the birthplace'

Salvation arrived in the person of John Shakespear – note the variant spelling – an eighty-two-year-old Hindustani scholar from the colourfully named Leicestershire market town of Ashby-de-la-Zouch. Retired on a generous pension from the East India Company, where he had taught South Asian and Middle Eastern languages to new cadets, but still earning steady royalties from his English-Hindustani dictionary, the elderly bachelor had money to spend but no one to spend it on. Inspired by the possibility that he was descended from a branch of William Shakespeare's family, yet always careful to spell his surname without the final 'e', to avoid misleading anyone, John Shakespear told the Birthplace's trustees that he wanted to help pay for the renovations. In the spring of 1856, he travelled to Stratford to inspect the house, after which he engaged in a long correspondence with William Oakes Hunt, Stratford's town clerk, about how the renovations might proceed and how much they would cost. Evidently, the wealthy John Shakespear liked what he heard, because on 18 July he pledged the handsome sum of £2,500 – nearly as much as it had cost to buy the house at auction – for renovating and protecting the Birthplace:

> Whereas the said John Shakespear . . . being desirous of honouring the birthplace of the poet Shakespeare and of preserving the same from decay and injury, has agreed to appropriate and pay the sum of 2,500*l*. . . . [to] purchase the property adjoining the said birthplace with a view to pull the same down and isolate the birthplace from any adjoining building, and then to restore the whole house, as nearly as practicable, to what it is represented as having originally been.

He rejected a proposal to encase the Birthplace within a gigantic glass dome, though had it been built it would have realized one of P.T. Barnum's most extreme fantasies. John Shakespear died in 1858, leaving a further £2,500 to create a 'museum at Shakespeare's house in Stratford', along with funds to pay a resident custodian sixty pounds a year. His nephews successfully challenged the bequest in the Court of Chancery, which ruled that John Shakespear's directive in his will lacked precision; it was merely a 'personal wish' to aid the Trustees – dismissed, harshly, as a 'club of dilettanti' – rather than a formal donation to a recognized charity with a clear public mission. For now, at least, the Birthplace was trapped in legal limbo, no longer a private dwelling with a sideline in tourism but not yet an official heritage site run and maintained for the benefit of all.

'A lie from beginning to end'

John Shakespear's unexpected gift forced the Trustees to make up their minds about what they should do with the Birthplace and its surroundings. As with any historic building, the fundamental choice they faced was whether to *restore* it or to *preserve* it. This was the most consequential decision they would make and from it everything else followed. Yet the choice was far from straightforward because each option entailed its own benefits and risks.

To restore the Birthplace meant to return it to the structure, condition and appearance it had during Shakespeare's lifetime. That must, on the face of it, have seemed the right course of action. After all, the value of the Birthplace resided in a singular and precise history: William Shakespeare was born and grew up there. The house as it subsequently existed – post-Shakespearean, as it were – didn't matter at all. Indeed, that long intervening history had to be erased, or scraped away, altogether obliterated so that the birthplace could re-emerge in its original pristine state.

A fine sentiment, but a fraudulent one. The great English art critic John Ruskin, in his masterpiece *The Seven Lamps of Architecture* (1849), had denounced restoration as 'the most total destruction which a building can suffer', much preferring the charm, as he saw and felt it, of the architectural ruin. Any claim to return a structure to its original state, he asserted, was a 'lie from beginning to end', because every restored structure, precisely because it had been restored, ended up pretending to be that which it was not and could never be. Architectural restoration, he believed, was an inherent falsehood – not by any deceitful intent, but by the very nature of the undertaking. Because what could never be restored were the very things that everyone longed to restore: the life spirit of an old building, its soul, its beating pulse. All the vibrancy was gone, never to return. At least the ruin, decayed, but original, still possessed '*some* life, some mysterious suggestion of what it had been, and of what it had lost'. The ruin implied the lost whole, and truthfully so, while a restoration could at best only aspire to be a reasonable likeness of that lost whole, a model of it, but nothing more.

In pronouncing his firm verdict, Ruskin had in mind the hatchet jobs perpetrated on such grand historic sites in Italy and France as the Baptistery at Pisa, the Casa d'Oro in Venice and the cathedral of Lisieux. Even so, the Trustees of the Birthplace needed little prompting to apply Ruskin's opinion to their own domestic dilemma. Smearing one of the house's ancient oak beams in varnish wouldn't bring it back to life. The extra sheen would succeed only in making the house more delightful to modern visitors, creating an agreeable mirage of the past that, however beguiling, or however convincing, was still, and always, just a mirage. This is one way of thinking about the reconstructed Globe theatre on London's Southbank. It can replicate the original architecture, and it does; but it cannot resurrect the original performers and the original spectators, the people who made the theatre what it was in Shakespeare's time.

Still, if you were seduced by the promise of historical authenticity, it wasn't so clear how you would go about it. Which parts of the Birthplace would you remove? Which ones repair? Which put back in? Answering such questions, for they were inescapable, was difficult because no record survived as to what the house looked like in Shakespeare's time, inside or out. The earliest image dated only from the 1760s, two hundred years after Shakespeare's birth and so was hardly a reliable source. Worse yet, restoration entailed the risk that the house's original fabric – flagstone floor, wattle-and-daub, oak frame – might be damaged by negligence or, in a prospect too horrible to imagine, demolished entirely. In saving the house you might end up destroying it. The whole mission of architectural restoration was fraught, in both theory and in practice.

By contrast, to preserve the Birthplace meant to maintain its present state, neither returning it to the past nor undertaking further alteration. The house, frozen forever in time, would appear to all future generations exactly as it appeared in the year 1856. The learned John Payne Collier, soon to be exposed as a serial forger of Shakespeare documents, urged his fellow Trustees to keep the house 'as far as possible, in the state which it now is'. Preservation was the easier and less risky option, he argued, because no historical guesswork was required. No one had to decide which parts of the house would remain and which removed. Moreover, the Birthplace retained many of its original features, so that preserving it would, in fact, capture for posterity something of the house as Shakespeare knew it. Collier, for one, felt 'most anxious' that 'no scrap of the original fabric should be removed', as might accidentally occur during restoration works.

Yet the price to be paid for keeping the original features intact was also keeping intact the many additions, alterations and defacements, all those architectural layers that concealed the home of John and Mary Shakespeare. By common agreement, the most offensive of these later additions was the nasty red brick frontage to the Swan and Maidenhead Inn. Yet it, too, would remain *in situ*. Not for nothing was the preservationist view known colloquially as 'anti-scrape'.

If restoring the Birthplace was an impossible dream, then preserving it was a dull reality. The whole purpose of preventing the house from falling into private hands was to safeguard it forever as a shrine to Shakespeare. Yet there was little point in doing that if the house continued to bear the imprint of the many people who lived there over many years. Paradoxically, to preserve the Birthplace could mean to obscure – or worse, negate – the very reason you preserved it in the first place. How could anyone searching for Shakespeare find him if he were buried beneath the accumulated layers of other people's home improvement projects?

'If architecture it can be called'

Faced with this quandary, the Trustees sought advice from architect Edward Barry, son and colleague of Sir Charles Barry, who had designed the new Houses of Parliament in an elaborate neo-Gothic style. In 1857, the younger Barry, aged twenty-seven, had only a few commissions under his belt, but one of them was decidedly high-profile: he had rebuilt Covent Garden Theatre and designed the adjacent (and still in use) Floral Hall, a spectacular glass enclosure inspired by the Crystal Palace at the Great Exhibition of 1851. Closer to Stratford, he designed the Birmingham & Midland Institute, an educational charity, then under construction on Paradise Street in Birmingham's city centre, the foundation stone laid by Prince Albert himself.

Edward Barry arrived in Stratford in the summer of 1857 to inspect the Birthplace and to convey his findings and recommendation to the Trustees. He recognized at once that, in appearance and layout, the house was a jumble of 'genuine relics of antiquity' and 'additions made in modern times and in the worst possible state'. Of course, that much was fully evident to the Trustees and, indeed, to any sharp-eyed tourist. Despite its Tudor origins, the Birthplace was not, he concluded, in present danger of collapse, although some of the wooden floor beams needed reinforcing. Such reassurance must have been welcomed, since it allowed the Trustees some time in which to plan, unhurriedly, how to use John Shakespear's gift.

In his final report, dated 29 June 1857 – original copies are held by the Shakespeare Birthplace Trust and the Folger Shakespeare Library – Barry framed the question of what should be done to the Birthplace as one less about architectural history than cultural history: Shakespeare's life and afterlife. Were it not the birthplace of William Shakespeare, he ventured, the house on Henley Street, although old, would command little attention from anyone, including those who were curious about old buildings:

> The interest which this lowly cottage has possessed, and appears still to possess in the eyes of all those who value the works, and respect the name of Shakespeare is of an archaeological and antiquarian nature alone. The architecture, if architecture it can be called, possesses no feature of interest, not to be found with far greater completeness in other structures, and we may fairly assume therefore that the visitors are drawn to it from the fact of its being the house in which Shakespeare lived, and not from its being an edifice of any architectural pretensions. Such being the case,

too great care cannot be taken, lest any steps, now resolved upon, should appear to deduct from the historical interest of this celebrated spot, in favour of a restoration too strictly architectural.

Barry had found the crux of the matter. The truth that no one would much care about this one particular house had Shakespeare not been born there – in Stratford alone, other Tudor dwellings were more architecturally impressive – must guide the Trustees in deciding what to do next. Their loyalty was owed not to the house itself, he clarified, but to its most famous occupant; or rather, to the one through the other. Whatever was to be done to the Birthplace must be done for Shakespeare's sake alone, making him once again a tangible, not phantom, presence in the place of his nativity. It wasn't the house that would be restored; it was Shakespeare himself.

The only way, Barry concluded, to make the Birthplace the 'nucleus' of the Shakespeare trade was

To remove with a careful hand all those excrescences which are decidedly the result of modern innovation, to uphold with jealous care all that now exists of undoubted antiquity, not to destroy any portion about whose character the slightest doubt may exist but to restore any parts needing it in such a manner that the restorations can never be mistaken for the old work, though harmonizing with it, and lastly to adopt such measures as modern science enables us to bring to our aid, for the perfect preservation of the building, and perhaps to make Shakespeare's House a nucleus of such an institution as might prove eventually not unfit to bear so illustrious a name.

John Ruskin would have been horrified by such unbridled zeal, however carefully executed, for architectural restoration. Yet such criticism would have mattered little to Edward Barry, who knew that never had an English architect received so idiosyncratic a commission: to use what was there to make manifest what was not there.

'According to the oldest Print extant'

Other than literary historian John Payne Collier, who declared himself a lifelong 'enemy' of architectural restoration, the Trustees agreed with Barry; and so, they voted to restore the Birthplace, not to preserve it. Their decision was no sudden change of heart, nor, for that matter, unexpected – because the deed of gift they had drawn up the previous year stipulated that John Shakespear's money would be used to 'restore the whole house'.

In theory, restoring the Birthplace was a straightforward matter of stripping away all that was not original. Remove the confusing layers of 'modern ugliness' and then stand back and let the house of 'undoubted antiquity' shine through. In practice, it proved a tricky business. To restore the Birthplace meant returning it to an earlier condition and appearance: but which condition? and what appearance? Granted, enough of the original oak timber frame survived to give a rough impression of how the house had looked in the 1560s and 1570s, when the young William Shakespeare lived there. Nearby houses of similar size and age offered comparable details. Beyond that, however, it was pure conjecture, as no record from Shakespeare's time described or depicted the house where he was born.

The silence of the archive did not deter the Trustees. With no image of the Birthplace from Shakespeare's time to guide them, they relied instead on the next best thing: the oldest surviving image of the house, even if it dated from long afterwards. As William Oakes Hunt, Stratford's town clerk, explained to the Earl of Carlisle when seeking the peer's blessing for the proposed works, the goal was to 'restore the House to the state it is supposed to have been at the birth of the Poet according to the oldest Print extant and as it appeared at the time of Garrick's Jubilee in 1769'.

This 'oldest print extant' – we have seen it before – was the one published in *Gentleman's Magazine* in July 1769 and based on a drawing by antiquarian Richard Greene, whose brother Joseph was headmaster of Stratford's grammar school. This well-known engraving purported to depict the Birthplace as it stood in the 1760s, a full century and a half after Shakespeare's death. Yet as we know from contemporary accounts, including Samuel Winter's 1759 map of Stratford, the image was more fantasy than fact. Greene's drawing shows a well-maintained detached house with dormer windows and a porch in the middle of a field. Its only correct details were the most generic ones, the timber frame and the plastered walls.

And yet, this engraving was, despite its errors and anachronisms, taken as gospel truth. Applicants for supervising architect were instructed to study it. When Edward Barry made the detailed plans for restoring the Birthplace, anxious Trustees spotted where his blueprints deviated from it: What happened to the charming dormer windows? Why had the porch disappeared? They insisted, as the minutes of their meetings confirm, that Barry adhere to whatever was shown in the 'old drawing'. He did and so it has been ever since. In the 1920s, when tiles on the porch roof were replaced – the very porch that Barry's plans initially left out – the Shakespeare Birthplace Trust instructed that it be restored in accordance with Greene's picture. Even today, in the twenty-first century, the Birthplace still looks very much like that fanciful drawing made in the eighteenth century.

'An attractive site to the visitors of Stratford'

But no matter. As Edward Barry had intuited early on, restoring Shakespeare's birthplace was not fundamentally about honouring a work of Tudor architecture; it was, rather, about honouring a man of timeless genius,

Shakespeare the poet and playwright. That Greene's drawing offered little
accuracy mattered but little because accuracy was not needed. What was
needed was a version of the Birthplace that lived up to the nineteenth-
century's idolatrous worship of Shakespeare. This rickety 'cottage of
humility' had to be transformed, and speedily, into what it had never been:
a grand residence, charmingly picturesque, dominating its surroundings; in
short, a landmark. When it came to the Birthplace, optics trumped historical
facts.

Hence, the Trustees' insistence that the old houses flanking the Birthplace,
houses of equal architectural value, should be demolished. Nominally, this
'clearance', captured step-by-step in photographs now in the collection of
the Shakespeare Birthplace Trust, was to reduce the risk of fire. Such was the
fear that the Birthplace would burn to the ground that gas flames were
banished from it. By 1857 the house was, unlike most buildings at the time,
heated by hot water pipes. But an even larger consideration came into play.
The adjacent houses, themselves of historical interest, were pulled down in
the name of Shakespeare. Nothing must crowd or spoil the view of the
house where he was born. Indeed, the Trustees believed that the surrounding
cottages 'injured the appearance' of the Birthplace by making it look too
ordinary, just one more house in a row of similar houses. Like the Eiffel
Tower or the Washington Monument, though on its own more intimate
scale, the Birthplace had to stand out from its surroundings to make the
most lasting impression on those who visited it. The paramount imperative
was, as John Payne Collier remarked at the time, to make the house an
'attractive site to the visitors of Stratford'.

This was paradox in action. On the one hand, the Birthplace needed to be
anchored in its native setting, blending in with the seductive Elizabethan
look that streets in Stratford-upon-Avon still have. To dismantle the house
and move it elsewhere, as P.T. Barnum had intended, would diminish its
value by separating Shakespeare from the town of his birth. Yet on the other
hand, the house needed to be the sole attraction on Henley Street, just as it
was in Richard Greene's fictional drawing, the one site to which all eyes
turned and to which all steps led.

Distanced, now, from its surroundings, the Birthplace changed how
people thought about Shakespeare's own life. A freestanding house, with its
aura of prosperity and social cachet, upended Shakespeare biography,
transforming the son of a town glovemaker into the heir of a landed
gentleman, a blessed youth destined for fame and success in the wider world.
When Charles Knight journeyed to Stratford in the early 1840s to seek
materials on Shakespeare's life he searched in vain for evidence that the
playwright had grown up in ease and comfort, not 'obscure . . . and servile
employments'. Had he waited another decade, Knight would have found the
evidence he sought. Found it not secreted in dusty archives but on plain view
in the open streets, in the imposing way that the Birthplace stood out, in
bold relief. With its independent air of settled prosperity, the house, simply

by its altered appearance, made it seem that Shakespeare's everlasting fame as a poet and playwright was written in the stars – when, in fact, it was about the least likely path in life that the son of a Warwickshire town craftsman in the 1580s could have followed.

By 1864, when a slew of new biographies marked the 300th anniversary of Shakespeare's birth, an event known formally as the Tercentenary, his life story had been rewritten to conform to his house's changed appearance, a case of fact adapting to fiction. 'There can be little doubt', one chronicler enthused, 'that during his childhood, and up to his eleventh or twelfth year, little William Shakespeare lived in careless plenty, and saw nothing in his father's house but that style of liberal housekeeping, which has always distinguished the upper yeomanry and rural gentry of England.' It was a complete myth. But, like all myths, it answered a need; in this instance, the need for Shakespeare's house to be worthy, not of Shakespeare himself, but of how the Victorians thought about Shakespeare, the unrivalled god of their idolatry.

13

W.S.

Richard Greene's drawing of the Birthplace, because it depicted the exterior only, proved useless to the Trustees when planning the internal renovations. The oldest image of the house's interior dated from 1792, when Samuel Ireland sketched the vast kitchen hearth – we have met this image before – for his *Picturesque Views on the Upper, or Warwickshire Avon*. Ireland did not claim to depict the house as the young Shakespeare knew it, but only as it appeared to the artist himself two centuries later. His drawing of the cosy inglenook, even though that part of the house was added after Shakespeare lived there, was in itself not so far-fetched: in Elizabethan houses, large open hearths were common. But the devil lurked in the details. The pewter tankards arrayed so tastefully on the massive oak mantlepiece and the upright cupboard standing sentry nearby, to say nothing of the little straw basket dangling from a ceiling hook, made the Birthplace look as if it were Anne Hathaway's charming cottage in Shottery. Little wonder that his sketch became so popular; for it licenced the easy, sentimental view that Shakespeare enjoyed a happy, warm and nurturing childhood. But as a guide for restoring the house's interior, it was worthless.

With no credible images or historical records to rely on, the Trustees adhered to the strict directive of any architectural restoration: remove all distorting modern accretions, thus exposing the building's original fabric, and then repair what was damaged and restore what was missing. Top of the list for elimination was the brick frontage to the Swan and Maidenhead Inn, derided for making Shakespeare's birthplace resemble, in the snobbish words of the illustrator and antiquary Frederick Fairholt, a 'modern residence for a laboring man'. Original parts of the house that had fallen into disrepair could be fixed. Sagging oak beams could be supported with iron braces. Crumbling wattle-and-daub could be reinforced with Portland cement mixed with sand and gravel and then given a fresh plastered surface. Buffed up, but still genuine. Yet where a part of the original house was missing – a lattice window smashed long ago, a door lock rusted away – a replica had to be installed.

'To stain, and polish, and varnish'

In explaining the plan of work, I've made it seem easier and less problematic than it actually was. To their frustration, Barry and his team discovered that it was frequently impossible to be certain which parts of the house were modern additions and which original. So difficult was it to determine the true extent of John Shakespeare's backyard, which had, over the centuries, been supplanted by a brewery and other outbuildings, that the Trustees settled for a barefaced anachronism: a fragrant flower garden with broad gravel walks and sheltering lime trees of the sort once found at Tudor country estates like Charlecote Park but never at the back of a tradesman's townhouse. Not just any garden, but one blossoming with all the plants and flowers – rosemary, pansies, fennel, columbine and daisies – that the doomed Ophelia gives to her brother, Laertes, not long before her death by drowning. One visitor mocked it for resembling a polite, if incongruous, 'tea-garden'.

The garden remains much the same today, with the added formality of parterre planting and box hedges, further historical fancies chosen to evoke a status and affluence that the Shakespeare family did not, in fact, possess. To truly restore the garden, which was an extended workplace for the entire family, not a pastoral retreat, you would need to plant fruit trees, keep a few well-fattened pigs and light a fire under the vats for boiling and dying animal hides.

Even the most straightforward tasks proved controversial. Any rotted original floorboards had, obviously, to be replaced. But it wasn't a matter of simply laying down a new floor or slotting in a few new planks because while the Tudor oak beams had darkened over time any new replacements would be much lighter in hue. So garish a juxtaposition of past and present would spoil the overall effect, calling unwanted attention to modern infringements on the house's original fabric. Precisely to avoid that result, Edward Gibbs, the local surveyor and architect charged by Barry with the day-to-day works, sourced oak timber from other houses of the period, so that as nearly as possible the replacements would match the originals. Gibbs was well-suited to the task, for he lived in the Shrieve's House on Sheep Street (now Tudor World, an immersive tourist attraction), site of the oldest continually occupied home in Stratford.

Yet this alternative was little better. If the sourced floorboards did match the originals then their inclusion would pass unnoticed, allowing visitors to wrongly believe that they were walking across the same floorboards that William Shakespeare had, in his boyhood, also walked across. The same was true for the antique door latches that were added to give the Birthplace the right period look. Yet no matter however authentic they seemed (if they seemed that way at all) they were not the latches lifted a thousand and more times by Shakespeare himself. A certain amount of well-meaning fakery had to be tolerated, for such was the inevitable consequence of architectural restoration.

Not wishing to hoodwink future visitors, the Trustees declared that all replicas and replacements throughout the Birthplace would be marked as 'new'. So explained a local newspaper, *The Royal Leamington Spa Courier and Warwickshire Standard*, in April 1858: 'new features ... shall be distinctly stamped as new, and not be allowed to mislead the pilgrims who may visit the shrine of an intellect so vast and noble'.

Not that anyone at the shrine was in danger of being categorically misled, because so many of the added features stood out already because they were so obviously added. The palpable newness of the restored Birthplace – the gleam of new timber, the smell of fresh varnish, the unrusted iron ceiling braces – caused discerning eyebrows to rise. 'A spick-and-span new villa' one disgruntled visitor put it. 'Old lace treasured up with lavender or jasmine', in the American drama critic William Winter's account of just how daintily the Birthplace had been restored. How his image of good Victorian housekeeping would have pleased Miss Maria Chataway and her sister Miss Caroline – cosy names, straight out of Dickens – the house's kindly custodians. In a satiric travelogue published in *All the Year Round*, playwright Andrew Halliday, who visited Stratford in 1864 to mark the Shakespeare Tercentenary, found himself unmoved by the Birthplace precisely because it 'had been restored out of all its antiquity' – upgraded, as it were, to modernity, looking 'trim, and neat, and angular, and varnished'. Writing more seriously, but with equal savagery, was the Rev John Mounteney Jephson, vicar of Childeritch parish in Essex, who made a pilgrimage to the Birthplace only to be dismayed that the old house looked 'so smug and new':

> Many of the old timbers remain, and the house is, indeed, substantially the same house as it was; but new timbers have been inserted where the old were decayed, everything has been scraped and polished up, and the place looks as if it had been 'restored,' a word to strike terror into the heart of an antiquary, not to speak of a man of taste. The propensity to stain, and polish, and varnish, and substitute new work for old unnecessarily, is much to be deprecated. Perhaps the committee, who hold the property in trust for the nation, could not avoid giving to Shakspere's birthplace its present holiday appearance; but how often is the artistic eye offended by seeing a fine old building vulgarised by restorers! ... Perhaps a few years' exposure to the weather may tone down the 'neat' look of the house in Henley Street.

The architect himself was wary of relying on modern replicas. Years later, when delivering a lecture to the Royal Academy, Barry conceded that modern imitations of original features on historic buildings, especially when unmarked and thus allowed to pass silently as authentic, were but an 'elaborate forgery'. Yet there was no way to make the Birthplace look as it did in Shakespeare's time without substituting new works for old, without scraping and polishing, without staining and varnishing. Otherwise, you were left with the bare ruin of a house, a melancholy edifice that, while pleasing preservationists like the vicar of Childeritch, or the sagacious John Ruskin himself, would defeat the purpose of celebrating and commemorating Shakespeare. Ay, there's the rub!

'To my loving good friend'

Before the restoration works started, the only parts of the Birthplace shown to the public were the upstairs birthroom, the back kitchen and the former butcher's shop. The custodian's residence on one side (where for many years the Harts had lived) was then strictly private, while, on the other side, the Swan and Maidenhead Inn remained open to the public, but as a tavern not a Shakespeare tourist site. Edward Barry's plan, which has never been reversed, was to merge these three distinct segments into a unified whole, bestowing upon the entire property a conjoined grandeur, an amalgamated heft, that it had previously lacked.

The Swan and Maidenhead's brick frontage was removed to reveal part of the Tudor half-timber façade, which blended easily with the rest of the house's exterior, much of its timber being original and so gave the whole property a seamless appearance along Henley Street. It then looked, and still does look, as if it were one building, not three.

The same unifying principle was applied to the house's interior, with modifications mostly limited to what was needed to turn the cottage, the butcher's shop and the pub into a single structure. To link the different parts of the house, a new staircase was built in the middle, a downstairs partition wall and fireplace were removed from the Swan and Maidenhead Inn, while an oak side door (the one through which visitors today enter) was added to what had been the custodian's tiny cottage. Upstairs, in the area opposite the birthroom, the wattle-and-daub infill was removed from between the timber frames to create an airy, open space. The walls were never put back; and the light-filled rooms with whitewashed floors are still used for displaying historical artefacts about Shakespeare and his birthplace, including those scratched windowpanes bearing the signatures of so many visitors from long ago. Timber beams were repaired throughout, sagging floorboards reinforced with iron laths and old plasterwork made good. The result was, for most visitors, a convincing impression of a large and well-maintained Elizabethan house, rendering invisible its actual history as three different structures with three different purposes.

But a house is not a home. The restored Birthplace presented itself to the public as a formal museum and not as the place where William Shakespeare was born and raised. In years prior, the birthroom, denied adornment and refused its domestic purpose, focused all attention on the large white bust of Shakespeare set on a rickety table against the back wall. The restoration works preserved this air of sacred austerity and then extended it throughout the house. Gone was the Swan and Maidenhead Inn, its noisy conviviality replaced by the hushed reverence of a museum and library, those twin pillars of cultural respectability that signalled the Birthplace's worth and value. In the open loft near the birthroom were exhibited the artefacts and documents collected by the late Robert Bell Wheler, the esteemed Stratford local historian, and donated by his sister. One of them was the only surviving letter addressed to Shakespeare – 'To my Loveinge good ffrend & contreymann Mr. Wm Shackespere' – written by Stratford resident Richard Quiney on 25 October 1598. It survived because it was never delivered into Shakespeare's hands and so remained with Quiney's papers. Robert Bell Wheler had 'borrowed' the letter when working in the Corporation of Stratford archives and never troubled himself to return it. Those were the days.

'Rules and regulations'

Such was the controlling intent of the trustees 'to make such rules and regulations for the government, protection and preservation of the said house'. Their stewardship of the Birthplace was formalized in 1891 when a special Act of Parliament incorporated the Shakespeare Birthplace Trust. This independent charity continues to exercise its custodial role, which now extends to other Shakespeare sites in and around Stratford, including New Place, Hall's Croft and Anne Hathaway's Cottage. The signs of the Victorian times certainly called for regulations and rules. After several years of prudent restoration, the Birthplace reinvented itself as an official museum and library. In 1873, the first librarian, Charles Jackman, was appointed to look after the new and growing collection of documents and artefacts relating to Shakespeare's life and times. All visitors were looked after by the sisters Chataway.

More visitors than ever arrived at the Birthplace – by the 1860s, more than six thousand people a year – now that Stratford had joined Britain's rail network as a branch of the popular London to Birmingham line. Affordable fares, no more than a penny a mile, were offered on all train routes, thus putting Stratford and many other destinations all within easy reach of working-class travellers. By the 1890s, tourists arriving at the town's railway station found horse-drawn coaches waiting to take them to the Birthplace, Holy Trinity Church or the Shakespeare Memorial Theatre. Built on the banks of the Avon in 1879, and since then twice remodelled, the theatre is now home to the Royal Shakespeare Company. By the first decade of the twentieth century, visitors could see all the sites of Stratford from the relative discomfort of a motorcar, slowing down for a good look but never actually having to stop and get out, walk around or go anywhere inside. The age of hurried, perfunctory tourism had arrived.

It was all so different from George Vertue's casual visit to the Birthplace back in 1737, when he struck up a conversation with Shakespeare Hart himself. Or Washington Irving, in the early nineteenth century, watching

Mary Hornby in action three times before capturing her in print. Or even Phineas T. Barnum, the huckster who threatened to dismantle the Birthplace and ship it to New York City, laughing and blustering his way through the house in the 1840s. Now, it was all a question of what the Trust, in exercising its sober fiduciary responsibility, 'thought proper'. The Trustees spent a great deal of time bickering over which documents to collect, where to store them, how to catalogue them and how much to study them. 'Old documents', they finally decided, 'cannot, as a rule, be satisfactorily catalogued until every word in them has been carefully read.' Such fastidious academic concerns never bothered Shakespeare Hart, who gladly showed to George Vertue a legitimate copy of his legendary namesake's will.

'It will not harm the visitor to accept it'

Ironically, the new museum displayed its share of doubtful relics, although nothing close to what the scheming Mary Hornby had exhibited in the house at the beginning of the nineteenth century. In her time, anyone was welcome to sit upon and occasionally to depart with a sliver from the chair allegedly carved from Shakespeare's mulberry tree. More restraint prevailed in the 1860s: visitors were permitted to look at, but not touch, a desk purporting to be the one that Shakespeare used at the town grammar school and a gold signet ring (unearthed half a century earlier from a field near Holy Trinity Church) on whose decorative bezel the engraved confirmatory initials – 'W.S.' – were entwined in a true lovers' knot. The desk, of uncertain age, but which had definitely been in the town's grammar school, was donated in 1863. Robert Bell Wheler had bought the signet ring for thirty-six shillings; after his death, his sister gave it to the Birthplace. Although the desk was an imposture, the gold signet ring, still in the collection of the Shakespeare Birthplace Trust, was possibly genuine. 'It may have belonged to Shakespeare', William Winter informed the American readers of *Harper's Magazine* in May 1879. 'It will not harm the visitor to accept it.' Indeed, ever since the ring was discovered, in 1810, town folklore insisted not only that it belonged to Shakespeare but that he had lost it while mourning the death of his only son, Hamnet, who in 1596 was laid to rest in the churchyard.

Whether the items were genuine relics or counterfeit presentments mattered less than the effect they had upon the viewer. Upon first impression, the desk and the ring come across as highly personal objects: Shakespeare the boy sat *there*, Shakespeare the man wore *this*. But if we think about how those objects were first used, we can see how they place Shakespeare not in the confining comforts of home but actually in the public realm and the wider world. The desk on display, even if it were genuine, would never have been found in the house on Henley Street. It belonged rather on Church Street, in the King's New School. Seated at his grammar school desk, Shakespeare the boy acquired his small Latin and less Greek, read plays for the first time and likely first realized his gift for language and literature. Though the desk had been imported, so to speak, into the Birthplace, it still conjured in the visitor's mind an image of young William Shakespeare being *somewhere else* – at school – the place where he discovered poetry and drama and so felt his future in the instant.

The ornamental signet ring, no mere piece of jewellery, was used originally to brand a letter or a document's wax seal with its authenticating initials. When the ring's bezel was pressed into warm wax, the imprint would take and remain visible in the hardened seal, bearing true and durable witness that 'W.S.' (whoever that actually was) had written, dictated or sanctioned the words on the page. The letters on the ring were reversed, so that they would appear correctly in the wax imprint. Here, again, the private object escorts Shakespeare from his home into the public realm: no longer a schoolboy, but now a man active in worldly affairs, someone who writes confidential letters, draws up legal documents and keeps business records. Someone busy and important enough to wear on his thumb or index finger a gold signet ring.

The only assuredly genuine relic, the tiny letter from Richard Quiney to William Shakespeare, measuring just three inches long and two inches wide, was encased between sheets of glass and covered with a cloth to prevent sunlight from fading the ink. Visitors were allowed a glimpse, but not long enough to read it. Even if they had been permitted more time, it's still doubtful that they could read the letter because it was written in the distinctive Elizabethan script called 'secretary hand'. It's a standardized form of writing widely used at the time, but whose loops, flourishes and archaic spellings would in later centuries defeat most readers. Fret not, for Miss Caroline Chataway, younger of the sister-custodians, gladly recited it by heart to all beseeching visitors, her 'fervent spirit' and the letter's 'quaint phraseology', so reported William Winter, mingling to give her performance 'a delicious old-fashioned flavor'.

The epistolary contents were, however, unappetizingly prosaic. Quiney, a Stratford alderman, journeyed to London to ask William Shakespeare for a loan of thirty pounds; not for himself, but to help the town pay its accumulated debts. He wrote the letter when staying at the Bell Inn in Carter Lane, a neighbourhood in the heart of the City of London, near where Shakespeare lived and worked. Famously, it was never delivered; likely because Quiney ran into the letter's recipient at or near the Bell Inn before he could dispatch it. Whatever the story's precise sequence, all its action takes place in London. Yet again, an object on display in the Birthplace redirected attention *away* from the Birthplace, inviting visitors to focus instead on a Shakespeare who was always somewhere else.

'W.S.'

And so, what the restored Birthplace never did restore was Shakespeare at home. He was always missing, not so much hiding as busy somewhere else.

At the grammar school in Church Street, reading Horace and Seneca. At New Place, signing and (with that gold ring?) sealing property deeds. At Holy Trinity Church, grieving over his son's premature death. Or in London, writing plays for the Lord Chamberlain's Men and being asked by a friend for a loan. Little wonder, then, that the Birthplace, having finally become a museum, a repository (not always trustworthy) of documentary and material history, forgot that it had ever been Shakespeare's home.

Indeed, once restored, the Birthplace no longer looked like a home; no longer was a home. It was not decorated, as it is now, in an Elizabethan style, with painted and stencilled cloths hanging on the walls, a four-poster bed dominating the birthroom and the tools of the glover's trade – aprons hanging on wooden pegs, knives laid carefully out on the worktable, animal hides stretched on racks – close to hand in John Shakespeare's recreated workshop. The everyday possessions listed in so many Elizabethan household inventories, from green bolster pillows to yellow tablecloths, and from joint stools to copper kitchen pots, were oddly missing from the scene. Not until the 1940s, nearly a century after the house was first restored, did the Birthplace present itself as Shakespeare's family home, an agreeable simulation effect that it strives for still today, now enhanced by the presence of genial guides in period costume.

Photographs taken at the Birthplace in 1864, after the initial restoration works finished, show a house with little furniture, apart from the random side table or spindly chair pushed up against the walls, leaving the rooms uncluttered as visitors wandered upstairs to the birthroom, over to the museum on the other side of the landing and then back downstairs for a last look at the front hall and back kitchen hearth before heading outside for a stroll in the manicured garden. The cold bleakness of the nearly empty birthroom easily overpowered the dainty decorative pelmet that hung so absurdly over the front window, a last vestige of an otherwise erased domesticity.

Perhaps it's the rudimentary aspect of on-site photography – in the 1860s most photographs were taken in studios – but I can't help feeling that these images lend stark credence to a theme that had been quietly emerging in travelogues, in journalism and in letters written and diaries kept by sundry tourists: the Birthplace had lost its charm. A quirky, lively home once overflowing with dubious relics – a tourist trap, yes, but one of enchantment and warm delight – had grown cold and pale. What had once been a playful encounter with hoaxes and frauds, provided that, like Washington Irving, you suspended your disbelief, had converted into a solemn shrine to a distant deity. Shakespeare the godhead was gone, but his ghostly icon remained: the large white bust displayed in the birthroom, a holy image compelling silent adoration. The Victorians were nothing if not steadfast in their devotion to the Bard of Avon; and in the restored Birthplace they found – no, created – the hallowed space where their sanctified rituals of Bardolatry could be observed; but observed with finicky reverence, not reckless joy. The age of romance was over and dull modernity loomed on the horizon.

'He won't come back'

In 1891, after just two years in the job, Joseph Skipsey resigned as the Birthplace's custodian, fed up with pretending that the relics were genuine and tired of feeding nonsense to hungry gullible tourists, especially the Americans who expected him to play the charismatic showman. After resigning he wrote a secret letter, which remained sealed during his lifetime, declaring that the 'so-called tradition and legends' of the Birthplace were 'an abomination and must stink in the nostrils of every true lover of our divine poet'. Although Skipsey was himself a poet, best known for his ballad 'The Hartley Calamity', composed after 204 men and boys died in a coal mining accident in 1862, he took a strictly literal approach to his role as custodian of the house where Shakespeare was born. There, he believed, poetic licence was never to be welcomed.

When the letter was made public in 1903, after Skipsey's death, it captured the attention of Henry James, whose story 'The Birthplace' was published just a few months later. In the story, Joseph Skipsey becomes Morris Gedge, the fictional, but equally tormented, custodian of what is clearly meant to be Shakespeare's birthplace. Yet instead of resigning in frustration, Gedge resolves to perform his 'showman's song' with more gusto than ever, half-hoping that the sheer extravagance of his deceit would be its own betrayal. Henceforth, he would be so shameless in his performance, so unscrupulous in choosing his words – 'if we could look close enough, we should find the hearth stone scraped with His little feet' – that the pilgrims gathered so attentively around him would surely get wise to his scam. But his audience laps it up, more visitors than ever line up outside the door and the house's coffers overflow with coinage in unexpected abundance. The show's a hit. Gedge, to his astonishment, is rewarded with a higher salary for telling tall tales with the straightest of faces.

James's story, like the events that inspired it, is usually read as a critique of claims that Shakespeare's Birthplace is historically authentic, whether that be in its architecture, its collection or it legends, and therefore capable of delivering us into the very presence of the great author himself. That is, after all, what an author's house museum promises to do.

But I wonder if we haven't somewhat misperceived the story's emphasis. The real issue, it seems to me, isn't the house's authenticity but rather our insistent hunger for it. Visitors crowd to gaze upon the spurious relics and, like children clamouring for a favourite bedtime story, without the telling of which they cannot rest, demand to hear falsities recited to them with the utmost gravity. 'They want everything', Gedge complained to his wife. And the reason they want everything, such reason being but half-understood, and begrudgingly conceded, is that they know, deep down, there is nothing here on offer. The true object of their desire, Shakespeare himself, escaped long ago like a fugitive into the night's darkness, never to be glimpsed again, let alone recaptured. 'People pretend to catch Him like a flown canary and put Him back in the cage', one canny visitor admits to Gedge. 'He won't *go* back; he won't *come* back.' That's the grown-up moral of James's story. The moral that a reverential posterity has done its level best to deny, downplay and altogether distance itself from.

Epilogue: 'Memorials of the Marvellous Man'

The young English painter Henry Wallis scored a personal triumph in 1854 when three of his canvases, each on a Shakespearean theme, were exhibited at the prestigious Royal Academy in London. They were 'The Font in which Shakespeare was Christened', 'The Room in which Shakespeare was Born' and 'Shakespeare's House, Stratford upon Avon'. As Nicola Watson writes, all three paintings 'meditate on Shakespeare's increasing status as national genius'. What gave these watercolours their meditative feel was that no people and few objects appeared in them. All three depicted vacant yet implicitly intentional spaces: a baptismal font, the birthroom, a twisting staircase.

Who would redeem all that emptiness? Who would lend their active intention? Perhaps it was meant to be us, the onlookers, who could through our imagination insert ourselves into the space that was waiting for us to occupy it; that had been created for that very purpose.

Such an invitation feels implicit in Wallis's painting of the empty back staircase, the winding narrow passage lit only by a small, high window. Like the accompanying painting of the birthroom, the room to which the stairs lead (but only indirectly), the image is cold and austere. Yet because it shows a staircase, the picture suggests movement: taking the first step, and then a few more, until reaching the top of the turning stairs, just beyond the picture's edge. Now, we contemplate the end of the pilgrim's path, those final few strides in the long, questing journey to the Birthplace, the journey in search of Shakespeare that terminates in the room where his life started. Yet such is the genius of Wallis's image that the very desolation of the path calls into question the ardour of those who commit themselves to following it. Was it worth all the effort to reach the Birthplace? What, after all, was there to see? In a final irony, unbeknownst, perhaps, to the artist himself, the staircase depicted in the painting was built decades after Shakespeare had lived in the house. It was a staircase he never climbed.

Sir Edwin Landseer, famed for sculpting the four bronze lions at the foot of Nelson's Column in Trafalgar Square, objected to Wallis's painted staircase. Not because the actual staircase dated from after the time when William Shakespeare resided in Henley Street; but because the depicted staircase was barren. He asked his friend John Forster, in whose dining room the painting first hung – Forster had a personal stake in the Birthplace, having chaired the London committee that bought it at the 1847 auction – for permission to make a few changes. Forster consented, as did Wallis himself, and Landseer set about altering the canvas.

When the retouched version was exhibited in 1867 it was accompanied by a facsimile of a letter from Forster to Landseer, congratulating the second painter for adding 'memorials of the marvellous man himself'. He meant, of course, the William Shakespeare who does not appear on the staircase that he never climbed. What do appear, instead, are potent signs and symbols of him, the traces left behind of his life and works. The faithful spaniel waits for the absent master at the now-opened door. The wall-mounted breastplate and circular shield recall the armour-clad ghost of Hamlet's father, the role tradition claims had been acted first by the author himself. The spade leaning against the doorframe belongs to the same play's two gravediggers. The single glove draped over a lower step evokes Shakespeare's father, whose workshop was in the next room over. Perhaps we are meant to think also of the missing glove – like twins, gloves come in pairs – and call to our minds Shakespeare's grief over the early death of his only son, Hamnet, twin brother to Judith. Signs in varied abundance of William Shakespeare, the family man from Stratford who found fame and wealth in London. Yet still, no sight of him.

And then, there's the skull. The most famous skull in the history of Western drama. The one turned up by the gravediggers as they made room in the ground for Ophelia's fresh corpse. They tell Hamlet that it's the remains of Yorick, his father's court jester, dead and buried for some twenty-three years. Reconnecting the bones to the flesh that once covered them, Hamlet recalls a fellow of infinite jest, of most excellent fancy, who befriended him as a boy. Holding the freshly unearthed skull in his hands, Hamlet the man reflects on the death and decay that await all mortal beings, be they kings or clowns, princes or gravediggers, murderers or avengers. This was the dramatic moment that Landseer doubtless sought to evoke in the viewer's mind when he chose to place a skull on the stairs.

Yet I believe that this *memento mori* tells another tale. As we imagine ourselves about to climb the stairs to reach, eventually, the birthroom, we might also imagine that we pause to pet the dog at the door, inspect the armour on the wall or even retrieve the glove dropped on the floor. No sooner do we take our first step than we stumble over the skull blocking our way. Like Hamlet, we might pick it up, reflecting, as did he, on death the great leveller. Perhaps we hear inside our head Shakespeare's own words sung hauntingly in *Cymbeline* over the corpses of Cloten and Fidele: 'Golden lads and girls all must / As chimney-sweepers, come to dust' (4.2.261–2). Fidele turns out to be the heroine Imogen disguised as a boy and very much alive. Though the Birthplace, in its name, speaks the arrival of bawling new life, it feels, as William Winter recalled, as 'hushed as death'. No one, in this scene of 'mystical desolation', rises from the grave. As we behold the decaying skull, turning it slowly over in our hands, we realize that we are mourning over Shakespeare's own death. His the skull, ours the grief.

Forster, after setting eyes on the repainted painting, chose his words carefully in his letter to Sir Edwin, praising the artist for his 'memorials' to Shakespeare. In other words, signs of his death. For what is a memorial but a lasting tribute to the dead? That winding set of stairs, like the one taken by Friar Laurence at the end of *Romeo and Juliet*, delivers us not to a birthroom, but to a burial chamber. Alas, poor Shakespeare.

That Shakespeare is dead – the skull on the stairs – ought to come as no surprise. Because episodes of disappearance and loss colour much of what we know, and what we don't know, about him. The glover's son from Stratford-upon-Avon drops out of the historical record in 1585 and does not reappear until 1592 – the so-called 'lost years' – when he pops up in London, a hundred miles away, satirized as the 'upstart crow' of the late-Elizabethan theatrical world. If the First Folio had never been printed, and it was far from certain in 1623 that so expensive a work would be printed, then our knowledge of Shakespearean drama would be cut in half, because eighteen of the plays in that large volume had not previously been published. And just how much time did he really spend in Stratford once his playwriting career took off? The imponderables are truly imponderable.

Writing this book has taught me that instead of regretting all the ways in which Shakespeare is lost to us, we actually do prefer it that way. We prefer a Shakespeare who is lost; not wholly, not irretrievably, but just enough to let us play our part in recovering him. Because when we go out searching for Shakespeare we can be pretty confident that we will find the Shakespeare we seek. Like those Victorians who remodelled the Birthplace to make it convey their own exalted view of the playwright, we, too, are always making him our contemporary. Shakespeare conforms to *us*, not the other way around, because we make him do it. That's what the Birthplace taught me. Which is another way of saying, although for a radically different set of reasons than Ben Jonson had in mind when he composed his prefatory verse to the First Folio, that Shakespeare is 'not of an age, but for all time'.

BIBLIOGRAPHIC ESSAY

The literature on Shakespeare and Stratford-upon-Avon is vast. Spanning several centuries, it embraces everything from academic monographs based on primary and archival research to more resolutely popular genres like biography and travelogue. A full survey of these works lies beyond the scope and the purpose of this book. What follows, instead, is an account of the varied materials that I have consulted in my own research and writing – books, manuscripts, letters, newspaper and magazine articles, drawings, pictures and engravings – so that anyone who wishes to follow up on these sources can do so.

Readers interested in works devoted entirely or substantially to Shakespeare's Birthplace and Stratford-upon-Avon are well advised to start in the nineteenth century, when such works, invariably addressed to a popular readership, were first written. Chief among them and in chronological order are: Robert Bell Wheler, *An Historical Account of the Birth-Place of Shakespeare* (Stratford-upon-Avon: J. Ward, 1824), William Rider, *Views in Stratford-upon-Avon and its Vicinity* (Warwick and Leamington: J. Merridew, 1828), F.W. Fairholt, *The Home of Shakspere Illustrated and Described* (London: Chapman and Hall, 1847), Charles Vaughan Grinfield, *A Pilgrimage to Stratford-upon-Avon, The Birthplace of Shakspeare* (London, 1850), George Markham Tweddell, *Shakespeare: His Times and Contemporaries* (Bury, 1861), John R. Wise, *Shakspere: His Birthplace and Its Neighbourhood* (London, 1861), Rev J.M. Jephson, *Shakespere: His Birthplace, Home, and Grave* (London, 1864), Samuel Neil, *The Home of Shakespeare* (Warwick: H.T. Cooke, 1871), Charles Roach Smith, *Remarks on Shakespeare, his Birthplace, Etc.* (London: George Bell and Sons, 1877), Joseph Hill, *Shakespeare's Birthplace and Adjoining Properties* (Stratford-upon-Avon: n.p., 1885), Sidney Lee, *Stratford-on-Avon from the Earliest Times to the Death of Shakespeare*, new edn. (London: Seeley & Co, 1890), Emma Marshall, *Shakespeare and his Birthplace* (London: E Nister, 1890), W. Salt Brassington, *Shakespeare's Homeland* (London: J.M. Dent, 1903), and Henry C. Shelley, *Shakespeare & Stratford* (New York: Little, Brown, 1915).

In the twentieth century, the publication of book-length works on the topic declined dramatically, reflecting both a saturated market in touristic accounts of Shakespeare and Stratford and a growing awareness that the 'Shakespeare trade', the 'Shakespeare industry' and 'Bard biz', as the money-making apparatus of Shakespeare heritage sites has been variously called, was itself a legitimate topic of critical scrutiny. Although the 'humbug' of Shakespeare worship had been ridiculed in the Victorian era it was not until the twentieth century that it became fully possible to write about Shakespeare and Stratford with an appropriately detached scepticism and ever-increasing amounts of irony.

A pioneering text in this regard is Ivor John Carnegie Brown and George Fearon's *Amazing Monument: A Short History of The Shakespeare Industry* (London: W. Heinemann, 1939). In a more academic vein, its successor works include *The Shakespeare Myth*, ed. Graham Holderness (Manchester: Manchester University Press, 1988) and Barbara Hodgdon, *The Shakespeare Trade* (Philadelphia: University of Pennsylvania Press, 1998). At the same time, scholars like Levi Fox, a former Director of the Shakespeare Birthplace Trust, continued to offer expert documentary accounts of the Birthplace's history. See, for example, his essay 'The Heritage of Shakespeare's Birthplace' in *Shakespeare Survey* (1948). Julia Thomas's *Shakespeare's Shrine: The Bard's Birthplace and the Invention of Stratford-upon-Avon* (Philadelphia: University of Pennsylvania Press, 2012) is a serious academic study of the Birthplace and the town of Stratford-upon-Avon in the Victorian period. Her book intersects productively with my own.

Where I refer to particular facts or circumstances in Shakespeare's life I have relied upon the standard documentary sources: E.K. Chambers, *William Shakespeare: Facts and Problems*, 2 vols (Oxford: Clarendon Press, 1930), Samuel Schoenbaum, *William Shakespeare: A Documentary Life* (Oxford: Oxford University Press, 1975) and the same author's *William Shakespeare: Records and Images* (London: Scolar Press, 1981). An earlier work, James Orchard Halliwell-Phillipps' *Outlines of the Life of Shakespeare* (London: Longmans, Green & Co, 1881), has also been useful. Quotations from the poems and plays, except for references to the First Folio, are taken from *William Shakespeare: Complete Works*, eds Richard Proudfoot, Ann Thompson, David Scott Kastan and H.R. Woudhuysen (London: Arden Shakespeare, 2021).

Prologue

In developing my theme on the symbolic value of Shakespeare's house, I have been much indebted to works on the phenomenology and philosophy of domestic space, most especially Gaston Bachelard's *The Poetics of Space* (London: Orion Press, 1964) and Witold Rybczynski's *Home: A Short History of an Idea* (New York: Viking, 1988). More recent works on houses, homes and our fascination with them that have influenced my thinking include Julie Myerson's *Home: A History of Everyone Who Ever Lived in Our House* (London: Harper, 2005), Bill Bryson's *At Home: A Short History of Private Life* (London: Penguin, 2011) and Lucy Worsley's *If Walls Could Talk: An Intimate History of the Home* (London: Faber & Faber, 2012).

Academic works on the subject of authors' homes have also been greatly helpful. Chief among them include Nicola J. Watson's superb *The Author's Effects: On Writer's House Museums* (Oxford: Oxford University Press, 2020), Simon Goldhill's wryly insightful *Freud's Couch, Scott's Buttocks, Brontë's Grave* (Chicago: University of Chicago Press, 2011), Aaron Santesso's 'The Birth of the Birthplace: Bread Street and Literary Tourism before Stratford', *ELH: English Literary History* (2004), *Writers' Houses and the Making of Memory*, ed. Harald Hendrix (New York: Routledge, 2008), *Literary Tourism and Nineteenth-Century Culture*, ed. Nicola J. Watson (Basingstoke: Palgrave, 2009) and *Lives of Houses*, eds Kate Kennedy and Hermione Lee (Princeton: Princeton University Press, 2020). These works have influenced at every level my approach to writing the history of Shakespeare's Birthplace.

Chapters 1 and 2

In the account of Shakespeare's grandfather and father, I have relied on, apart from the documentary records compiled by Chambers and Schoenbaum (see above), some important recent Shakespeare biographies: Park Honan, *Shakespeare: A Life* (Oxford: Oxford University Press, 1998), Stephen Greenblatt, *Will in the World* (New York: Norton, 2005), René Weis, *Shakespeare Revealed: A Biography* (London: John Murray, 2007) and Jonathan Bate, *Soul of the Age* (London: Viking, 2009). David Bevington's *Shakespeare and Biography* (Oxford: Oxford University Press, 2010) is a compact but deeply learned account of the history of Shakespeare biography. Lena Cowen Orlin's *The Private Life of William Shakespeare* (Oxford: Oxford University Press, 2021) contains much new documentary material on John Shakespeare. See also the impressive online database 'Shakespeare Documented', maintained by the Folger Shakespeare Library.

For the history of Stratford, I have relied upon Robert Bell Wheler, *History and Antiquities of Stratford-upon-Avon* (Stratford-upon-Avon: J. Ward, 1806), Charles Isaac Elton, *William Shakespeare: His Family and Friends* (London: John Murray, 1904), Levi Fox, *Borough Town of Stratford-upon-Avon* (Stratford-upon-Avon: Corporation of Stratford-upon-Avon, 1953), Mark Eccles, *Shakespeare in Warwickshire* (Madison: University of Wisconsin Press, 1961), Robert Bearman, ed. *The History of an English Borough: Stratford-upon-Avon 1196–1996* (Stroud: Sutton Publishing, 1997) and Schoenbaum, *Documentary Life* (1975). John Leland's *Itinerary*, written in manuscript for Henry VIII, and from which I have quoted, may be easily consulted in a modern edition: *John Leland's 'Itinerary': Travels in Tudor England*, ed. John Chandler (Stroud: Sutton Publishing, 1993). On references in Stratford records to Shakespeare and his family, see *Minutes and Accounts of the Corporation of Stratford-upon-Avon and Other Records 1553–1620*, eds Richard Savage and Edgar I. Fripp, vol. 4 (Oxford: Clarendon Press,

1930) and Robert Bearman, *Shakespeare in the Stratford Records* (Phoenix Mill: Sutton Publishing, 1994). The court document regarding the fine levied upon John Shakespeare in 1552 does not specify that he then lived in Henley Street although that is the obvious implication. He would hardly have carted his refuse from a dwelling somewhere else only to dump it illegally by the side of the road when there was a legal compost heap at the end of the same street. The legal document regarding John Shakespeare's fine was first printed in Joseph Hunter's *New Illustrations of the Life, Studies, and Writings of Shakespeare* 2 vols. (London: J.B. Nichols and Son, 1845).

For the evolution of British domestic architecture in the early modern periods, see W.G. Hoskins, 'The Rebuilding of Rural England, 1570–1640', *Past and Present* 4 (1953): 44–59, Ralph Dutton, *The English Interior 1500 to 1900* (London: B.T. Batsford, 1948), John Summerson, *Architecture in Britain 1530 to 1830* (New Haven: Yale University Press, 1953), Maurice William Barley, *Houses & History* (London: Faber & Faber, 1987), *British Architectural Theory 1540–1750*, ed. Caroline van Eck (Burlington, VT: Ashgate, 2003), Paula Henderson, *The Tudor House and Garden* (New Haven: Yale University Press, 2005) and Maurice Howard, *The Building of Elizabethan and Jacobean England* (New Haven: Yale University Press, 2007). A modern facsimile of Andrew Boorde's *The boke for to lerne a man to be wyse in buyldyng of his house* (London, 1540) can be found in the 1971 DaCapo Press edition of his *The breviary of helthe*.

For John Shakespeare's neighbours in Henley Street, see Chambers, *Facts and Problems*, Schoenbaum, *Documentary Life*, Bearman, *Shakespeare in the Stratford Records* and Kate Emery Pogue, *Shakespeare's Family* (Westport, CT: Prager, 2008).

Chapters 3 and 4

Anyone studying the material and ideological aspects of Elizabethan domestic life will find immense value in the work of Lena Cowen Orlin. Her insights have helped me to build up my argument about what 'house' and 'home' would have meant to William Shakespeare the boy and the man. In particular, Orlin's richly informative anthology *Elizabethan Households* (Washington, DC: Folger Shakespeare Library, 1995), derived from an exhibition of the same name that she curated at the Folger, guided me towards important primary texts.

The core primary sources that I have drawn upon in this chapter – namely, Elizabethan domestic advice manuals – are rare in their original editions but are all available in modern print or electronic versions. William Harrison's 'An Historicall Description of the Land of Britaine' can be found in an edition published by the Folger under the title *The Description of England: The Classic Contemporary Account of Tudor Social Life*. A facsimile edition of Henry Wotton's *The Elements of Architecture* was published in 1970 by the DaCapo Press. A facsimile of *The Rich Cabinet Furnished with Varietie of Excellent Discriptions* was published in 1972, also by the Da Capo Press. John Dod and Robert Cleaver's *A Godlie Forme of Householde Government* has not been reprinted but is available electronically through Early English Books Online (EEBO). Valerie Wayne's scholarly edition of Edmund Tilney's *A Briefe and Pleasant Discourse of Duties in Mariage* was published in 1992 by Cornell University Press.

My discussion of the patriarchal structure of Tudor domestic life, and how that would have been manifested in Shakespeare's childhood, has profited from, in addition to the above-referenced primary sources, Orlin's *Elizabethan Households* and Matthew Johnson's *English Houses 1300– 1800: Vernacular Architecture, Social Life* (London: Routledge, 2010). See also Delia Garratt and Tara Hamling's beautifully illustrated volume *Shakespeare and the Stuff of Life: Treasures from the Shakespeare Birthplace Trust* (London: Arden Shakespeare, 2016), Jeanne Jones's *Family Life in Shakespeare's England: Stratford-upon-Avon 1570–1630* (Stroud: Sutton Publishing Ltd, 1996), Katherine Scheil's edited collection *Shakespeare & Stratford* (New York and Oxford: Berghahn, 2019) and Jane Shuter's *Visiting the Past: Shakespeare's Birthplace* (Oxford: Heinemann Library, 2002). In these chapters, as indeed throughout the book, I have relied upon Chambers and Schoenbaum for the specifics of key events in Shakespeare's life, especially the family's attempts to secure a coat of arms. For her insightful readings of how domestic objects and physical spaces operate in Shakespeare's plays, I am indebted to Catherine Richardson's richly informed *Shakespeare & Material Culture* (Oxford: Oxford University Press, 2011).

I have learned much about the material history of the Birthplace and its environs from Roz Sklar, former Acting Head of Collections at the Shakespeare Birthplace Trust. She also kindly shared with me Nicholas Molyneux's superb architectural and historical report on the Birthplace (1997, revised 2004) commissioned by the Shakespeare Birthplace Trust.

Transcriptions of household inventories for John Shakespeare's neighbours in Stratford-upon-Avon in the late-sixteenth century can be found in James Orchard Halliwell-Phillipps' 'Old Stratford on Avon Inventories, 1576–1874', now in the Folger Shakespeare Library, ms. Z.e.10. The inventories for Henry Field and Anne Hiccox can be found in Folger ms. W.b.193. For the dramatization of the inventory of a deceased person's property, I am indebted to Johnson's *English Houses 1300–1800*.

As in the previous chapters, Orlin's research has been influential. Other helpful works addressing the themes of domesticity, private life and hospitality in Shakespeare's time – and in Shakespeare's plays – include Heather Dubrow, *Shakespeare and Domestic Loss* (Cambridge: Cambridge University Press, 1999), Natasha Korda, *Shakespeare's Domestic Economies* (Philadelphia: University of Pennsylvania Press, 2002), Wendy Wall, *Staging Domesticity* (Cambridge: Cambridge University Press, 2002); Geraldo U. deSousa, *At Home in Shakespeare's Tragedies* (Burlington, VT: Ashgate,

2010) and Emma Whipday, *Shakespeare's Domestic Tragedies* (Cambridge: Cambridge University Press, 2019). On masculinity and childhood, my thinking has been influenced by Gina Bloom's excellent essay '"Boy Eternal": Aging, Games, and Masculinity in *The Winter's Tale*', *English Literary Renaissance* 40.3 (November 2010). On the decoration and furnishings of Elizabethan homes I have drawn upon the works cited for Chapter 1.

Thomas Heywood's *A Curtaine Lecture* is available through EEBO, while extracts from it have frequently been included in textbook anthologies on Elizabethan and Jacobean social history. Caleb Dalechamp's *Christian Hospitalitie*, another rare text, is also available through EEBO.

On early modern theatrical activity in Stratford-upon-Avon, see J.R. Mulryne's 'Professional Players in the Guild Hall, Stratford-upon-Avon, 1568–1597', *Shakespeare Survey* 60 (2007), 1–22.

On the irresistible and insoluble question of the marriage between Anne Hathaway and William Shakespeare, I have drawn inspiration from Bate's *Soul of the Age*, Katherine Duncan-Jones, *Ungentle Shakespeare: Scenes from his Life* (London: Arden Shakespeare, 2001), Germaine Greer, *Shakespeare's Wife* (London: Harper, 2007), Katherine West Scheil's *Imagining Shakespeare's Wife: The Afterlife of Anne Hathaway* (Cambridge: Cambridge University Press, 2018) and my fellow participants in a lively seminar on 'Shakespeare and Biography' expertly convened by Jonathan Crewe of Dartmouth University for the 2012 meeting of the Shakespeare Association of America.

Chapters 5 and 6

The full title for the work commonly known as the First Folio is *Mr. William Shakespeares comedies, histories, & tragedies: published according to the true originall copies*. It was compiled by John Heminge and Henry Condell, friends of Shakespeare and his colleagues in the King's Men theatrical company. It was printed in London in 1623 by Isaac Jaggard and Edward Blount. About 228 copies have survived, nearly a third of which are in the Folger Shakespeare Library. The First Folio is an extremely well-known work, with facsimile and digital editions readily available. Its prefatory verses are routinely reprinted in editions of Shakespeare's plays and poems. For the editorial and publication history of the First Folio I have relied upon Peter W.M. Blayney, *The First Folio of Shakespeare* (Washington, DC: Folger, 1991) and Emma Smith, *Shakespeare's First Folio: Four Centuries of an Iconic Book* (Oxford: Oxford University Press, 2016).

Shakespeare's will, the contents of which were not publicly known for over a century after his death in 1616, is preserved in the National Archives in London. Transcriptions of it can be found in Chambers, *Facts and Problems* and Schoenbaum, *Documentary Life*. For the ownership of the Birthplace over the following two centuries, see 'Pedigree in the hand of

Robert Bell Wheler of the Shakespeare and Hart families of Stratford', 1813–14, Folger ms. S.b. 123. See also 'Register of wills and probates of the parish of Stratford-upon-Avon, Peculiar, 1699–1849', Folger ms. W.b.272. On the tenancy of the eastern portion of the Birthplace, see Jeanne E. Jones, 'Lewis Hiccox and Shakespeare's birthplace', *Notes and Queries* 41 (1994), 497–502. On the occasionally resurfacing controversy over whether Shakespeare was actually born in the house on Henley Street see Halliwell-Phillipps, *New Evidences in Confirmation of the Traditional Recognition of Shakespeare's Birth-Room A.D. 1769–1777* (Brighton: n.p., 1888).

A digital facsimile of William Dugdale's *The Antiquities of Warwickshire Illustrated* (1656) is available through EEBO. His comments on Shakespeare and the grave and funerary monument in Holy Trinity are routinely excerpted in Shakespeare biographies.

John Dowdall's letter to Mr Southwell, dated 10 April 1693, is in the Folger Shakespeare Library, ms. V.a.74.

On the rise of literary tourism in the eighteenth century, see Santesso, 'The Birth of the Birthplace'.

Nicholas Rowe's 1709 'Some Account of the Life, &c. of Mr. William Shakespear' has been reprinted several times in the modern era, mostly recently by Pallas Athene Publishers in 2009 to mark the 300th anniversary of the original edition. John Aubrey's *Brief Lives* (c. 1681) was not published until 1898. A Penguin paperback edition of this enduringly popular work is readily available. Charles Gildon's *The Lives and Characters of the English Dramatick Poets* (1699) is largely a reworking of Gerard Langbaine's *An Account of the English Dramatick Poets* (1691), the latter work available in a facsimile version printed in 1973 by Garland Publishers. Lewis Theobald's Preface to his *Works of Shakespeare: In Seven Volumes* (London: A. Bettesworth et al., 1733) was reprinted in facsimile by the University of California Press in 1949 in the Augustan Reprint Series. On the history of Shakespeare biography, see Bevington, *Shakespeare and Biography* and Schoenbaum, *Shakespeare's Lives* (Oxford: Oxford University Press, 1970 and 1991).

New Place, the Stratford home of the mature William Shakespeare, of which only the foundations remain, has been largely overshadowed by the Birthplace. One of the best purely factual accounts of the property, and one that I have turned to repeatedly, is James Orchard Halliwell-Phillipps, *An Historical Account of the New Place* (London: J. E. Adlard, 1864). Halliwell-Phillipps had a particular attachment to this property and was largely responsible for establishing a trust to purchase New Place in the early 1860s (ownership was transferred to the Shakespeare Birthplace Trust in 1872) and for conducting the first archaeological dig on the premises shortly thereafter. For recent scholarship, see Robert Bearman's masterful essay 'Shakespeare's Purchase of New Place', *Shakespeare Quarterly* 63.4 (Winter 2012), 465–86. On David Garrick and Charles Macklin's alleged visit to New Place, see Samuel Ireland's *Picturesque Views on the Warwickshire Avon* (London: R. Faulder and T. Egerton, 1795), Fairholt's *The Home of*

Shakspere, Halliwell-Phillipps' *Outlines of the Life of Shakespeare* and Christian Deelman's *The Great Shakespeare Jubilee* (London: Michael Joseph, 1964). George Vertue's sketch of New Place is in the British Library, MS Portland Loan 29/246, 1737. Reactions to the felling of the New Place mulberry tree are also found in Benjamin Victor's *History of the Theatres of London and Dublin* (London: G. Faulkner and J. Exhshaw, 1761). See also the testimony of the retired Stratford shoemaker Richard Grimmitt (b. 1682), 'Account of New Place by Joseph Greene, 1767', Folger ms. S.a.115. A fascinating collection of essays on the recent archaeological work conducted at the site is *Finding Shakespeare's New Place: An Archaeological Biography*, eds Paul Edmondson, Kevin Colls and William Mitchell (Manchester: Manchester University Press, 2016).

The original unpublished manuscript of Samuel Vince's 'A tour through part of England and North Wales in the summer of 1777' is Folger ms. M.a. 208. Original prints of Samuel Winter's 1759 map of Stratford-upon-Avon are held by the Shakespeare Birthplace Trust and the Folger Shakespeare Library. Richard Greene's watercolour of Shakespeare's Birthplace, made in 1762 and subsequently turned into a much-reprinted engraving, is now in the Folger Shakespeare Library, Art Vol. d75.

For accounts of the Birthplace during and immediately prior to the 1769 Shakespeare Jubilee, I have relied upon the following sources: 'Extract of a Letter from a Lady on a Journey at Stratford upon Avon in Warwickshire', *Gentleman's Magazine* (1760); 'Letter from the Place of Shakespear's Nativity', *British Magazine, or Monthly Repository for Gentlemen and Ladies* 3 (1762); 'The House in Stratford in which Shakspeare was born', engraving, *Gentleman's Magazine* 39 (July 1769); James Boswell, 'A Letter from James Boswell, Esq., on Shakespeare's Jubilee at Stratford-upon-Avon', *London Magazine* (September 1769); Samuel Richardson's continuation of Daniel Defoe's *A Tour Thro' the Whole Island of Great Britain* 4 vols (London: W. Strahan et al., 1769); David Garrick, *Ode upon Dedicating a Building and Erecting a Statue to Shakespeare* (London: T. Becket and P.A. De Hondt, 1769); James Solas Dodd, 'A Detail of the Whole Diversions of the Jubilee at Stratford Upon Avon', in *Essays and Poems, Satirical, Political, Moral and Entertaining* (Cork: Eugene Swiney, 1770) and Thomas Davies, *Memoirs of the Life of David Garrick* (London: T. Davies, 1780). On the alleged walnut tree at the Birthplace, see *The Annual Register. . .for the Year 1765* (London: J. Dodsley, 1784). The literature on the Shakespeare Jubilee is extensive but the best works are Deelman, *The Great Shakespeare Jubilee* and Michael Dobson, *The Making of the National Poet* (Oxford: Clarendon Press, 1993).

Chapters 7–9

For the general outline of the history and ownership of the Birthplace from the 1769 Shakespeare Jubilee to the 1847 auction I have relied upon Wheler's

Historical and Descriptive Account of the Birth-place of Shakspeare, Halliwell-Phillipps' *Outlines of the Life of* Shakespeare and Fox's essay 'The Heritage of Shakespeare's Birthplace'. Informative as these works are, I have found much more detailed – and more interesting – information in the archives of the Folger Shakespeare Library, which contain (1) the correspondence between the Hart family and their Stratford lawyer, Robert Wheler, between 1793 and 1806 (ms. W.a.62), (2) the receipts and rental notices of Mary Hornby, who leased the Birthplace from 1793 to 1820 (ms. Y.d.804), (3) 'Pedigree in the hand of Robert Bell Wheler of the Shakespeare and Hart families of Stratford' (ms. S.b.123), (4) 'Register of wills and probates of the parish of Stratford-upon-Avon, Peculiar, 1699–1849' (ms. W.b.272), (5) the draft conditions of the sale of the Birthplace by the Hart family in 1805 (ms. W.b.16), (6) Mary Hornby's announcement of her 'Genuine reliques of Shakespeare, the poet' (PR2932.H75 Cage) and (7) Jane Hart Iliff's 1822 'certificate of authenticity' for the relics owned by Mary Hornby (ms. Y.d.83).

At the Shakespeare Birthplace Trust, I have consulted (1) Edmond Malone's letters to John Jordan in the 1790s on the history of Shakespeare's family (ER1/15), (2) a scrapbook relating to the 1847 sale of the Birthplace (ER1/29) and (3) correspondence of Stratford town clerk William Oakes Hunt regarding the restoration of the Birthplace in the 1850s (ER1/45), including letters to and from the benefactor John Shakespear (TR46/1/114). These archival documents have added more detail to my account of the Birthplace's history than is normally found in secondary works.

Washington Irving's account of Mary Hornby can be found in his *The Sketchbook of Geoffrey Crayon, Gent.* (New York: C. S. Van Winkle, 1819–20), a book still in print. Nathaniel Hawthorne's description of the Birthplace can be found in his essay 'Recollections of a Gifted Woman', which first appeared in the *Atlantic Monthly* 11 (1863), 43–58. The essay later appeared in his book *Our Old Home: A Series of English Sketches* (Boston: Ticknor and Fields, 1866). The quotation from Mary Hornby's poetry is from her edited 'collection' *Extemporary Verses, Written at the Birth Place of Shakspeare, at Stratford-upon-Avon, by People of Genius* ... [Stratford: n.p., 1818]. See also J. Norris Brewster's *Histrionic Topography: or, the Birth-Places, Residences, and Funeral Monuments of the Most Distinguished Actors* (London: J. Cole, 1818) and Nathan Drake's *Shakspeare and His Times: Including the Biography of the Poet* (London: T. Cadell and W. Davies, 1817).

Samuel Ireland's illustration and depiction of the Birthplace can be found in his *Picturesque Views on the Warwickshire Avon*.

The scrapbooks of the Shakespeare scholar and collector James Orchard Halliwell-Phillipps, now in the Folger Shakespeare Library (ms. Y.d.1119–1414), contain a wealth of material that I have drawn upon in writing these chapters in particular. Scrapbook 72 (ms Y.d.1147), devoted to the Birthplace, includes various drawings and illustrations, cuttings from contemporary magazines and newspapers, a transcript of a letter dated 3 September 1795 from Thomas Hunt of Stratford-upon-Avon to Samuel Ireland (the original is British Library Add Ms 30,348, fol. 158) on the proposed sale of the house for £350, the architect Edward Barry's 1857 report on options for preservation and restoration of the Birthplace, correspondence between Halliwell-Phillipps and W.O Hunt (the latter a trustee of the Birthplace) at the time of the restoration work and a copy of Edmond Malone's letter on the Hart family's poverty. Many similar archival documents, including other Halliwell-Phillipps scrapbooks, can be found, not surprisingly, in the library at the Shakespeare Birthplace Trust. Robert Southey's proposal to aid the Hart family is found in his long essay *Colloquies on Society* (London: John Murray, 1824).

Chapters 10 and 11

On the auction of the Birthplace in 1847 my sources, almost entirely, have been contemporary periodicals and newspapers: the *Athenaeum*, *Bentley's Miscellany*, *Fraser's Magazine*, *Gentleman's Magazine*, *Howitt's Journal*, *Illustrated London News*, *The Penny Magazine*, *The People's Journal* and the *Spectator*. From these original materials, which I read in the University of London Library in Senate House, can be pieced together a week-by-week account of the campaign to rescue the Birthplace from falling into the hands of a private speculator and the activities undertaken subsequent to the sale to raise additional funds. For a contemporary account, see William Howitt, *Homes and Haunts of the Most Eminent British Poets* (London: Richard Bentley, 1847). An efficient summary of these events can also be found in Thomas, *Shakespeare's Shrine*.

The Shakespeare Birthplace Trust contains a wealth of memorabilia and journalistic accounts of the 1847 auction, including (1) Shakespeare Miscellanies, vol. 3 (ER1/112), (2) appeal for funds to purchase the Birthplace (ER25/3/29/5, TR46/1/41), (3) tickets for charity theatrical performances in aid of the fundraising appeal (ER25/3/29/6), (4) a copy of the conditions of sale and letter of sale, May 1847 (TR46/1/43), (5) the deed of conveyance of the Birthplace to the Stratford and London Committees (TR46/1/50) and (6) Robert Bell Wheler's correspondence relating to the sale, including with the Court family's trustee (TR46/1/81).

J. Stirling Coyne's play is *This House to be Sold; (The Property of William Shakspeare) Inquire Within* (London: National Acting Drama Office, 1847). On P.T. Barnum's interest in the Birthplace, I have relied upon Albert Smith, 'A Go-A-Head Day with Barnum', *Bentley's Miscellany* 21 (1847), 522–7; Barnum's *The Autobiography of P.T. Barnum* (London: Ward and Lock, 1854) and *Life of P.T. Barnum* (Buffalo, NY: Courier Company, 1886) and Mark Twain, *Following the Equator: A Journey Around the World* 2 vols (New York: American Publishing Company, 1897), 2:336ff.

Chapters 12 and 13

For the restoration of the Birthplace undertaken in the 1850s I have relied upon the primary materials cited above (especially those collected by Halliwell-Phillipps) and contemporary accounts such as J.M. Jephson's *Shakespere: His Birthplace, Home, and Grave* (London: Lovell, Reeve & Co., 1864). Additionally, I have consulted materials in the Shakespeare Birthplace Trust collection, including Edward Gibb's 1851 report on the Birthplace's exterior (TTDI/116), Edward Barry's 1857 report to the Trustees (ER1/45/3) and the 1857 contract for the restoration works (TTD1/116). Supplementary information can be found in Fox, 'The Heritage of Shakespeare's Birthplace' and Thomas, *Shakespeare's Shrine*.

To mark the 1864 Shakespeare Tercentenary, *All the Year Round* published a series of satiric accounts of the Birthplace and Stratford-upon-Avon, including 'The Sensational William' (12 February 1864), 'Shakespeare, Not a Man of Parts' and Andrew Halliday's 'Shakespeare Mad' (21 May 1864). For a scholarly account of these same events, see Richard Foulkes, *The Shakespeare Tercentenary of 1864* (London: Society for Theatre Research, 1984). On the Birthplace in the late-nineteenth century, after the restorations were completed, see William Winter, 'Shakespeare's Home', published in *Harper's Magazine* (May 1879) and *Shakespeare's England* (Boston: Joseph Knight Company, 1893).

Henry James's short story *The Birthplace* was first published in his collection *The Better Sort* (New York: Charles Scribner's Sons, 1903). A newspaper cutting about Joseph Skipsey's resignation as the Birthplace's custodian can be found at the Shakespeare Birthplace Trust (ER25/3/28/30).

On the institutional history of the Birthplace in the twentieth century, see Fox's *The Shakespeare Birthplace Trust: A Personal Memoir* (Stratford-upon-Avon: Shakespeare Birthplace Trust, 1997).

Epilogue

Henry Wallis' painting *Shakespeare's House* (*c.* 1854), as repainted by Sir Edwin Landseer, is now in the Victoria and Albert Museum in London; a digital copy can be seen on the V&A's website. The Shakespeare Birthplace Trust collection includes a copy of Wallis's painting before it was altered.

ACKNOWLEDGEMENTS

My greatest debt of thanks is to the Shakespeare Birthplace Trust and its staff for supporting this book and for making archival materials available to me. I wish particularly to thank Rosalyn Sklar, former Acting Head of Collections, for her commitment to this book, for sharing with me her deep knowledge of the Birthplace's history and for providing valuable feedback on a draft manuscript. This book is all the better for her timely interventions. Paul Edmondson, the Trust's Head of Research, has offered both expert insight and sustaining friendship during the many months I spent researching and writing this book. During my time in Stratford-upon-Avon, I was fortunate to be appointed a Visiting Fellow at the Shakespeare Institute, a position kindly arranged by the Institute's Director, Michael Dobson. Tiffany Stern and Robert Stagg welcomed me to the Institute's legendary Thursday seminars and provided genial company. I had the pleasure of getting to know Min and David Willoughby de Broke, who I admire for their devotion to Warwickshire and for whose warm hospitality I remain grateful. I also thank Queen's University Belfast for granting the sabbatical leave that enabled me to complete this book.

Much of this book was also researched at the Folger Shakespeare Library in Washington, DC. Among the Folger's outstanding staff, I particularly thank Owen Williams, Camille Seerattan, LuEllen DeHaven and the late Betsy Walsh for their guidance, expertise and encouragement. Garland Scott and Esther French kindly invited me to write a short piece about the Birthplace for the Folger's blog series 'Shakespeare and Beyond'. I am especially grateful to the Folger for providing most of this book's images and for generously allowing them to be reproduced under a Creative Commons Licence.

Mark Dudgeon, my editor at Arden Shakespeare, has offered enthusiastic and unfailing support for this book, including recognizing its potential to reach an audience beyond academia. I thank him and his editorial colleagues at Bloomsbury for their collective vote of confidence. Ella Wilson, also at Arden, deserves my sincerest thanks for seeing the manuscript through its editorial preparation. My thanks and gratitude also go to Merv Honeywood at RefineCatch for managing the overall production process, to Paul King for his expert copy-editing and to Heather Dubnick for once again compiling a superb index. David Forrer at Inkwell Management has been the best of literary agents, and I remain grateful for his support, knowledge and perseverance.

To this book's dedicatee belong the respect and admiration of all those who have been inspired by William Shakespeare.

INDEX

PLATE 1. *Shakespeare's Birthplace, view from Henley Street, Stratford-upon-Avon, photograph, late-nineteenth century. Folger Shakespeare Library, ART File S899h1 no.76.*

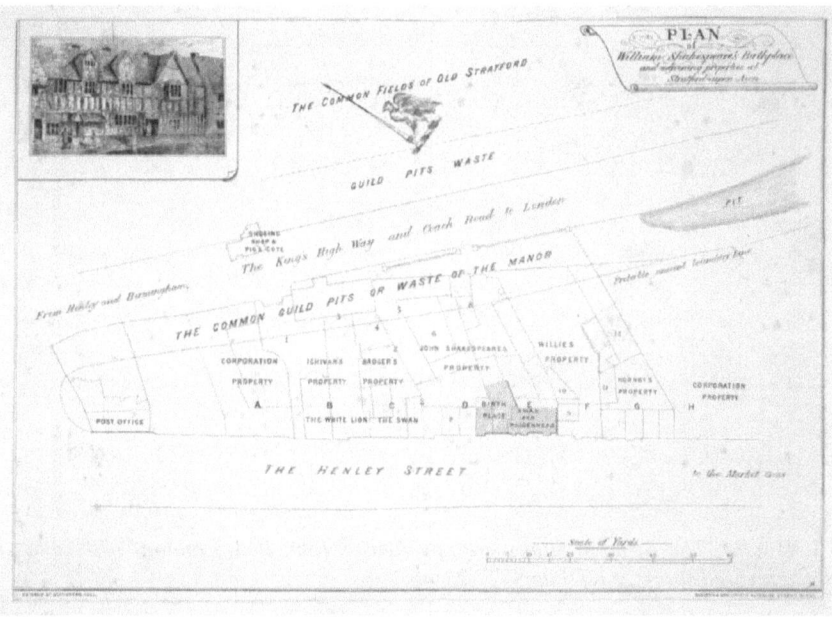

PLATE 2. *Plan of William Shakespeare's birthplace and adjoining properties on Henley Street, Stratford-upon-Avon, print by Joseph Hill, c. 1850. Folger Shakespeare Library, ART Vol. d79 no.9.*

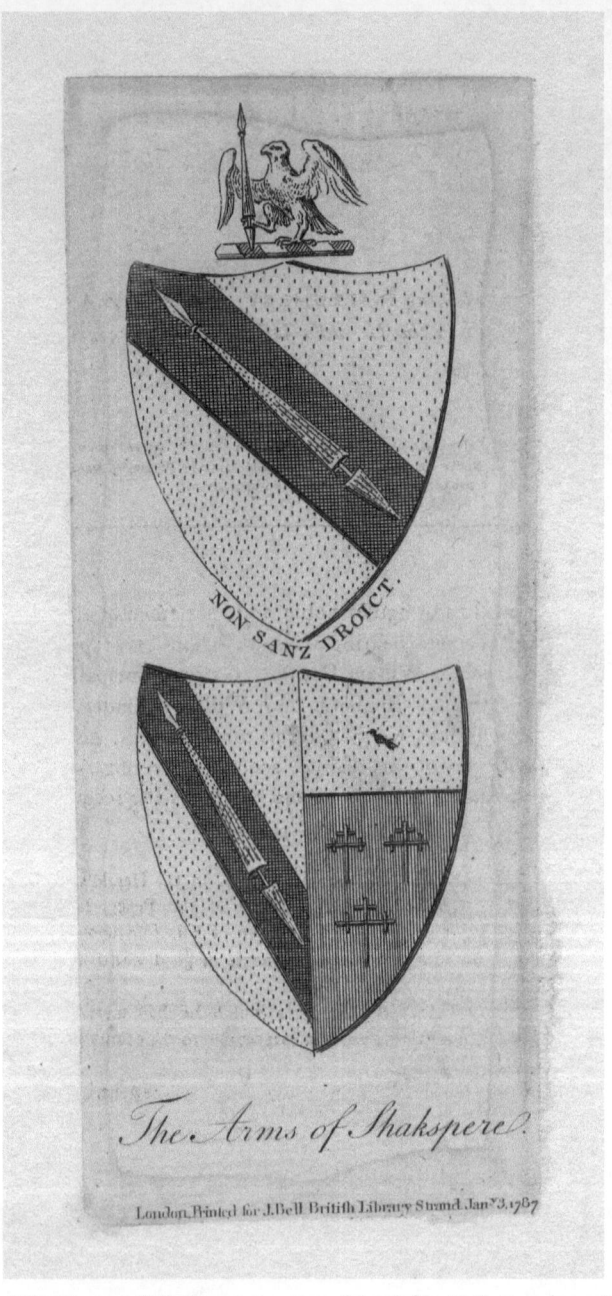

The Arms of Shakspere.

London, Printed for J. Bell British Library Strand Jan.ʳ 3, 1787

PLATE 3. 'The Arms of Shakspere', printed by John Bell, London, 1787. Folger Shakespeare Library, ART File S527.21 no.1

Mr. WILLIAM
SHAKESPEARES
COMEDIES,
HISTORIES, &
TRAGEDIES.

Publiſhed according to the True Originall Copies.

Martin Droeshout sculpsit London.

LONDON
Printed by Iſaac Iaggard, and Ed. Blount. 1623.

PLATE 4. *Title page, Mr. William Shakespeares Comedies, Histories, & Tragedies. Published according to the True Originall Copies. London, Printed by Isaac Jaggard and Edward Blount, 1623. Folger Shakespeare Library, STC 22273 fo.1 no.23.*

PLATE 5. *Chancel, Church of the Holy Trinity, Stratford-upon-Avon, showing Shakespeare's gravesite and funerary monument, photograph, n.d. Folger Shakespeare Library ART File S898c1 no. 82.*

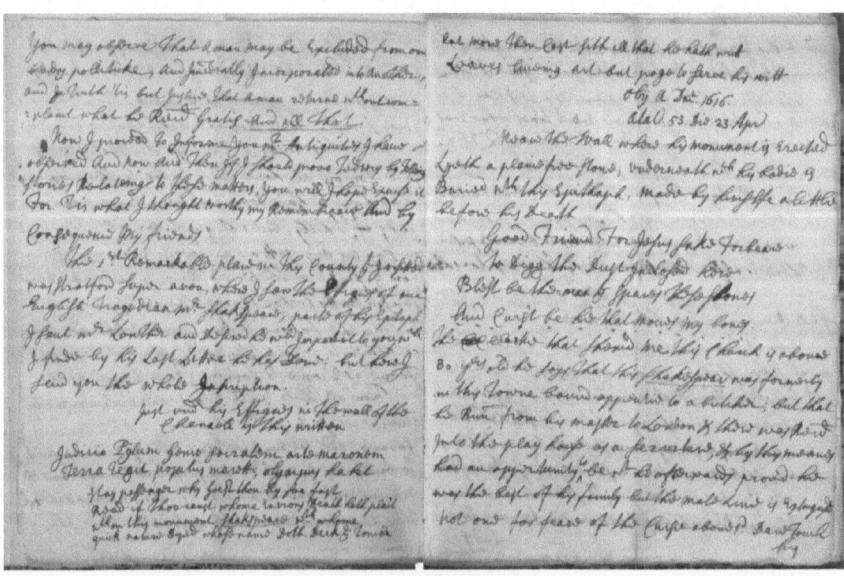

PLATE 6. *John Dowdall, manuscript letter to Mr Southwell, 10 April 1693, fol. 3 verso and fol. 4 recto. Folger Shakespeare Library, ms V.a.74.*

PLATE 7. *New Place gardens and The Guild Chapel of the Holy Cross, Stratford-upon-Avon, photograph, n.d. Folger Shakespeare Library, ART File S899h1 no.63 pt.3.*

Shakspere's House, New Place, Chapel & Grammar School.

PLATE 8. *'Shakspere's House, New Place, Chapel, & Grammar School', Stratford-upon-Avon, conjectural engraving by Samuel Ireland, printed by R. Faulder and T. Egerton, London, 1795. Folger Shakespeare Library, ART File S899h1 no.52.*

PLATE 9. 'New Place. Chapel. Guild-hall &c', Stratford-upon-Avon, drawn by Robert Bell Wheler, engraved by Francis Eginton and printed by J. Ward, 1806. Folger Shakespeare Library, ART File S899h1 no.51.

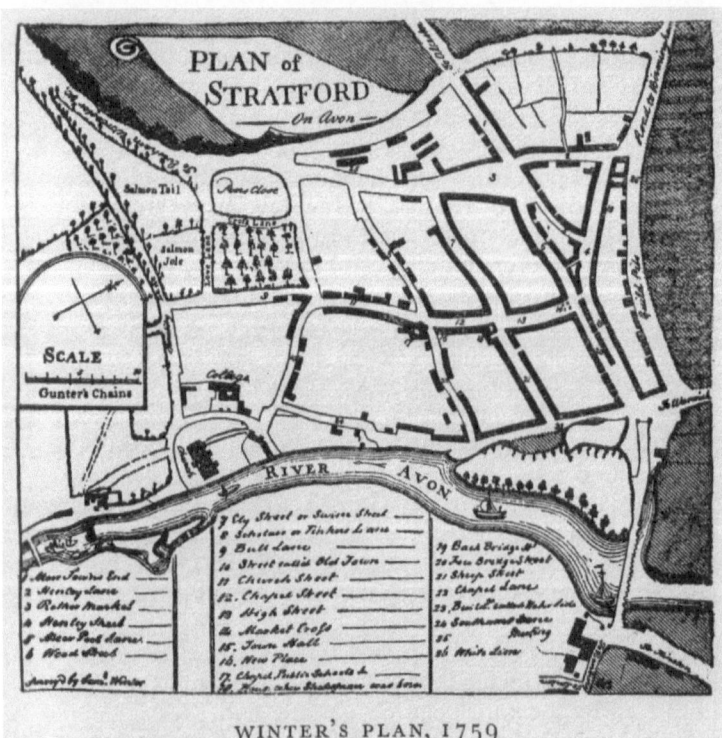

PLATE 10. Plan of Stratford-upon-Avon, watercolour drawing by Samuel Winter, 1759. Folger Shakespeare Library, ART Vol. d74 no.1a.

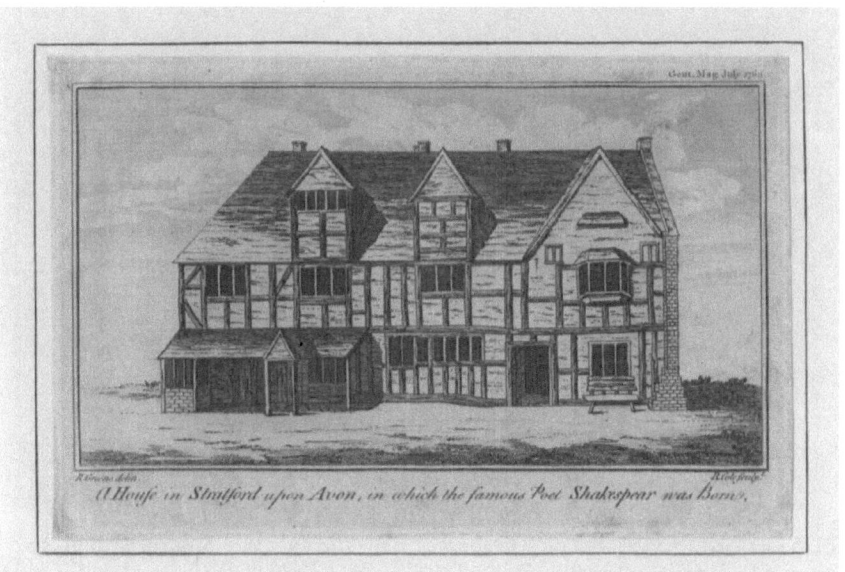

PLATE 11. 'A House in Stratford upon Avon, in which the famous Poet Shakespear was Born', drawn by Richard Greene and engraved by Benjamin Cole, Gentleman's Magazine, July 1769. Folger Shakespeare Library, ART File S899h1 no.65 copy 1.

PLATE 12. 'Kitchen of the House in which Shakspere was born', Stratford-upon-Avon, etched by Samuel Ireland, in his Picturesque Views on the Upper, or Warwickshire Avon . . . London: R. Faulder and T. Egerton, 1795. Folger Shakespeare Library, ART File S899h1 no.48.

PLATE 13. *Exterior of Shakespeare's Birthplace, Stratford-upon-Avon, watercolour drawing by Phoebe Dighton, 1834. Folger Shakespeare Library, ART Vol. d61 no.22a.*

PLATE 14. *'The Birthplace of Shakspere', Stratford-upon-Avon, drawn by John Brandard, printed in Leamington, England, by C. Elston, c. 1830s. Folger Shakespeare Library, ART File S899h1 no.3.*

PLATE 15. 'The Room in which Shakespere was Born', drawn and printed by George Rowe, published by F. & G. Ward, Stratford-upon-Avon, c. 1840s. Folger Shakespeare Library, ART File S899h1 no.40.

PLATE 16. Shakespeare's Birthplace, Stratford-upon-Avon, exterior, photographed and published by Samuel E. Poulton, London and Reading, England, c. 1840s. Folger Shakespeare Library, ART File S899h1 no.58.

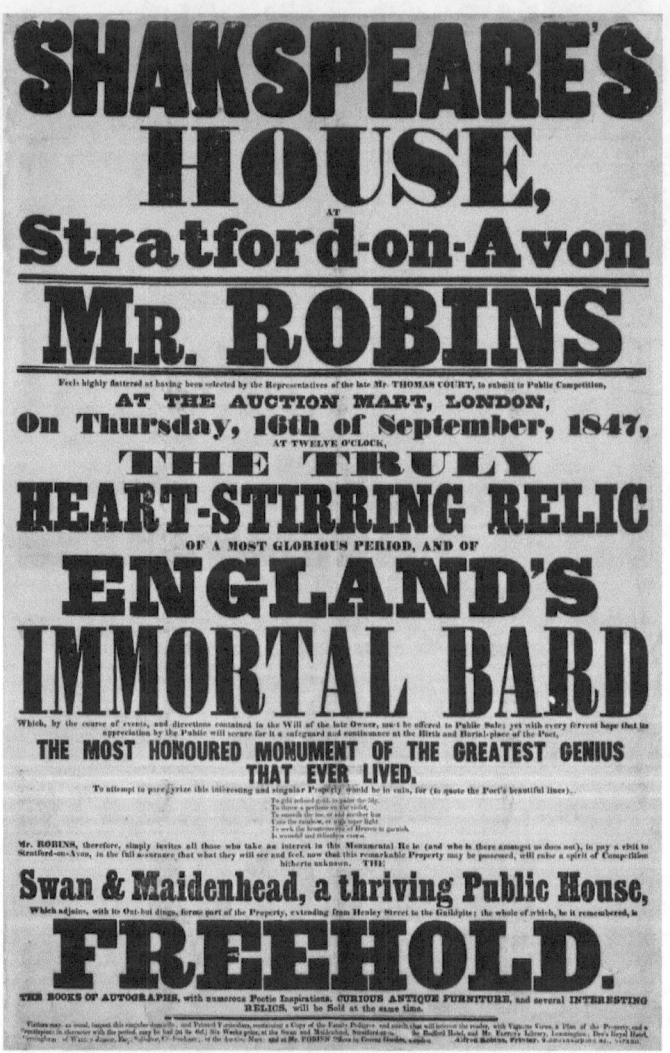

PLATE 17. *Broadside, auction of Shakespeare's Birthplace, Stratford-upon-Avon, held at the Auction Mart in Covent Garden, London, on 16 September 1847, printed by Alfred Roberts, London. Folger Shakespeare Library, Y.d.1147.*

PLATE 18. *View of Henley Street, Stratford-upon-Avon, looking northeast, photograph, c. 1870. Folger Shakespeare Library, ART File S899h1 no.57 part 18.*

PLATE 19. *Attic staircase, Shakespeare's Birthplace, Stratford-upon-Avon, pencil and watercolour sketch by John Thomas Blight, 1864. Folger Shakespeare Library, ART Vol. d69 no.13b.*

PLATE 20. *Birthroom, Shakespeare's Birthplace, Stratford-upon-Avon, pencil and watercolour sketch by John Thomas Blight, 1864. Folger Shakespeare Library, ART Vol. d69 no.13a.*

PLATE 21. *Birthroom, Shakespeare's Birthplace, Stratford-upon-Avon, photograph by Francis Bedford, c. 1870s. Folger Shakespeare Library, ART File S899h1 no.60 part 12.*

PLATE 22. *Interior, Shakespeare's Birthplace, Stratford-upon-Avon, pencil and watercolour sketch by John Thomas Blight, 1864. Folger Shakespeare Library, ART Vol. d69 no.23a.*

PLATE 23. *Desk and chair, Shakespeare's Birthplace, Stratford-upon-Avon, pencil and watercolour sketch by Paul Braddon, late-nineteenth century. Folger Shakespeare Library, ART Box B798 no.23.*

PLATE 24. *Exterior, Shakespeare's Birthplace, Stratford-upon-Avon, photograph, c. 1900. Folger Shakespeare Library, ART File S899b1 no.57 part 7.*

PLATE 25. *Henry Wallis, 'Shakespeare's House, Stratford-upon-Avon', oil painting, c. 1854, as repainted by Sir Edwin Landseer. Victoria and Albert Museum, London, accession number F.38. © Victoria and Albert Museum, London.*

Illustration 25 is reproduced courtesy of the Victoria and Albert Museum, London. All other illustrations are reproduced courtesy of the Folger Shakespeare Library, Washington, DC, under a Creative Commons Attribution-ShareAlike 4.0 International License.